# TRANSLATIONS AND CONTINUATIONS: RICCOBONI AND BROOKE, GRAFFIGNY AND ROBERTS

T0347272

# Chawton House Library Series:
# Women's Novels

*Series Editors:*   Stephen Bending
Stephen Bygrave

## Titles in this Series

## Forthcoming Titles

*Translations and Continuations: Riccoboni and Brooke, Graffigny and Roberts*

EDITED BY

Marijn S. Kaplan

Routledge
Taylor & Francis Group

LONDON AND NEW YORK

First published 2011 by Pickering & Chatto (Publishers) Limited

Published 2016 by Routledge
2 Park Square, Milton Park, Abingdon, Oxfordshire OX14 4RN
711 Third Avenue, New York, NY 10017, USA

First issued in paperback 2016

*Routledge is an imprint of the Taylor & Francis Group, an informa business*

BRITISH LIBRARY CATALOGUING IN PUBLICATION DATA

Translations and continuations: Riccoboni and Brooke, Graffigny and Roberts.
– (Chawton House library series. Women's novels)
1. Epistolary fiction, French.
I. Series II. Riccoboni, Marie Jeanne de Heurles Laboras de Mezieres, 1713–
1792. Letters from Juliet, Lady Gatesby to her friend Lady Henrietta Campley.
III. Grafigny, Mme de (Francoise d'Issembourg d'Happoncourt), 1695–1758.
Letters from a Peruvian woman. IV. Roberts, Rose. Letters to and from a Peruvian princess. V. Kaplan, Marijn S.
843.5'08-dc22

ISBN 13: 978-1-138-23538-0 (pbk)
ISBN 13: 978-1-8489-3026-1 (hbk)

Typeset by Pickering & Chatto (Publishers) Limited

# CONTENTS

# ACKNOWLEDGEMENTS

This project, an effort in international collaboration just like its texts, would not have come to fruition without the assistance of numerous people and the support of several institutions.

I am grateful for the fall 2010 semester of faculty leave my American home institution, the University of North Texas in Denton, Texas, awarded me and which allowed me to complete this book. Also at UNT, I would like to thank Pamela Johnston and Lynne Wright in the Interlibrary Loan Department of Willis Library for their help in locating and obtaining several hard-to-find editions, and my graduate student Katlyn Crawford for her research assistance with them. Still in Denton, I would like to acknowledge Dawn Letson, the now-retired Coordinator of Special Collections at The Woman's Collection at Texas Woman's University Library, who sent me a digital copy of Brooke's first edition overnight.

In Canada, my gratitude goes to Edward (Ted) Pitcher and Isobel Grundy for their willingness to share their work on the elusive Miss Roberts.

Across the pond in England I would like to express my appreciation to Chawton House Library and the School of Humanities at the University of Southampton for awarding me a Visiting Fellowship at Chawton House Library in October 2010, which allowed me to complete the research for this book. Sincere thanks go in particular to Jacqui Grainger, Librarian at Chawton House Library, for her help in getting the first editions to the United States, Mark Pollard at Pickering & Chatto Publishers for his support of the project, Gillian Dow, for her advice and encouragement, and last but certainly not least, Stephen Bygrave and Stephen Bending, series editors, for their helpful suggestions and insights.

# INTRODUCTION

## I.

Through the motif of translation and continuation this book connects four Enlightenment women writers from two countries and affecting three national literatures, thus partaking in the relatively recent trend within academia for recuperating from silence the voices of forgotten women writers and tracing the networks among them.[1] It presents English translations of two of the most popular eighteenth-century French novels written by women, Marie Jeanne Riccoboni's 1759 *Lettres de Milady Juliette Catesby à Milady Henriette Campley, son amie* translated by Frances Brooke as *Letters from Juliet Lady Catesby to her Friend Lady Henrietta Campley* (1760) and Françoise de Graffigny's 1747 *Lettres d'une Péruvienne* translated by Miss R. Roberts[2] as *Letters Written by a Peruvian Princess* (1774). The latter is followed by a second volume containing Roberts's translation of an anonymous 1748 French continuation to Graffigny's novel, *Suite des Lettres d'une Péruvienne* (*Continuation to the Letters from a Peruvian Woman*),[3] as well as her own continuation.

## II.

Françoise de Graffigny, née d'Happoncourt (1695–1758), the only one of these authors born during the seventeenth century, wrote one novel in addition to some stories, fables and plays. Married young and unhappily, Graffigny had three children who all died young. Separated from her abusive husband, she had a sixteen-year relationship with an officer who eventually abandoned her.[4] Having moved to Paris from her native Lorraine, she started to write and opened a salon visited by such male luminaries as Diderot, Montesquieu, Rousseau and Voltaire. She became famous mostly for her one novel entitled *Lettres d'une Péruvienne* (*Letters from a Peruvian Woman*). This epistolary novel published in 1747 became a bestseller in France and was reprinted forty-six times over the next three decades. The *Nouvelles littéraires* stated that 'Il y a longtemps qu'on ne nous avait rien donné d'aussi agréable que les *Lettres d'une Péruvienne*. Elles contiennent tout ce que la tendresse a de plus vif, de plus délicat et de plus passionné' ('It has been a long time since we have seen anything as pleasant as the *Lettres d'une Péruvienne*. They contain the most intense, delicate and passionate features of love').[5] *Cinq années littéraires* similarly found in the novel a 'variété de beaux détails, d'images vives, tendres, ingénieuses, riches, fortes, légères, singulièrement tracées; de sentimens délicats, naïfs, passionés' ('a variety of beautiful details, of vivid, tender, ingenious, rich, strong, subtle and exceedingly well drawn images; delicate, naïve, passionate sentiments').[6] Graffigny's novel is currently relatively well known since in the opinion of one critic 'No work of eighteenth-century French literature has benefited more clearly from American experiments in canon revision'.[7] The author is nowadays also of great scholarly interest because of the very extensive correspondence she left and which the Voltaire Foundation has been publishing since 1985.[8] It offers a fascinating glimpse of French Enlightenment society and culture reminiscent of what Madame de Sévigné's correspondence achieved for the previous century. Graffigny became quite familiar with the concept of continuations for the unconventional proto-feminist ending to her novel so dissatisfied her contemporaries that they rewrote it repeatedly.[9] The author published an expanded edition of her novel in 1752, but always refused to change its ending. Although the oeuvres of Graffigny and her French colleague Riccoboni overlap thematically through their proto-feminism, their lives appear not to have coincided much. It is uncertain whether they ever met, but Graffigny – being eighteen years older – did know Riccoboni's parents-in-law.[10] She died the very month Riccoboni's *Lettres de Milady Juliette Catesby* came out.[11]

Marie-Jeanne Riccoboni, née de Heurles de Laboras (1713–92) became an immensely popular French author of short stories and novels of sensibility once retired from her less successful career as an actress with the Parisian theatre company, Comédie Italienne. Unhappily married and childless, she separated from her husband and after being abandoned by a lover, cohabited with a fellow actress for nearly forty years until her death.[12] Translation and continuation played important roles in her literary career as it was launched when she wrote a continuation to Marivaux's *Vie de Marianne* in 1751; she translated Fielding's *Amelia* in 1762 and various English plays in 1769. Her third novel, *Lettres de Milady Juliette Catesby à Milady Henriette Campley, son amie*, became a sensational bestseller that appeared in twenty-one editions and, based on re-editions, ranked second only to Rousseau's *La Nouvelle Héloïse* (*The New Heloise*) (1761) in eighteenth-century French literature. Diderot was among the first to read Riccoboni's manuscript in late 1758. He did not like it initially, but changed his mind upon rereading it.[13] The *Observateur littéraire* shared his later opinion calling it 'un des plus ingénieux, des mieux écrits & des plus intéressans qui aient été faits depuis bien des années' ('one of the most ingenious, the best written and the most interesting (novels) that have been written in many years').[14] The *Mercure de France* concurred with 'L'esprit, la chaleur, le naturel & l'élégance, caractérisent [cet ouvrage] et justifient [son] succès' ('imagination, warmth, naturalness and elegance characterize this work and justify its success').[15] A play entitled *Cécile* was adapted from the novel and performed at the Comédie Italienne in March 1780.[16] Riccoboni displays Anglophilia – a love for everything English – in this novel, even though ironically she never left France. She did however correspond across national borders with David Hume and David Garrick, among others,[17] and it is her relationships with them that affected her connection with her English translator Frances Brooke.

Frances Brooke (née Moore) (1724–89) started her literary career in 1755 writing for the weekly periodical the *Old Maid*. Having translated Riccoboni's novel in 1760, which was a great success in England where it saw seven editions during Brooke's lifetime and established Riccoboni's reputation, she went on to publish her own first novel in 1763, the successful *History of Lady Julia Mandeville*.[18] It showed Riccoboni's influence and she signed it as 'the translator of *Lady Catesby's letters*'. She subsequently authored several plays, additional translations from the French, and more novels. After a five-year stay in Quebec where her husband, the Reverend John Brooke, with whom she had one son, was a Church of England chaplain to the British forces, she also published what is considered to be the first Canadian novel, *The History of Emily Montague*, in 1769.

They had never met, but Brooke contacted Riccoboni after the appearance of *Letters from Juliet Lady Catesby* and tried to establish a professional translator–author relationship with her.[19] In a May 1765 letter to Garrick, Riccoboni recounts how Brooke offered her respects in a letter and asked for permission to send her works. Riccoboni acknowledges that she had intended to have Brooke translate her 1764 *Histoire de Miss Jenny*, but since Hume did not know Brooke, he personally arranged for a different translator.[20] Garrick responds a month later and basically forbids her to work with Brooke: 'You will be civil to her & no more, all this is Entre nous'. He had refused to produce Brooke's play *Virginia* in 1756 and she had attacked him in the *Old Maid*.[21] Riccoboni complies and writes the following month that 'Eût-elle tous les talens du monde, Mistress Brooke n'aura jamais mes ouvrages' ('Even if she had all the talent in the world, Mrs Brooke will never have my works').[22] She remains loyal to Garrick in 1777 when Brooke's *Excursion* vilifies him again, swears never more to read anything by Brooke, throws her book across the room and writes 'Je hais à la mort cette méchante créature' ('I hate this mean woman to death').[23] It is unfortunate that Riccoboni refused to continue her professional affiliation with Brooke since her translation is generally considered the best of any of Riccoboni's novels.

Brooke was acquainted with Miss Roberts (*c*. 1730–88), the translator of – and author of a continuation to – the *Peruvian Letters*. In a letter to her friend Richard Gifford, Brooke reveals Roberts to be the translator of *Elements of the*

*History of France* when speaking of her own *Elements of the History of England*, both by the Abbé Millot and both to appear in 1771: 'There is a history of France, translated by an acquaintance of mine from the same author; a very good book, but not so well translated as mine; I tell you so, but I wd not any body else; it's done by a Mrs. Roberts, sister to the High Master of St. Pauls School'.[24] Brooke's son Jack was a student at St Paul's School[25] and the never-married Miss Roberts lived with her younger brother Richard, High Master there from 1769 to 1814.[26] In her Preface to the *Elements of the History of France*, Roberts also refers to Brooke and her translation: 'the History of England, translated from the same author, by the ingenious Mrs. Brooke'.[27] Brooke and Roberts shared the same publishers during the 1770s and 1780s, Dodsley and Cadell. Earlier, while living in Gloucester, Roberts had already published another French trans-lation and in 1770 it was followed by *Sermons written by a Lady* in London. It was undoubtedly her religious background that inspired her continuation to Graffigny's work, her first fiction. In it, she rewrites the French novel's controver-sial ending – merely confirmed in its initial French continuation also translated by Roberts – in a more traditional, conformist manner. She subsequently pub-lished a translation of a text by Jeanne Marie Le Prince de Beaumont, a tragedy and some legendary tales; it has been suggested that Roberts may have also contributed to *Lady's Magazine* and other periodicals.[28] In addition to Brooke, Roberts likely knew Hannah More and her immediate circle as it included her two nieces, Mary and Margaret Roberts, whom More called affectionately 'my counsellors, *not* solicitors; for they give more than they take'.[29] More in turn also knew Brooke (and was friends with David Garrick and his wife Eva) for whom she attended a farewell party when Brooke left for Quebec in 1763.[30]

## III.

Both French novels belong to the genre of epistolary fiction; specifically, they are monovocal novels, that is, composed of letters written by one primary correspondent who is, in both cases, a young woman. Readers do not see the addressee's response, unless it is 'quoted' by the primary correspondent, a tool Riccoboni in particular uses profusely. The main topos connecting these novels is that of the abandoned woman, which appears in literature dating back to at least the first century BC when Virgil wrote the *Aeneid* where he recounts how the Trojan Aeneas travels to Italy to become the ancestor of the Romans after having abandoned his lover, Queen Dido of Carthage. The French epistolary fiction tradition offers a precursor for both novels incorporating the topos of the abandoned woman: in the first French epistolary novel, *Lettres de la religieuse portugaise* written in 1669 by Guilleragues, a Portuguese nun laments having been abandoned by her lover, a French officer. Incidentally, the theme also occurs in the two authors' lives[31] and both novels were written post-abandonment.

In Graffigny's *Lettres d'une Péruvienne*, set during the Spanish conquest of Peru, a Peruvian princess named Zilia is kidnapped by the French and taken – anachronistically –to Enlightenment France. Being a foreigner and thus incorporating the theme of translation into the novel's very foundation, she writes letters of love and longing to her fiancé and close relative Aza, a Peruvian prince, about her experiences in France and observations of the French. After converting to Christianity, Aza abandons Zilia because he can no longer marry a relative. Zilia is devastated yet refuses to marry Déterville,[32] her French captor, in spite of his admirable character and behaviour, and instead chooses to become an author and live alone. The novel raises questions about the woman as exotic Other, the roles of women, marriage and language, society's expectations and perceptions of women, incest, epistolarity and the abandoned woman.

Riccoboni's *Lettres de Milady Juliette Catesby à Milady Henriette Campley, son amie* centres on the mystery surrounding a young English widow named Juliette Catesby who is engaged to be married in a love match. On the eve of their wedding, however, her fiancé d'Ossery disappears, abandoning her and eventually marrying someone else. Before the inevitable reunion and happy ending, Juliette relates her love story's many surprising twists and turns in letters to her friend Henriette: she recounts how in a moment of weakness, her fiancé took advantage of a woman who became pregnant and whom he therefore felt obliged to marry instead. The text raises the issues of marriage, widowhood, friendship, betrayal and forgiveness, death, epistolarity and again, the abandoned woman.

The theme of the abandoned woman dominates contemporary reviews, infusing criticism into otherwise positive critiques. The almost exclusively male critics wrote gendered reviews of Graffigny's novel in which they expressed their disapproval of the ending; the abandoned Zilia's decision to stay single. Thus, *Cinq années littéraires* proposes a different ending to the novel claiming it is preferable for Zilia to be dead than abandoned: 'Il faut ici tuer quelqu'un ... C'est Zilia, la seule personne à qui vous vous intéressiez véritablement; il faut la tuer, afin qu'elle vous intéresse encore davantage' ('Someone has to be killed here ... It is Zilia, the only person who truly interested you. She has to be killed so that she will interest you even more').[33] *Observations sur la littérature moderne* states that 'Un degré de parenté de moins rendoit Zilia à son Amant, et épargnoit aux Lecteurs la douleur de la voir abandonnée' ('one lesser degree of kinship would have restored Zilia to Aza and would have spared readers the pain of seeing her abandoned'), continuing that Virgil can be forgiven for having Aeneas abandon Dido, because the continuation of his story is interesting and significant, but that Graffigny does not have Aza do anything of interest or importance after he abandons Zilia and that therefore, her abandonment is not justified.[34] Instead of yielding to the criticism regarding her ending however, Graffigny actually added to her subsequent 1752 edition elements underscoring the importance of Zilia's final choices of independence, authorship and spinsterhood. For Riccoboni's novel, critics focused on Juliette's fiancé d'Ossery, the perpetrator, rather than on his abandonment and rape victims, but instead of condemning his criminal behaviour, they praised his sense of honour and loyalty. Thus, the *Journal Ency-clopédique* calls the abandonment and rape 'un tort qui n'étoit pas même une infidélité' ('a wrong which was not even an infidelity')[35] and the *Observateur littéraire* terms the rape a 'petite aventure de l'après souper' ('small after-dinner adventure').[36]

More than two centuries later, modern critics, all of them writing after the emergence of feminism and many of them female, critique the novels and the topos quite differently. They render *overt* what Joan Hinde Stewart calls the '*covert* female rebellion'[37] of eighteenth-century French women writers by uncovering and decoding the authors' proto-feminist messages. Thus, rather than focusing on the male abandoners and rapist, they analyse the abandoned and raped female bodies on their own merit instead of as part of an incom-plete heterosexual couple. So whereas eighteenth-century readers and critics expected and demanded closure for abandoned Zilia – either marriage to Aza, to Déterville, or death – their modern counterparts interpret the lack thereof as feminist commentary on the status of women in eighteenth-century France and an opportunity for female choice and empowerment.[38] And while Juliette's marriage at the end of Riccoboni's novel undoubtedly pleased contemporary readers, one modern critic considers the symbolic act of d'Ossery taking Juliette's pen a reversal of the abandoned woman topos: when Juliette recovers her pen from her new husband in order to write to her friend Henriette, it is in fact her fiancé 'who gets (symbolically) abandoned ... [because] it is to express her desire for a woman that Juliette recaptures her pen.'[39]

The reception of Brooke's 1760 translation *Letters From Juliet Lady Catesby, To Her Friend Lady Henrietta Campley* differed from that of the original novel. Although overall also quite positive, reviews did not discuss the abandoned or raped woman and the perpetrator – the content – as much as the transla-tion's style and relation to the original.[40] Riccoboni herself wrote of Brooke's translation in a letter dated 31 August 1765 that 'Mistress Brooke s'est trompée lourdement en cinquante endroits de *Catesby*' ('Mrs Brooke made serious mis-takes in fifty places in *Catesby*').[41] As indicated in the Editorial Notes, I have identified about a dozen mistakes, not fifty. Beyond that, her translation remains quite faithful to the French original with occasional additions or deletions, sometimes due to the fact that Riccoboni 'translated' England without having been there, and other times to Brooke's interpretation. Brooke does not change the plot but makes some minor changes.[42] As Raeleen Chai-Elsholz points out in one of the rare studies of the translation, she criminalizes the rape scene,[43] thus reclaiming the voices and rights of the abandoned and raped victims more pointedly than the French original.

While Brooke's translation incorporates mainly subtle changes, the translation by Roberts presents a different story. Roberts states in her Preface: 'I was not indeed altogether satisfied with the conclusion, being desirous the Indian Princess should become a convert to Christianity, through conviction; and that so generous a friend as Deterville might be as happy as his virtues deserved. This thought determined me to add a second volume' (p. iv). In order to achieve these goals, Roberts takes liberties with her translation: she bases it on Graffigny's 1747 text, not the 1752 version that confirms Zilia's independence in the face of opposition through extra letters criticizing marriage, the treatment of women and the French love for the superficial and the superfluous. She also deletes Graffigny's preface including references to Zilia's life 'after' Graffigny's text which, the fictional editor implies, consists of writing and translating. Roberts thus eliminates part of Graffigny's feminist context. Her translation contains more religious overtones than the original, adjustments to the English readership, some omissions and corrections of the French.[44]

In Volume II, which starts with Roberts's translation of *Suite des Lettres d'une Péruvienne* and concludes with her own continuation, Roberts portrays Zilia as more assimilated, less Other and more traditional; she does not write much and translate although she continues to be an avid reader. The text raises the issues of religion, friendship, love, incest, bigamy, pre-romanticism, and the man as Other, that is Deterville appreciating and 'translating' England. The major formal transformation consists in the original epistolary monovocality becoming polyphony, already apparent from the volume's title, *Letters to and from a Peruvian Princess*, and Zilia and Deterville trading places as primary letter writers. Deterville writes twenty-two letters in this volume, most of which are addressed to his fellow Knight of Malta, Dubois, and therefore *Letters about a Peruvian Princess* would have been a more appropriate title. Zilia's loss of epistolary voice correlates to the loss of her emotional, intellectual and spiritual independence as her marriage and conversion are discussed and brought about *for* her, but to a lesser extent *by* her.

Roberts introduces a new character and uses her – Maria, a friend of Zilia's – as a vehicle to reframe the abandoned woman topos. Maria is a melancholy young woman: her lover has abandoned her because he learned they had the same father. Both overcome their incestuous feelings through religion: he joins an order and later dies, while Maria retreats to a convent. In the original novel, Zilia and Aza were equally affected by the incest taboo and thus, this *mise-en-abyme* of the abandoned woman topos shows Zilia that incestuous love is a dead end, literally, with religion being the only salvation, literally and figuratively.

Roberts implies that once converted, Zilia can 'abandon' incestuous Aza and marry faithful Deterville (faithful in both senses: loyal and full of faith), which is what unfolds. While the topos of the abandoned woman makes Graffigny's ending proto-feminist, Roberts transforms it in her continuation to bring about Zilia's conversion and marriage, a decidedly traditional, unfeminist ending.

## IV.

Roberts and Brooke elucidate the relationship between translation and gender. Between 1760 and 1775, the two women published seven translations from French three of which, including those discussed here, came from female-authored originals. Of the seven, Brooke's *Letters From Juliet Lady Catesby* is the only text without a preface or dedication in the translator's voice. In these metatextual documents, Roberts and Brooke remark not only on the translation at hand but also on the relationship between translation and gender.

The two translators agree that their primary role is to transmit the French original as accurately and completely as possible into English. Interestingly, both make this comment not in their fiction translations but in their 1771 translations of Millot's study of history. Brooke says in her Advertisement that 'she has endeavored to transfuse the spirit and perspicuity of her author's style into the translation'[45] while Roberts in her Preface distinguishes her role as a translator from that of Millot, the historian: 'the difference betwixt an historian and translator being, that the historian is allowed to make his own remarks, and express his own feelings, while the translator can only convey those of another'.[46] Brooke nevertheless expresses awareness that factors such as a translator's country of origin and religion may affect her work stating that 'she may possibly, as an Englishwoman, and a Protestant, be herself guilty in some degree of the very error [prejudice] she is presuming to charge on him [Millot]; she knows how difficult it is to break the ties of education, to change an habitual mode of thinking, and to become absolutely a citizen of the world'.[47] Although she uses 'Englishwoman' principally in order to contrast Millot's country of origin with her own and does not write 'English woman', Brooke hints nonetheless at the role gender plays in writing and translating.

The conflict between female virtue and 'going public' in early modern Europe has been studied extensively.[48] Various strategies to solve this dilemma emerge from the translations by Roberts and Brooke. Brooke publishes her *Letters From Juliet Lady Catesby* anonymously. Roberts divulges her gender ('a Lady') but not her name in *Select Moral Tales*. Roberts stresses female virtue by dedicating her texts to virtuous women and asking for their protection, like the Duchess of Devonshire 'a Young Lady in whose mind are centered those many Virtues which concur to adorn her Family and who would not disdain to patronize a

Work originally written, and since translated, by a Woman'.[49] There and elsewhere, Roberts also embodies female modesty: 'the translation ... being begun as an exercise in the French language, the partiality of my friends has induced me to publish it'[50] and 'Having already twice appeared in print ... it may be imagined I have lost that timidity which is natural to all young writers, especially of my sex, when they first expose themselves to the praise or censure of the Public: notwithstanding which, I ingenuously confess, I feel the contrary'.[51] In the *Peruvian Letters* she admits 'being fearful of deviating in the least from that strict delicacy which ought to be always observed by a woman's pen'.[52]

Yet, Brooke and Roberts also use their translations to champion female causes and defend women, especially from the 1770s onward when their careers were better established. Thus, Brooke criticizes a female character created by her male author, but does so 'with diffidence': 'there seems to be something like sex in the very soul. A well-educated woman ... might possibly have felt the passion of love to the *degree*, but not in the *manner*, our author describes: even vice itself, in the gentler sex ... retains the blushing veil of modesty. Perhaps, but this idea is offered with diffidence, woman alone can paint with perfect exactness the sentiments of woman'.[53] Roberts praises her female author and establishes the superiority of a female translator but using the eminent John Hawkesworth[54] as a vehicle: '[he] recommended it to me as a Novel of that delicate kind which was peculiarly adapted to a Female Writer; abounding with moral and religious truths; and being originally written by a Woman justly celebrated among the French Authors, [it] was the more suitable to a Translator of the same Sex'.[55] Lastly, Roberts supports women's education in her *Elements of the History of France* but with modesty and self-deprecation: 'the reading of history is now become a part of female education ... The translator, though a woman, hopes, that in thus facilitating the accomplishment of her sex, she has not gone out of her sphere; as she has only conveyed through one language what was produced in another'.[56] Thus, in spite of Roberts's reversal of Graffigny's ending, Brooke and Roberts actually advance the cause of proto-feminism using their gender and their translations subversively.

## Notes

1. For examples of this trend, see the electronic databases *Orlando: Women's Writing in the British Isles from the Beginnings to the Present* (http://orlando.cambridge.org) and *WomenWriters* (http://neww.huygens.knaw.nl/).

2. Isobel Grundy, chief editor of *Orlando*, lists 'Rachel' as the author's first name, but I have been unable to corroborate this.

3. Graffigny attributed the *Suite* to Charles de Fieux de Mouhy (1701–84). See Note on the Texts, n. 9.

4. For analyses of her later life (and death), including a relationship she had with a much younger man, see J. H. Stewart, *The Enlightenment of Age: Women, Letters and Grow-*

*ing Old in Eighteenth-Century France* (Oxford: Voltaire Foundation, 2010), pp. 69–91, 223–45.

5. *Nouvelles littéraires*, 1 (1747), p. 132.

6. *Cinq années littéraires*, 1 (1748), p. 20.

7. J. DeJean in her introduction to *Lettres d'une Péruvienne*, ed. J. DeJean and N. K. Miller (New York: Modern Language Association, 1993), p. ix.

8. *Correspondance de Madame de Graffigny*, ed. J. A. Dainard, M.-P. Ducretet, E. Showalter (Oxford: Voltaire Foundation, 1985–).

9. Next to the continuation translated by Roberts, the best known is *Lettres d'Aza ou d'un Péruvien* (*Letters from Aza or from a Peruvian*), published in 1748 by Hugary de Lamarche-Courmont. For information on the French continuations, see Appendix 2 in *Letters of a Peruvian Woman*, trans. J. Mallinson (Oxford: Voltaire Foundation, 2009) and E. Showalter Jr, 'Les *Lettres d'une Péruvienne*: composition, publication, suites', *Archives et bibliothèques de Belgique*, 54:1–4 (1983), pp. 23–8.

10. See H. Bostic, *The Fiction of Enlightenment. Women of Reason in the French Eighteenth Century* (Newark, DE: University of Delaware Press, 2010), p. 105.

11. Despite a 1759 publication date, the novel appeared in December 1758. See Note on the Texts, n. 1.

12. For an analysis of the relationship she had later in life with Robert Liston, her junior by twenty-nine years, see J. H. Stewart, *The Enlightenment of Age*, pp. 132–52.

13. *Oeuvres complètes de Diderot*, ed. J. Assézat (Paris: Garnier, 1875), vol. 7, p. 408.

14. *Observateur littéraire*, 1 (1759), p. 332.

15. *Mercure de France* (June 1759), p. 73.

16. F. M. Grimm, *et al.*, *Correspondance littéraire, philosophique et critique*, ed. M. Tourneux (Paris: Garnier, 1880), vol. 12, p. 378.

17. For an analysis of Riccoboni's famous correspondence with her compatriot Laclos, author of *Liaisons dangereuses* [*Dangerous Liaisons*], in the context of women and aging, see J. H. Stewart, *The Enlightenment of Age*, ch. 8.

18. Riccoboni owned a copy of this book (E. Crosby, *Une Romancière oubliée: Madame Riccoboni, sa vie, ses oeuvres, sa place dans la littérature anglaise et française du XVIIIe siècle* (Genève: Slatkine Reprints, 1970), p. 171).

19. On this unusual phenomenon, see M. H. McMurran, *The Spread of Novels: Translation and Prose Fiction in the Eighteenth Century* (Princeton, NJ: Princeton University Press, 2010), pp. 60–2.

20. *Mme Riccoboni's Letters to David Hume, David Garrick and Sir Robert Liston: 1764–1783*, ed. J. C. Nicholls (Oxford: Voltaire Foundation and Taylor Institution, 1976), p. 45.

21. *Mme Riccoboni's Letters*, ed. J. C. Nicholls, p. 48.

22. Ibid., ed. J. C. Nicholls, p. 51.

23. Ibid., ed. J. C. Nicholls, pp. 416, 422, 426.

24. As cited in L. McMullen, *An Odd Attempt in a Woman: The Literary Life of Frances Brooke* (Vancouver, British Columbia: University of British Columbia Press, 1983), p. 128.

25. McMullen, *An Odd Attempt in a Woman*, p. 121.

26. In 1775, Roberts published another translation from the French of Jeanne Marie Le Prince de Beaumont, *The Triumph of Truth, or Memoirs of Mr. De La Villette*. It was dated 'St. Paul's Churchyard, Jan. 12, 1775'.

27. *Elements of the History of France, translated from the Abbé Millot ... by the translator of Select tales from Marmontel, and Author of Sermons by a Lady* (London: Dodsley and Cadell, 1771), p. vi.
28. E. W. Pitcher, 'The Miscellaneous Periodical Works and Translations of Miss R. Roberts', *Literary Research Newsletter*, 5:3 (1980), pp. 125–8, and unpublished files Ted Pitcher graciously shared.
29. *The Letters of Hannah More*, ed. R. Brimley Johnson (London: John Lane The Bodley Head Ltd., 1925) p. 159.
30. S. Brown, P. Clements, I. Grundy (eds), Frances Brooke entry: Life screen within *Orlando: Women's Writing in the British Isles from the Beginnings to the Present* (Cambridge: Cambridge University Press Online, 2006) http://orlando. cambridge.org/ 20 November 2010.
31. Graffigny and Riccoboni were both abandoned by a lover, as described in section II. In addition, Riccoboni's father was found to be a bigamist and forced to abandon her mother and her in order to return to his first wife.
32. Although rare, a famous earlier refusal to marry can be found in Madame de Lafayette's 1678 *La Princesse de Clèves* (*The Princess of Cleves*).
33. *Cinq années littéraires*, 1 (1748), p. 21.
34. *Observations sur la littérature moderne*, 1 (1749), p. 49.
35. *Journal Encyclopédique* (May 1759), p. 123.
36. *Observateur littéraire*, 1 (1759), p. 332.
37. J. H. Stewart, *Gynographs: French Novels by Women of the Late Eighteenth Century* (Lincoln, NE and London: University of Nebraska Press, 1993), p. 1.
38. See notably E. J. MacArthur, 'Devious Narratives: Refusal of Closure in Two Eighteenth-Century Epistolary Novels', *Eighteenth-Century Studies*, 21:1 (Autumn 1987), pp. 1–20: 'If women preferred the epistolary form, and were considered especially talented in using it, perhaps it was because the openness of the form corresponded to the openness of the stories they wished to tell, stories in which women's lives were less circumscribed and defined than in the real, extra-fictional world of the time' (pp. 18–19).
39. S. S. Lanser, 'The Rise of the Novel, the Fall of the Voice: Juliette's Catesby's Silencing', *Fictions of Authority: Women Writers and Narrative Voice* (Ithaca, NY and London: Cornell University Press, 1992), p. 39.
40. See Note on the Texts for contemporary reviews.
41. *Mme Riccoboni's Letters*, ed. J. C. Nicholls, p. 54.
42. See Editorial Notes.
43. R. Chai-Elsholz, 'Textual Allusions and Narrative Voice in the *Lettres de Milady Juliette Catesby* and Its English Translation', in A. Cointre, A. Rivara, F. Lautel-Ribstein (eds), *La Traduction du discours amoureux 1660–1830* (Metz: Centre d'Etudes de la Traduction, Université de Metz, 2006), pp. 119–42.
44. See Editorial Notes.
45. *Elements of the History of England* (London: Dodsley and Cadell, 1771), p. v.
46. *Elements of the History of France*, p. iv.
47. *Elements of the History of England*, p. vi.
48. See E. C. Goldsmith and D. Goodman (eds), *Going Public* (Ithaca, NY and London: Cornell University Press, 1995) and E. C. Goldsmith (ed.), *Writing the Female Voice. Essays on Epistolary Literature* (Boston, MA: Northeastern University Press, 1989).
49. *The Triumph of Truth* (London: Cadell, 1775), p. vi–vii. *Select Moral Tales* (Gloucester: R. Raikes, 1763) is dedicated to Elizabeth Montague.

50.  *Select Moral Tales*, p. vii.
51.  *Elements of the History of France*, p. iii.
52.  *Peruvian Letters* (London: Cadell, 1774), p. iv.
53.  *Memoirs of the Marquis de St. Forlaix* (London: Dodsley, 1770), p xi–xii.
54.  See Editorial Notes, *The Peruvian Letters*, Volume I, n. 11.
55.  *The Triumph of Truth*, p. x.
56.  *Elements of the History of France*, p. vi.

# SELECT BIBLIOGRAPHY

## Anonymous

[de Mouhy, Charles de Fieux?], *Suite des Lettres d'une Péruvienne* (Peine [Paris]: 1748).

## Frances Brooke

### Reviews

*Critical Review*, 9 (May 1760), p. 420.

*Daily Advertiser*, 23 April 1760.

*London Magazine, or, Gentleman's Monthly Intelligencer*, 29 (April 1760), p. 224.

*Monthly Review*, 22 (June 1760), p. 521.

### Works

*Virginia a Tragedy, with Odes, Pastorals, and Translations* (London: A. Millar, 1756).

*Letters from Juliet Lady Catesby, to her friend Lady Henrietta Campley, translated from the French* (London: R. and J. Dodsley, 1760).

*History of Lady Julia Mandeville* (London: R. and J. Dodsley, 1763).

*The Old Maid. By Mary Singleton, Spinster* (London: A. Millar, 1764).

*History of Emily Montague* (London: J. Dodsley, 1769).

*Memoirs of the Marquis de St. Forlaix: translated from the French of Mons. Framery* (London: J. Dodsley, 1770).

*Elements of the History of England: from the Invasion of the Romans to the Reign of George the Second, translated from the French* (London: Dodsley and T. Cadell, 1771).

*The Excursion* (London: Cadell, 1777).

*The Siege of Sinope, a Tragedy* (London: Cadell, 1781).

*Rosina, a Comic Opera in Two Acts* (London: Cadell, 1783).

*Marian, a Comic Opera in Two Acts* (London: Cadell, 1788).

*History of Charles Mandeville* (London: W. Lane, 1790).

# Françoise de Graffigny

## Reviews

*Cinq années littéraires*, 1 (1748), pp. 18–24.

*Nouvelles littéraires*, 1 (1747), p. 132.

*Observations sur la littérature moderne*, 1 (1749), pp. 33–54.

## Works

*Lettres d'une Péruvienne* (Peine [Paris]: 1747).

*Letters Written by a Peruvian Princess, translated from the French* (London: J. Brindley, 1748).

*Cénie* (Paris: Cailleau, 1751).

*Lettres d'une Péruvienne* (Paris: Duchesne, 1752).

*La Fille d'Aristide* (Paris: Duchesne, 1759).

*Oeuvres posthumes de Madame de Grafigny* (Paris: Segaud, 1770).

'La Nouvelle Espagnole' (1745), in *Oeuvres badines complètes du comte de Caylus* (Amsterdam, Paris: Visse, 1787), vol. 6, p. 13–68.

'La Princesse Azerolle ou l'excès de la constance' (1745), in *Oeuvres badines complètes du comte de Caylus* (Amsterdam, Paris: Visse, 1787), vol. 9, p. 243–302.

*Les Saturnales* (1752), ed. E. Showalter, *SVEC*, 175 (1978), p. 113–80.

*Lettres portugaises, Lettres d'une Péruvienne, et autres romans d'amour par lettres*, ed. B. A. Bray, I. Landy-Houillon (Paris: Flammarion, 1983).

*Correspondance de Mme de Graffigny*, eds J. A. Dainard, M.-P. Ducretet, E. Showalter (Oxford: Voltaire Foundation, 1985–).

*Lettres d'une Péruvienne*, ed. C. Piau-Gillot (Paris: Côté-femmes, 1990).

*Letters from a Peruvian Woman*, trans. D. Kornacker (New York: Modern Language Association, 1993).

*Lettres d'une Péruvienne*, ed. J. DeJean and N. K. Miller (New York: Modern Language Association, 1993).

*Françoise de Graffigny: Choix de lettres*, ed. E. Showalter (Oxford: Voltaire Foundation, 2001).

*Lettres d'une Péruvienne*, ed. J. Mallinson (Oxford: Voltaire Foundation, 2002).

*Lettres d'une Péruvienne*, ed. T. Corbeau (Paris: Flammarion, 2005).

*Letters of a Peruvian Woman*, trans. J. Mallinson (Oxford: Voltaire Foundation, 2009).

# Marie Jeanne Riccoboni

## Reviews

*Année littéraire*, 8 (December 1758), pp. 289–302.

*Correspondance littéraire* (April 1759), pp. 98–9.

*Journal Encyclopédique* (May 1759), pp. 112–27.

*Mercure de France* (June 1759), pp. 73–87.

*Observateur littéraire* 1 (1759), pp. 314–32.

## Works

*Lettres de mistriss Fanny Butlerd à milord Charles Alfred de Cailombridge, comte de Plisinthe, duc de Raflingth. Ecrites en 1735. Traduites de l'anglais en 1765 par Adélaïde de Varançai* (Amsterdam [Paris]: 1757).

*Histoire de M. le marquis de Cressy*, Traduite de l'anglais par Mme de *** (Amsterdam [Paris]: 1758).

*Lettres de Milady Juliette Catesby à Milady Henriette Campley, son amie* (Amsterdam [Paris]: 1759).

*L'Abeille* in *Le Monde*, ed. J.-F. de Bastide (Paris: 1761), vol. 3, pp. 9–42, 121–47, 287–91; vol. 4, pp. 38–69.

*Amélie: sujet tiré de Mr. Fielding* (Paris: Brocas & Humblot, 1762).

*Histoire de Miss Jenny, écrite et envoyée par elle à milady, comtesse de Roscomonde, ambassadrice d'Angleterre à la cour de Dannemark* (Paris: Brocas & Humblot, 1764).

*Histoire d'Ernestine* in *Recueil de pièces détachées* (Paris: Humblot, 1765), pp. 169–302.

*Suite de Marianne* in *Recueil de pièces détachées* (Paris: Humblot, 1765), pp. 1–111.

*Lettres d'Adélaïde de Dammartin, comtesse de Sancerre, au comte de Nancé, son ami* (Paris: Humblot, 1767).

*Le nouveau théâtre anglois*, 2 vols (Paris: Humblot, 1769).

*Lettres d'Élisabeth-Sophie de Vallière à Louise Hortence de Canteleu, son amie* (Paris: Humblot, 1772).

*Lettres de Milord Rivers à Sir Charles Cardigan entremêlées d'une partie de ses correspondances à Londres pendant son séjour en France* (Paris: Humblot, 1777).

*Histoire d'Aloïse de Livarot* (Paris: 1780).

'Histoire de deux jeunes amies', in *Mercure de France*, 1 April 1786, pp. 5–42, 8 April 1786, pp. 64–88.

'Correspondance de Laclos et de Madame Riccoboni au sujet des *Liaisons dangereuses*', in *Laclos: Oeuvres complètes* (Paris: Gallimard, La Pléiade 1959), pp. 686–98.

*Mme Riccoboni's Letters to David Hume, David Garrick and Sir Robert Liston: 1764–1783*, ed. J. C. Nicholls (Oxford: Voltaire Foundation and Taylor Institution, 1976).

*Lettres de Milady Juliette Catesby à Milady Henriette Campley, son amie,* pref. S. Menant (Paris: Desjonquères, 1997).

*Trois histoires amoureuses et chevaleresques,* ed. P. Bolognini-Centène (Reims: Presses Universitaires de Reims, 2005).

*Lettres de la princesse Zelmaïde au prince Alamir, son époux, 1765. Lettre de la marquise D'Artigues à sa soeur, 1785,* ed. M. S. Kaplan (Paris: Éditions Indigo & Côté-femmes, 2009).

## R. Roberts

### Reviews

*Critical Review,* 39 (June 1775), pp. 473–8.

*Daily Advertiser,* Monday, 18 April 1774.

*London Review,* 1 (1775), p. 516.

*Monthly Review,* 51 (August 1774), pp. 161–2.

*Town & Country Magazine,* 7 (August 1775), p. 436.

### Works

*Select Moral Tales translated from the French by a Lady* (Gloucester: R. Raikes, 1763).

*Sermons written by a Lady, the translatress of Four Select Tales from Marmontel* (London: J. Dodsley, 1770).

*Elements of the History of France, translated from the Abbé Millot ... by the translator of Select Tales from Marmontel, and Author of Sermons by a Lady* (London: J. Dodsley, T. Cadell, 1771).

*The Peruvian Letters, translated from the French. With an Additional Original Volume* (London: T. Cadell, 1774).

*The Triumph of Truth; or, Memoirs of Mr. De La Villette. Translated from the French [of Jeanne Marie Le Prince de Beaumont].* (London: T. Cadell, 1775).

*Malcolm, a Tragedy* (London: printed for the author, 1779).

*Albert, Edward and Laura, and The Hermit of Priestland; Three Legendary Tales* (London: Cadell, 1783).

### Secondary Material

Abbott, J. L., 'John Hawkesworth: Friend of Samuel Johnson and Editor of Captain Cook's *Voyages* and of the *Gentleman's Magazine', Eighteenth-Century Studies,* 3:3 (Spring 1970), pp. 339–50.

Altman, J. G., *Epistolarity: Approaches to a Form* (Columbus, OH: Ohio State University Press, 1982).

Blain, V., P. Clements, I. Grundy (eds), *The Feminist Companion to Literature in English: Women Writers from the Middle Ages to the Present* (London and New Haven, CT: Yale University Press, 1990).

Bostic, H., *The Fiction of Enlightenment. Women of Reason in the French Eighteenth Century* (Newark, DE: University of Delaware Press, 2010).

Chai-Elsholz, R., 'Textual Allusions and Narrative Voice in the *Lettres de Milady Juliette Catesby* and Its English Translation', in A. Cointre, A. Rivara, F. Lautel-Ribstein (eds), *La Traduction du discours amoureux 1660–1830* (Metz: Centre d'Etudes de la Traduction, Université de Metz, 2006), pp. 119–42.

Cook, E. H., *Epistolary Bodies: Gender and Genre in the Eighteenth-Century Republic of Letters* (Stanford, CA: Stanford University Press, 1996).

Crosby, E., *Une Romancière oubliée: Madame Riccoboni, sa vie, ses oeuvres, sa place dans la littérature anglaise et française du XVIIIe siècle* (Genève: Slatkine Reprints, 1970).

Dijk, S. van, 'Lire ou broder: Deux occupations féminines dans l'oeuvre de Mmes de Graffigny, Riccoboni et de Charrière', in J. Herman, P. Pelckmans (eds), *L'Epreuve du lecteur: Livres et lectures dans le roman d'Ancien Régime* (Louvain: Peeters, 1995), pp. 351–60.

Goldsmith, E. C. (ed.), *Writing the Female Voice: Essays on Epistolary Literature* (Boston, MA: Northeastern University Press, 1989).

Goldsmith, E. C., and D. Goodman (eds), *Going Public: Women and Publishing in Early Modern France* (Ithaca, NY and London: Cornell University Press, 1995).

Grimm, F. M. *et al.*, *Correspondance littéraire, philosophique et critique ...* , ed. M. Tourneux (Paris: Garnier, 1880).

Kaplan, M. S., 'Epistolary Silence in Françoise de Graffigny's *Lettres d'une Péruvienne* (1747)', *Atlantis: A Women's Studies Journal / Revue d'Études sur les Femmes* 29.1 (2004), pp. 106–12.

—, 'Marie Jeanne Riccoboni's *Lettres d'Elisabeth Sophie de Vallière*: A Feminist Reading', *Women In French Studies*, 13 (2005), pp. 25–36.

—, 'Widows and Riccoboni's *Lettres d'Adélaïde de Dammartin*', in N. Bérenguier, C. R. Montfort and J. Rogers (eds), *Eclectic Expressions: Women's Triumphs, Past and Present. Selected Essays from Women in French International Conference 2006, Women In French Studies* (special issue 2008), pp. 58–65.

Lanser, S. S., 'In a Class by Herself: Self-Silencing in Riccoboni's *Abeille*', *Fictions of Authority: Women Writers and Narrative Voice* (Ithaca, NY and London: Cornell University Press, 1992), pp. 45–60.

—, 'The Rise of the Novel, the Fall of the Voice: Juliette's Catesby's Silencing', *Fictions of Authority: Women Writers and Narrative Voice* (Ithaca, NY and London: Cornell University Press, 1992), pp. 25–41.

*The Letters of Hannah More*, ed. R. Brimley Johnson (London: John Lane The Bodley Head Ltd., 1925).

MacArthur, E. J., 'Devious Narratives: Refusal of Closure in Two Eighteenth-Century Epistolary Novels', *Eighteenth-Century Studies*, 21 :1 (Autumn 1987), pp. 1–20.

Mallinson, J., 'Reconquering Peru: Eighteenth-Century Translations of Graffigny's *Lettres d'une Péruvienne*', *SVEC*, 6 (2007), pp. 291–310.

Martin, M., *Selling Beauty. Cosmetics, Commerce, and French Society, 1750–1830* (Baltimore, MD: Johns Hopkins University Press, 2009).

McMullen, L., *An Odd Attempt in a Woman: The Literary Life of Frances Brooke* (Vancouver, British Columbia: University of British Columbia Press, 1983).

McMurran, M. H., *The Spread of Novels: Translation and Prose Fiction in the Eighteenth Century* (Princeton, NJ: Princeton University Press, 2010).

*Oeuvres complètes de Diderot*, ed. J. Assézat (Paris: Garnier, 1875).

*Orlando: Women's Writing in the British Isles from the Beginnings to the Present*, eds S. Brown, P. Clements, I. Grundy (Cambridge: Cambridge University Press Online, 2006).

Pitcher, E. W., 'The Miscellaneous Periodical Works and Translations of Miss R. Roberts', *Literary Research Newsletter*, 5:3 (1980), pp. 125–8.

Pollak, E., *Incest and the English Novel, 1684–1814* (Baltimore, MD and London: Johns Hopkins University Press, 2003).

Rivara, A., 'Les *Lettres d'une Péruvienne* traduites en Angleterre et en France', in J. Mallinson (ed. and introd.), *Françoise de Graffigny, femme de lettres: Ecriture et réception* (Oxford, England: Voltaire Foundation, 2004), pp. 272–87.

—, 'Les *Lettres d'une Peruvienne* de Mme de Graffigny et leur traduction par Miss Roberts (1774)', in A. Cointre, A. Rivara and F. Lautel-Ribstein (eds), *La Traduction du discours amoureux 1660–1830* (Metz: Centre d'Etudes de la Traduction, Université de Metz, 2006), pp. 65–77.

Showalter, E. Jr, 'Les *Lettres d'une Péruvienne*: Composition, Publication, Suites', *Archives et bibliothèques de Belgique*, 54:1–4 (1983), pp. 14–28.

Sol, A., 'Violence and Persecution in the Drawing Room: Subversive Textual Strategies in Riccoboni's *Miss Juliette Catesby*', in S. Woodward (ed.), *Public Space of the Domestic Sphere/ Espace public de la sphère domestique* (London, ON: Mestengo, 1997), pp. 65–76.

Stewart, J. H., *Gynographs: French Novels by Women of the Late Eighteenth Century* (Lincoln, NE and London: University of Nebraska Press, 1993).

—, *The Enlightenment of Age: Women, Letters and Growing Old in Eighteenth-Century France* (Oxford: Voltaire Foundation, 2010).

Thomas, R., '"Ma Soeur, mon amie"': Friends as Family in Madame Riccoboni's Fiction', *New Perspectives on the Eighteenth Century*, 5:1 (2008), pp. 13–19.

—, 'Remarriage and its Discontents: Young Widows in Mme Riccoboni's Fiction', *Women in French Studies*, 17 (2009), pp. 54–65.

*Women Writers*, ed. S. van Dijk, http://neww.huygens.knaw.nl/.

# NOTE ON THE TEXTS

## *Letters from Juliet Lady Catesby*

Riccoboni published the first edition of her *Lettres de Milady Juliette Catesby à Milady Henriette Campley, son amie* anonymously in 1759[1] in Paris although the title page states 'Amsterdam'. Brooke published the first edition of her English translation on 23 April 1760 in London,[2] also anonymously; a second edition appeared later that same year. Five more editions followed during Brooke's lifetime, in 1763, 1764, 1769, 1780 and 1786; Dodsley in London published all seven editions. For this book, I have used the first edition of Brooke's translation dated 1760 and held at Chawton House Library, and compared it to Riccoboni's 1759 French original.

Brooke's translation of the novel was the first, but certainly not the last: eighteenth-century translations followed in German (1760), Italian (1769, and a noteworthy adaptation by Casanova in 1780), Danish (1780), Russian (1797), Swedish (1799) and Portuguese (1800). Like its French original, the English translation became a bestseller. Readers and critics generally liked it: the *Critical Review* claimed it was 'well executed, and the delicacy of thought and expression in the French original, happily preserved in the English version'[3] and the *London Magazine* said that 'the letters abound with fine sentiments, and contain the agreeable relation of the amours of Lady Catesby and Lord Ossory'.[4] The *Monthly Review* liked the letters less: 'they are too destitute, however, of both narrative or humour, to be very generally admired'.[5] Riccoboni herself wrote of Brooke's translation in a letter dated 31 August 1765 that 'il faut lui rendre une justice due, ce qu'elle entend elle l'exprime très bien' ('we have to give her credit, for what she understands, she expresses very well').[6] Her opinion of Brooke was undoubtedly negatively influenced, however, by her good friend David Garrick's deteriorating relationship with her translator.[7]

I have altered the first edition as little as possible, but in order to facilitate reading, I have curtailed the use of italics of which Riccoboni was quite fond and which Brooke also used profusely in her text: italics for the days of the week, place names, place indications and proper names have been eliminated. However, in an effort to be truer to the original, I have kept them for all quotations within letters. In later editions, starting in 1769, quotation marks are introduced. I have eliminated all capitals for regular (non-proper) nouns. I have not indicated punctuation changes in later editions, but they are included in the Errata listed in the first edition and reproduced as textual variants. A short list of silent corrections is also present. There, and for the textual variants, I use '1760a' to refer to Brooke's first 1760 edition and '1760b' to refer to her second 1760 edition. Textual variants other than the Errata are included if they are corrections or change the meaning of the original, but excluded if they are clearly typographical errors.

I have commented on the English translation only if it differs significantly from the French original. This excludes for instance cases where the words supposedly quoted do not correspond exactly to those in the original as well as cases where Brooke has chosen not to translate implied facts, such as when a letter is inserted and Riccoboni details who wrote it and to whom (e.g., 'Billet de Milord d'Ossery à Milady Catesby'; 'Note from Lord Ossory to Lady Catesby'), while Brooke only indicates the addressee ('To Lady Catesby') or when Riccoboni says specifically 'à Londres' ('to London') and Brooke says merely 'to town'. All translations in the editorial material are mine unless otherwise indicated.

## *The Peruvian Letters*

Graffigny published her first edition of *Lettres d'une Péruvienne* anonymously in late 1747 in Paris,[8] but the title page reads 'Peine' ('trouble, sorrow'), the author's nickname for the city. The following year, a seven-letter continuation to the novel appeared anonymously also in Paris: [Peine], *Suite des Lettres d'une Péruvienne* [*Continuation to the Letters from a Peruvian Woman*], which Graffigny attributed to Charles de Fieux de Mouhy (1701–84).[9] In response to criticism particularly of the ending, Graffigny published an expanded version of her novel in 1752, without however directly addressing the criticism or changing the ending. Roberts published the first and only edition of her translation and continuation on 18 April 1774 with Cadell in London[10] and placed her name on the title page, for the first time acknowledging one of her texts. For this book, I have used Roberts's translation and continuation held at Chawton House Library. Since Roberts based her translation on Graffigny's 1747 text (rather than the 1752 one which is now generally considered authoritative) and the anonymous 1748 *Suite* [*Continuation*], I have compared her translation to those two French originals.

Roberts's was not the first English translation of Graffigny's text, for it appeared much earlier in 1748.[11] Eighteenth-century translations into other languages include Italian (1754), Russian (1791) and Spanish and German (1792).[12] While the French original became a bestseller, Roberts's translation and continuation never appeared in a second edition, in spite of overall positive reviews. Thus, the *London Review* called it 'a spirited and easy translation'[13] without commenting on the continuation, and the *Monthly Review* stated that 'we shall not, in any probability, ever have a better translation of them [*Peruvian*

*Letters*], than the present'. About the continuation, it added that 'the design of converting the Indian princess to the Christian religion ... was commendable in Miss Roberts'.[14] The *Critical Review*, which apparently did not know the translator's sex, said: 'If the familiarity of the subject should be found to diminish, in some degree, the enthusiasm of a lover who is converted to Christianity, it must at least be acknowledged, that Mr. Roberts has written with a laudable regard to virtue, and that his supplement is calculated to instill religious sentiments, as well as to afford rational entertainment' (478).[15] *Town & Country Magazine* reiterated the concept of virtue: 'The second volume is written to make the Indian princess a convert to Christianity. The first volume is translated with spirit, and the latter is penned to advance the cause of virtue and religion'.[16]

I have altered Roberts's edition as little as possible. Thus, I have maintained the capitals she used for some common nouns such as Quipos, Mamas, Temple and Sun, as they were copied directly from Graffigny who had Zilia employ them as an expression of her cultural and linguistic alterity. I have commented on the English translation only if it differs significantly from the French original. Graffigny's text contains no less than forty-four footnotes about Peru and Peruvian culture. In order to distinguish them from my Editorial Notes, I have kept hers as footnotes marked with symbols (*†‡), while my Editorial Notes are marked with superscript numbers, starting with 1. The Editorial Notes are followed by a short list of silent corrections. All translations in the editorial material are mine unless otherwise indicated.

## Notes

1. It carried a publication date of 1759, but an early review actually came out in late 1758 in *L'Année littéraire*, 8 (December 1758), pp. 289–302.
2. *Daily Advertiser*, 23 April 1760.
3. *Critical Review*, 9 (May 1760), p. 420.
4. *London Magazine*, 29 (April 1760), p. 224.
5. *Monthly Review*, 22 (June 1760), p. 521.
6. *Mme Riccoboni's Letters,* ed. J. C. Nicholls, p. 54.
7. See Introduction, p. xi.
8. For a succinct publication timeline, see E. Showalter Jr, 'Les *Lettres d'une Péruvienne*: composition, publication, suites', *Archives et bibliothèques de Belgique*, 54:1–4 (1983), pp. 21–3.
9. E. Showalter, 'Les *Lettres d'une Péruvienne*: composition, publication, suites', p. 25.
10. *Daily Advertiser*, 18 April 1774.
11. *Letters Written by a Peruvian Princess, translated from the French* (London: J. Brindley, 1748). Chawton House Library holds this text as well.
12. J. Mallinson, 'Reconquering Peru: Eighteenth-century translations of Graffigny's *Lettres d'une Péruvienne*', *SVEC*, 6 (2007), p. 291.
13. *London Review*, 1 (1775), p. 516.
14. *Monthly Review*, 51 (August 1774), p. 162.
15. *Critical Review*, 39 (June 1775), p. 478.
16. *Town & Country Magazine*, 7 (August 1775), p. 436.

# LETTERS

FROM

## JULIET LADY CATESBY,

### TO HER FRIEND

## LADY HENRIETTA CAMPLEY.

Translated from the French.

LONDON,
Printed for R. and J. Dodsley, in Pall-Mall,
MDCCLX.

# LETTERS
## FROM
## JULIET LADY CATESBY,
## TO HER FRIEND
## LADY HENRIETTA CAMPLEY

### LETTER I.

Summer-Hill, Tuesday.

With six horses on full speed, relays properly disposed, and an air of the most eager haste, I fly, accompanied by persons for whom I have very little regard, to others, for whom I have no regard at all: I abandon my dearest friends; I leave you, you whom I love so tenderly: Ah! why this departure! this haste![1] why press to arrive, where I do not wish to be! To remove myself, – from whom? – From Lord Ossory.[2] Ah! my dear Henrietta, who would once have told me, I should ever have fled from him? Is he not the same object, whose loss, I imagined, would have deprived me of life; who, during two years, was always present to my idea, and, whom nothing has power to make me forget? I fly, then, that I may not meet those eyes, that mine have sought with so much pleasure; where my destiny seemed wrote,[a] and whose glance once ruled all the movements of my soul. Strange alteration! what different effects are produced by the same cause?[b] Heavens! what was my surprize at seeing him! How did his mourning, and his air of sorrow strike me![3] How ought his wife to regret the loss of life? What difficulty had I not to turn my head at parting! Into what a state did that sight! – But, could you conceive that he has dared to call at my door, – to insist on seeing me, – to write to me, – to imagine I would open his letters? How audacious is this man? But, are they not all so?[4]

I am still astonished at the step I have taken. I tell myself every moment I have acted rightly; I tell myself so, but I do not feel it sufficiently: I seek for reasons to applaud myself on the part I have pursued; I find them, but it is in my

pride only. I experience, my dear, that the heart has no taste for those weak lenitives, in which our vanity finds so much consolation.

In fine, I am gone: Behold me, fifty miles from London, and yet not *dead*;
assure my Lord Castle-Cary[5] of this. In spite of his predictions I did not *faint
away* at the foot of the first *beech*;[6] the *afflicted graces* have not yet raised for
me that *beautiful tomb* in which he already saw me laid. Tell him that I do not
repent: I can do violence to my sentiments; I can suffer; but I know not how to
repent. Adieu! my amiable Henrietta! When you have told his Lordship all this,
tell yourself, that no-body loves you so much as I do.


## LETTER II.

Wednesday, Sir John Aston's.[7]

We are going to leave a very disagreeable house, the master of which, is still more
disagreeable.[8] He is one of those troublesome people, one is so sorry to meet
with; the species of whom, is, however, too common; one of those men[9] who
fatigue one by their attention to please, and never speak, but in a strain of tedious compliment. He has given us a very plentiful, and a very bad supper; served
up with so much ceremony, and such an air of preparation, as could not fail of
making the whole company sensible how much trouble they had occasioned.

Sir John has been married six months, as you know; his lady is a young
woman, long, lean, pale, foolish, proud, with a termagant air;[10] a little head, set
upon a thin neck, and an eternal sneer, without the least trace of gaiety on her
countenance. This couple seemed to me,[a] extremely well paired.

Sir Harry[11] is very much attached to Lady Elizabeth; except my own, I have
seen few brothers so obliging. But, as our virtues borrow something from our
temperament, I have discovered that he is naturally attentive and officious; he
loves to mix in every thing, to make himself necessary. We have already had two
or three quarrels: He will stiffle me in the coach, for fear I should get cold; I let
down the glass, he pulls it up, and I again let it down; he makes grave represen-
tations to me on the subject; I, with all gentleness, explain to him my will; he
insists; I am obstinate; he gives it up with reluctance; and when I have put him
into a very bad humour, he chides, and I recover the liberty of breathing.

For Sir James, his character is sweetness, complaisance, and grace, united to
gaiety; he speaks just what he ought; he expresses himself agreeably, and what
he says amuses: Lady Elizabeth is enchanted with him: You know how lively
her approbations are; it is happy for her, they are not lasting enough to convert
themselves into tenderer sentiments.

I endeavour to busy myself about others, that I may drive away those woes
which bring me back to myself. Sometimes I flatter myself that I no longer love;

that what I felt at seeing my Lord Ossory was more owing to hatred, than to a softer passion. – I hate him, perhaps, – Ah! why should I not hate him? – I hope at least, that I shall become calm enough to see him, to speak to him, to treat him with the most mortifying disdain. – O, no – I will never speak to him, will never see him. – Here is Sir Harry, he teases me, he will not wait; this is one of his faults; not the least patience. Adieu! love me, love me as you know you are beloved by me.

## LETTER III.

Thursday, Lord Danby's.[12]

I write to you, from the most agreeable place, perhaps, in nature: From my window I have a view of woods, waters, meadows, the most beautiful landscape imaginable: Every thing expresses calmness, and tranquillity: This smiling abode, is an image of the soft peace, which reigns in the soul of the sage who inhabits it. This amiable dwelling carries one insensibly to reflect; to retire into one's self; but one cannot at all times relish this kind of retreat; one may find in the recesses of the heart, more importunate pursuers than those from whom solitude delivers us.

Lord Danby received us perfectly well; could one imagine a man like him would not think retirement a misfortune? It is rare, very rare, my dear, that persons born in a high rank, educated in the hurry of the world, in the toilsome inactivity of a court,[13] can find in themselves the resources against lassitude. The remembrance of the past, often offers nothing to their view but a chain of follies and weaknesses, which seen in cold blood, appear in their true colour. One must have all my Lord Danby's virtues, to find the examination of one's own heart a pleasing employment.

I have found out, that Sir Harry is as curious as he is attentive: He stopped our women an hour, to ask a thousand questions of Betty: He has remarked the sighs that escape me,[a] he fancies there is a secret in one of my boxes, he has offered her ten guineas to assure him of it. He is *astonished that I write to you every day; he cannot conceive the reason of so regular a correspondence. Is it really to you I write?* What think you of these impertinent enquiries? they cost me twelve guineas, for I fancy I ought to reward Betty's fidelity, for fear, upon reflection, she should repent of it.

The man knows not what he would have,[14] he wearies me, he displeases me. – I believe really, he intends. – Ah! how odious would he then be to me. – Don't I see him? – Heaven! what a look![b] – He certainly divines I am speaking of him. It is my letter which puts him[c] into this ill humour. – I promise you, Sir Harry, I shall write every day, therefore be so good to use yourself to it.[d] – But his sister comes, – I must leave you; my dear friend.[15] Adieu! tell my Lord Castle-Cary, I do not forget him.

## LETTER IV.

From the mansion of Sir George Howard, your humble adorer.
Friday.

I congratulate you, my Henrietta, on so obstinately refusing to become the mistress of this savage habitation. Miss Biddulph,[16] who, upon your refusal, has accepted the heart, the hand, and the whole immense person of Sir George our host, is a much properer person than yourself, to procure him that species of happiness, which he is capable of tasting.

Lady Howard is a very little woman, handsome enough, and not coquet;[17] she manages his family, governs his tenants, scolds his servants;[18] brings him children, works tapestry for his rooms, does not read for fear of spoiling her eyes, consults the chaplain, interdicts love in all her dominions, marries her dependants, treats the most trifling affairs seriously, and makes an important business of the least thing in the world.

Let us, however, see a little nearer this happy woman, this woman, who will laugh till her last hour: If she laughs, my dear, we should weep, we, who so little resemble her. We should think it strange, if this notable woman had more merit than we; it is, however, certain, she has more happiness. Her life is simple and uniform; but she is quiet and useful; To-morrow will produce no painful change in her situation; her soul is always open to the impression of pleasure. But what pleasure, you will say? Ah! my dear Henrietta, are there, then, so many kinds? A long study of ourselves, reason, and knowledge, do they render us more happy? I know not what idea others have of this light we call, understanding; it appears to my imagination like a torch, which the first breath of air may extinguish: It brightens the darkness a little, but does not half dissipate it; its weak light is sufficient to show us, that we walk on the edge of a precipice, but not to point out the slippery path where our feet may fail us; we fall, my dear, and when at the bottom of the abyss, have the advantage of reflecting that if we had seen clearer, we had not been there.

I am not absolutely unhappy: I begin to believe, that the misfortunes we bring on ourselves, are easier to support than those we owe to others. A kind of, I know not what secret emotion assists us to support them; I wish it may not be vanity. Adieu! my amiable friend! How does my Lord Castle-Cary in my absence? I am no longer present to make up your quarrels, therefore, you ought to engage in them the seldomer. When he vexes you a little, remember he is my relation and my friend: He has many estimable qualities, he is worthy of your heart, – If, however, there is a man in the world, worthy the tenderness of a woman, who thinks justly.

## LETTER V.

Saturday, Mortimer-House[19]

We are now, my dear Henrietta, at a most delightful seat; during two months, gaiety has presided here: It belongs to a widow,[20] scarce twenty. Enchanted with her new state, she comes to pass the year of her mourning here, only to meditate in peace on her future choice, when decency will permit her to make herself amends for what she suffered with an old husband, whom she hated with all her heart. She has the most beautiful face you can conceive, a fine heighth, an air of dignity, and a most engaging sincerity; in giving an account of her sufferings, she scarce can smother her laughter. *The old Lord was jealous, and she could have overreach'd him, she could.* – This agreeable silly creature[a] has just as much sense, as is necessary to amuse herself, and to please.

Miss Annabella, her sister, is a very different creature: Was never out of this magnificent seat, where she has always lived with her father only. Her figure is noble, and interesting, her air sweet and delicate; she has a great deal of breeding, and more sentiment. She wants nothing, in short, but knowledge of[b] the world; but if she has not all the graces which that bestows, she is free from the vices to which it leads; Vices, which, it is so difficult to avoid in polite circles,[21] where they have found the contemptible art of forgiving mutually every defect of the heart. I am always enraged, when I hear this criminal indulgence, honoured with the name of softness of manners, knowledge of human nature, and a condescension indispensable in society. O! this Sir Harry; – he is insupportable; every thing displeases him.[22] – I thought him of a more equal temper: People must be very amiable to appear so to those who see them every day; I am out of patience with him;[23] he advises me to throw away a nosegay[24] that Sir James has gathered himself, and has just given me; Sir Harry has not breathed since I have had it; he brings me twenty examples of illness, occasioned by the too strong perfume of jonquills; he assures me they are very bad for the head. As I see his impertinent jealousy, I shall keep the nosegay; I would keep it, if it gave me a thousand headachs. I shall be at Winchester to-morrow, I shall find your letters there, it is the only pleasure I promise myself. Adieu! My tenderest respects to my Lord Castle-Cary.

## LETTER VI.

Sunday, Winchester.[25]

I received your letters, as soon as I arrived here; you cannot doubt, my dear Henrietta, of the sincere pleasure I felt in reading them. Every moment of my life, your friendship has been dear to me: For a long time my heart was satisfied with it: How happy was I then! If my soul is now possessed, too feelingly possessed, by less voluntary, and more tumultuous sentiments, believe me, they have not weakened that tender and solid affection, which attaches me to you: The amiable qualities, which gave birth to this friendship, owe nothing to illusion; nor can[a] either time or absence destroy it!

My firmness astonishes you. Ah! my good God! This effort, which you admire, would, if I was able to examine it without passion, lose much of the value we both set upon it. What is it that I sacrifice? Of what good do I deprive myself? Of the sweetness, perhaps, of being again deceived! But can I abandon myself to this pleasure, when I have lost that of deceiving myself?

You bid me pardon my Lord Ossory, or think no more of him. Pardon him? Ah! never! think no more of him! I think of him certainly as little as I can; I no longer think of him with pleasure: I no longer think of him with regret; – I think of him. – Alas! my dear! Because it is impossible for me not to think of him. Remembrance will not leave us; we fancy we lose it in the world, but a moment of solitude restores all its force, which dissipation seemed to have taken away. When alone, that idea, once so dear to me, is ever present to my imagination; I see again that form. – How did the soul, which, I believed, animated that ungrateful man, embellish all his features! What a perfect creature did it offer to my eyes! Ah! why, why has it torn away the amiable veil which hid his vices, and his falshood, from me? – So much candor in that countenance, and so much perfidy, so much ingratitude, in that heart! Oh! that he is not as noble, as generous as I believed him? – Yes, my greatest misfortune is, being forced to despise him. Adieu! my good, my beloved friend! I am not in a state to reply to all you ask. – How weak am I still! – Ought I to speak of him![26] – I can fly him, renounce, hate, detest him: But to forget him. – Alas! I cannot forget him.

## LETTER VII.

Wednesday,[27] Winchester.

I have this instant received a letter from my Lord Castle-Cary, which he certainly has not communicated to you. He treats my flight, as a piece of female cunning; he does not absolutely tell me so, but that is what he *would* say. He thinks my intention is to mortify *poor Lord Ossory*, to try him, to make him miserable, and at last to pardon him. The idea which he has of my designs, does not give me a high opinion of the manner in which he himself pardons. Let this suffice, till I am in a humour to answer him. I should, indeed, despise myself, if I was capable of so low an artifice; if, believing I could forgive him – forgive him, Henrietta! – If I could, and had the cruelty to make him wait for my forgiveness, and to play with the suspence of a man, that I meant to make happy. I should despise myself indeed.[28] No, my dear Henrietta, I will never oblige any one to purchase a benefit

I intend them. Either I know myself very ill, or it is not in my nature to pardon him. I should promise it in vain. The sorrows I have felt, are forever engraven on my memory: I am very far from desiring it should be in my power, to inflict an equal share of misery on him: My hatred is as generous as my friendship was tender: I shall confine its effects to flying the presence of the ingrate. My Lord Castle-Cary pretends, that all resentment ought to yield to a sincere repentance. With my inferiors, I will govern myself by this maxim, but never with my friends.[29] But, my dear, it will not be useless to make a little remark here. It is, that men only establish this principle, in hopes to take advantage of it: Accustom yourself to think, with my Lord Castle-Cary, that repentance effaces all faults, and, depend on it, he will provide himself of sufficient occasions to repent. – His letter displeases me, I confess: I renounce his approbation: It would cost me too dear, if I must buy it by a weakness, which would degrade me in my own eyes: I have always regarded as the greatest of all misfortunes, the loss of one's own good opinion: One may enjoy the esteem of others, without deserving it. We may owe it to dissimulation; but what must become of our internal peace, when we can no longer esteem ourselves? My Lord Castle-Cary is very singular to expect I should submit to his decision, an affair of which he knows so little. Reprimand him, reprimand him heartily, I beg of you.

## LETTER VIII.

Tuesday, Winchester.

You ask me, how I spend my time, with whom I am, and who of my present companions are most agreeable to me. Alas! I am weary of myself; I am with all the world, and no-body pleases me enough to engage my attention. We are here, fifteen, or sixteen of us from London, without counting the neighbouring people of fashion, of whom the house is always full. This continual crowd rather distracts than amuses me.

Lord Wilton[30] has a violent passion for the fine arts: He has laboured hard to acquire them, but Nature has denied him the talents which bring them into view, and that taste, which only can give them perfection. With a strong voice, he sings disagreeably; and dances with a bad grace, though industriously exact in the steps. He designs correctly, paints little screens, which are neither pretty nor ugly; and makes detestable verses with great facility. Every day gives birth to a thousand couplets, and madrigals, in which Cupid, Venus, Hebe, all Olympus,[a] find themselves,[31] whether they will or no, at the feet of the terrestrial divinities of the castle. – You assume, when you arrive, the name which rhyme[32] is pleased to confer on you. As to the rest, my Lord is a worthy man; I do not believe he has a fault, except that of desiring to be what he is not. Born with simplicity, courtesy, and a moderate understanding, if he had not pretended to superiority, he had escaped the mortification of seeing himself ridiculous. His lady. – But some-body comes. – Who is it? – Ah! who can it be but Sir Harry! – But who has subjected me to Sir Harry's importunities? Why must I suffer them? What right has he to weary me thus? Ah! my dear Henrietta, what enemy to the human race, invented that falshood, which, under the name of politeness, commands our civilities, and forces us to constrain ourselves? – This troublesome creature gets admittance into my closet; insensibly he gains ground; he is always at my side.[33] – He almost reads what I am writing. – I wish he read this, to teach him. – I continue writing on purpose – *Sir Harry, be so obliging, – give me leave.* – He bows, sighs, and stays; he stays indeed. In the humor I am in, I wish he would speak, that he would tell me, he loves me. – I would give a thousand guineas, he would make that confession. – Since my ill stars will fix him here, I must leave you.

Tuesday night.[34]

As I was going to tell you this morning, Lady Wilton is very amiable; she thinks justly, behaves with decorum, and without affectation; she is handsome, well made; by her bloom, one would imagine her younger than Lady Elizabeth her sister. She loves her Lord, sees his weak side, never laughs at it herself; and by her serious air, prevents others from rallying him. Devout towards God, she serves him without ostentation; severe to herself, complaisant to her friends, easy and gentle to all the world, she claims little attention, but attracts the highest, and possesses the respect and sincere admiration of all who know her.

We have here the new Countess of Ranelagh,[35] a little giddy-brain, who loves nothing but noise and play; she is pretty, but without character; How disagreeable a state! I have observed, that this species of people adopt the faults of every body they converse with.

But she, who pretends to the glory of eclipsing all, of conquering all hearts, is the beautiful Countess of Southampton;[36] always lovely, lovely from morning till night, ever in the attitude of sitting for her picture, she thinks of nothing but how to appear most beautiful, and talks of nothing, but the effects of her charms. If any man[37] addresses his conversation to her, she is so convinced he is going to make her a compliment, that an air of thanks precedes her attention to what he is to say. All our ladies are busied in rallying her; in spite of every thing they can say, the Countess pleases all eyes, but, she pleases the eyes only.

We have Sir William Manly,[38] gay, agreeable, simple, plain; a true Englishman, attached to the manners, to the laws, to the customs of his country. He is of a very ancient family, but little distinguished by court-favour; and, thinks his birth infinitely preferable to new, though higher titles. Possessor of the finest estate in the county, he lives in the midst of his dependants, like a tender father, surrounded by his children, who adore him; without ever thinking he is above them, except when his superiority can remove their miseries, or procure them any advantages. In the commission of the peace for a large county, he has laboured to instruct himself, in what so many others neglect, the duties of this trust,[a] and joins knowledge to the most equitable integrity. This is a man, my dear; and the only one here, who deserves that appellation.

But the idol of all our ladies,[b] is Sydney,[39] the youngest of those Sydneys you are acquainted with: He is a young baronet, not very rich, but infinitely proud notwithstanding; he is tall, well made, has the finest hair in the world, admirable teeth, some wit, very little sense, and a great deal of trifling jargon. He knows nothing, talks of every thing, lies with impudence; is knowing in dogs, horses, baubles, despises every body, admires himself sincerely, decides without ceasing, tires people of taste, shines amongst fools, and passes here for a charming fellow: Adieu! my dearest friend! I embrace my Lord Castle-Cary, though I do not pardon him.

## LETTER IX.

Wednesday, Winchester.

They have brought me two of your letters; I ought to have received them yesterday; I was very uneasy about them: Sir Harry thought they must have been forgot, he went seven miles to enquire for them. I believe I have a bad heart, for I am angry at having this obligation to him.

What you tell me of the rupture between Sir Charles and Lady Selby, appears to me incredible. What? that lover, so passionate, who adored her, who could not live without seeing her, and who threatened in his jealous furies,[c] to stab himself before her eyes? He has quitted her, and with that unconcernedness, that eclat, without troubling himself either about her, or the world! – Happy men! what advantage does difference of education, prejudice, and custom, give to that daring sex, who blush at nothing, say and do, whatever they please! What arts will man not practice, when impelled by interest, or by pride! He cringes at our feet, without being ashamed; our scorn does not abase him, our disdain can not repulse him: Mean when he desires, insolent when he hopes, ungrateful when he has obtained. Supple, and insinuating serpent; who, like that in Milton, takest every form, triest every art to engage our attention; and then conveyest thyself from the snare thou hast spread for us![40] – Poor Lady Selby! How I pity her! How bitter is it[d] to be abandoned! Ah! my dear Henrietta! with what levity you speak of her situation! If you had ever felt that tormenting misery. – May you never feel it! – This relation has recalled to my memory those hours, when my erring heart – But I will think of it no more.

Have I told you, that we have here the famous Countess of Sunderland, so beautiful, so indifferent, so beloved, and so esteemed, not only in England, but in the northern courts, of which she was the admiration? She is near forty, and does not appear thirty.ª I cannot better paint her to you, than by sending you the copy of a letter she wrote to Sir William Manly: He has preserved it carefully ever since he received it, which is thirteen years. He has traced the outlines of it to me, which has given me a great desire to see it, and he has promised me to send for the box in which it is kept. This letter, he says, perfectly characterises the countess. He was in love with her, and cannot see her even now, without emotion. He had wrote her a declaration of love, and it is her answer to that declaration, which I am to see. As soon as I have this wonderful epistle, I will communicate it to you. Adieu! my charming friend.

## LETTER X.

Thursday, Winchester.

You are cruelly exact, my dear Henrietta: You promised me not to mention Lord Ossory, and you keep your word, with a punctuality that I admire. I did not wish you should entertain me with his sentiments, with my own, or the caprice which brings him back to me: But, to leave me in ignorance, whether he is yet in London, whether he intends staying there, what he is doing, whether he endeavours to see my Lord Castle-Cary; this is hard, yes, very hard, indeed. It is sometimes kind to fail a little in complying with one's request  – But, why this vain curiosity? – What interest have I? – Persevere, – Tell me nothing of him, my temper is grown very bad, every thing displeases me: Sir Harry makes this place disagreeable to me; he besets me, he fatigues me, wherever I turn I see only him;[41] he follows me, he meets me every-where. Scarce am I a moment in my closet, before he enters with an air of some important business: You would suppose, by his looks, something very interesting brought him there; he has nothing to say to me, but, perhaps, to bid me good-morrow. He goes out, he comes back, he seems disturbed, he takes out of Betty's hands, whatever she was going to bring me, disorders my books, throws them down, asks me for tea,[42] goes away without drinking it; returns to tell me he is ill, overwhelmed with anguish, that he is dying. He walks with his arms across, sighs, groans, does not die, and exhausts my patience to that degree, that I find it difficult to behave to him with politeness. How I hate love! How I hate all who entertain the cruel design of inspiring me with it! – Sir James desires a moment's conversation with me: He has formed a project, he says, which he will submit to my decision: He regards me with an air that – He speaks to me with such a tone of voice – What can he have to say to me? – I have one obligation to Lord Ossory, the remembrance of him will be my preservative, my eternal preservative, against all his sex. Who can appear amiable to me, after my Lord Ossory? Who can inspire me with confidence, when my Lord Ossory has deceived me? How different are all I see from him? – But, my dear, I must think no more of him.[43] – Alas! how difficult is it to forget him!

I enclose the letter I promised you: Sir William has allowed me to take a copy; you will have the goodness to send it me back?

To Sir William Manly.

My esteem for Sir William Manly engages me to explain myself to him, with a freedom, which I should, perhaps, dispense with myself, from using to another. You are amiable, well made, modest; you appear prudent, and I believe you discreet. So many perfections, if you join constancy to them, will render the woman, who loves you, happy. They would justify her choice in her own eyes,[44] as well as in those of others: An uncommon advantage, which would determine me in your favour, if love was a sentiment to which I chose to give up my heart. My reasons for avoiding this passion, are not founded on those prejudices, which have for a long time lost much of their influence: The present custom allows me to have a lover, and, perhaps, I should not esteem myself less, if my taste led me to admit one. What I owe to my Lord Sunderland, would, however, restrain me, if he had the generosity[45] to think our promises were mutual. He neglected me at a time, when the slightest complaisance would have engaged my most tender attachment: I sincerely thank him, for leaving me to that indifference, which he deserves I should feel for him: It is extreme, he knows it, and if I do not give publick marks of it, it is only from regard to myself, not thinking it decent to show contempt for the man, whose name I bear.

Left to my own reflections, I have long made it my employment to consider with a philosophick attention,[46] the world, the different seasons of human life; the duration, or, to speak with more propriety, the perpetual vicissitude, of all sublunary things. My most serious study has been to examine the virtues, and the failings of my own sex:[47] I have endeavoured to discover the guides which are given us, to lead us safely through the difficult paths in which we tread.[48] I have seen, Sir William, that coquetry, weakness, and pride, are the portion of both sexes; but particularly of my own. To pride, well understood, and turned towards its noblest object, women owe their virtue. Coquetry, in just bounds, makes them agreeable; Weakness makes some wretched, and others contemptible. Our taste ranks us indispensably in one of these classes; mine has decided for me, pride is my choice. Those who esteem nothing but the frivolous advantage of being lovely, pass one part of their lives, in applauding themselves on their charms, and the other in lamenting their loss. What a ridiculous part does a coquet play, when she has no longer those attractions she would still be thought to possess! Weak women are to be pitied; the sensibility of their hearts,[49] is a rock on which their reason is shipwrecked: Too often they preserve the habit of loving, long after they have lost the power to please: They become the jest of young ingrates, who address, deceive, and expose them to publick contempt and infamy.

Pride has none of these inconveniences; she enjoys the past, the present, and the future; has always the same pleasures, age cannot destroy them; she loves and admires herself forever. Is one not happier, Sir William, in indulging a sentiment, which one is certain, will always be pleasing,[50] than in giving way to those which captivate our wills, and make our happiness depend on the caprice and inconstancy of others? In whatever light my choice may appear to you, believe that nothing can make me renounce it. If my friendship is dear to you, abandon forever, the useless design of troubling the sweetness of my life; and by a conduct conformable to my principles, render yourself worthy of my confidence, and my esteem.

Behold[51] here a woman, who is the object of universal esteem and respect: And wherefore? Because she has loved herself, to such a degree, as to leave no room for the love of any other being. She has excited the admiration of all the world, but she has made the happiness of no-body, possibly, not even of herself. To oppose continually, that tender inclination, which carries us – To what, my dear! To lament one day, the loss of a blessing – which one moment may change into the bitterest anguish. Is tenderness then, so estimable? Are its pleasures great enough, to recompense the pangs with which its loss overwhelms us? I know not whether I see the Countess's virtues, and her reasoning, in a just light: But, her class of weak women, seems to me, that of good hearts.

## LETTER XI.

Friday, Winchester.

How! my dear Henrietta! he is gone! They know not whither! You fear he is in France. – And why fear it! – Ah! whether he stays, or goes abroad, what is it to me? – What interest ought I to take in it? – He is dead to me. – Yet it is sweet, however, to think he lives for no other than myself.[52]

I am afflicted, my dear friend; I know not what I would have: Disgust and insipidity are diffused around me; the manner of living here wearies me, without dissipating my chagrin. Ruinous gaming, long repasts, a great deal of musick, little repose, continual noise, none of those calm delights I promised myself in the country. – You are sure, my Lord Ossory is no longer in town; yet, if his family is there, – one would suppose. – In France? – Why in France? – The Marchioness of Dorchester,[53] whom he once loved, is just gone thither. – Perhaps, his passion for her is revived. – Does my Lord Castle-Cary hide nothing from you! The manner in which he writes to me, gives me suspicions. – Ah! what is all this to me? Why do I torment myself? – Lady Elizabeth begs you will send her a white domino,[54] very genteel, that is, very much adorned. Send me one also; let it be, – my God, whatever you please: It is for a masquerade,[55] that my Lord Wilton is to give: One is fatigued with pleasures here. – To go away without seeing Lord Castle-Cary, without endeavouring to be acquainted with you, to speak to you, – not to strive to find out where I am, to know from myself! – Strange, inconceivable creature! He appeared full of ardor: he *could not live without seeing me again, without appeasing me. – To recover his heart, or to die,* said he to Betty, the day that she came, all in tears, to beg I would receive his visit, and hear him! – And yet he is gone! He is gone, my dear, and has not seen my Lord Castle-Cary. Where-ever he is, I wish him all the happiness I desire for myself. But why, accuse me of cruelty, and reproach me for his departure? Ah! my dear Henrietta! You love Lord Castle-Cary more than you imagine! You adopt his style, without perceiving it. Adieu! Here is Sir Harry: I am very proper at present to converse with him.

## LETTER XII.

Saturday, Winchester.

I am weary to death of this place, my dear. How do I already regret your closet, my own, the sweetness of those conversations[a] which an unbounded confidence[b] rendered so animated, those simple amusements, those hours so usefully past in reading. If chagrin sometimes broke in upon our tranquillity, at least coldness never found a place in our hearts: One seems free here, and yet constraint is hid under that seeming liberty: Every one has the freedom of doing what he will, but not of speaking what he thinks. How little satisfaction does the great world, that brilliant society, called good company, give to those who examine it attentively! It is neither taste nor the heart, nor even the hope of pleasure, which draws together these fantastical beings, born to possess much, to desire more, and to enjoy nothing. They seek each other, without being impelled by affection; they meet without being pleased, and part without regret. What is it then, which unites them? Equality of rank, and of fortune, custom, weariness of themselves; that necessity of dissipation, which they feel perpetually, and which seems attached to greatness, riches, and splendor; in short, to all those goods, which Heaven has not equally distributed to all its creatures.

What bonds, my dear, and what friends for a heart like mine! Little accustomed to disguise my sentiments, what pleasure can I find amongst those to whom I cannot avow them, without reserve? One must be in a very happy situation to amuse oneself with those, for whom one has no tenderness; but I am too full of reflection: I weary you, perhaps. Adieu! in whatever humour I am, I love you always; yes, with all my heart.

## LETTER XIII.

Sunday, Winchester.

Two of your letters! – He is not come back. – They know not where he is – One from my Lord Castle-Cary – He tells me nothing; but he chides me, and in a style, that he would have me take for that of friendship – For that of reason – I will certainly answer him. He complains to me of the little complaisance you shew him: Why, my dear Henrietta, have you not told him what you know of me, what I consented you should communicate to him? *You will not let this man see to what an excess another has been beloved.* The excuse is disobliging; is he then to blame for being angry? Though he is my most esteemed friend, I have a kind of repugnance at confessing to him my weaknesses.[a] I will, however, tell him all: he will at least be convinced, that those caprices with which our sex is reproached, have no share in my resentment. You are not upon good terms with Sir Harry; it is a misfortune I cannot hide from you: he asked me yesterday, why you had deferred your marriage with Lord Castle-Cary till summer: I told him you chose to wait your uncle's return, who was to come back at that time from his embassy. A quarter of an hour after he repeated the same question, and I made him exactly the same reply. *Cruel woman,* he exclaimed, *to impose so hard a condition!* – *If I was Castle-Cary.* – If you were,[b] Sir? Said I, – *I believe.* – You believe? – *I hope your Ladyship is not offended.* – But pray, if you were[c] Castle-Cary? – *I dare not speak; – I have the unhappiness to displease you, – to be troublesome to you, notwithstanding, Madam* – Upon this, he rose[d] from his seat, took Heaven to witness to I know not what, walked about very fast, began a conversation with himself, and all this with an air so gloomy, so afflicted, so melancholy. – And has remained ever since so disconcerted – But here he comes more sad, more indisposed, more dying, than ever: He brings me some pamphlets, I am sure they are worth nothing, even before I see them.[56]

## LETTER XIV.

Monday, Winchester.

I write this post to Lord Castle-Cary, and give him that detail he could not obtain from you. His long friendship for my Lord Ossory[57] persuades him, that the usage of which I complain, cannot be[e] unpardonable. I flatter myself, he will judge otherwise; he shall no longer, at least, have an excuse for tiring me with commonplace arguments. To tell you the truth, my dear Henrietta, I would on no account, that any other person should see this history; it appears to me a disagreeable circumstance to have one, and if I was to think seriously, I should probably destroy this. I spent part of the night in writing it; I cannot express to you how much this

employment has disordered me. As soon as Lord Castle-Cary has read this pacquet, do me the favour to burn it. I cannot answer your letter; you were very gay,
my dear, when you wrote it; I am not enough so at present to reply.

To Lord Castle-Cary.

No, my Lord, I have not that spirit of obstinacy, which could lead me to afflict
myself, that another may share in my pains; but I have that noble firmness, which
distinguishes generous minds from those mean souls, always ready to receive any
impression you wish to give them. Determined in my resolutions by unalterable
principles, I am capable of those exalted efforts which honour demands; and what
I believe my duty, shall always regulate my conduct, and my ideas of happiness. *He
has wronged you*, you say, *he is sensible of it, he returns; you reject his submissions:
this proceeding is inconsistent with your character: you still love; you are still beloved;
you ought to pardon.* And why ought I, my Lord? You had a quarrel with Mr.
Sternill, he had insulted you in a moment of madness, he acknowledged his fault,
he offered you all the satisfaction in his power; you knew he loved you: notwithstanding this, you refused to hear him; nothing could prevail on you to consent
to an accommodation: and for a doubtful jest, a word escaped in the heat of a
foolish dispute, you stretched dead at your feet him, whom you had an hundred
times called by the tender name of friend. Did any one blame your inflexibility?
And why must I pardon? I, who have been insulted with cool reflection, with
premeditated design, under the veil of friendship, of love, of all those sentiments,
which have power to touch a grateful and tender heart? Ah! what right has one
sex to sport with the softness and sensibility of the other?

If custom has made the point of honour different between us, if I am not
forced to revenge myself publickly, ought my resentment to be the less lively?
Ought it to yield to the advances of an enemy, who must have expiated with
his life, a much less injury, had it been offered to your Lordship? What are your
pretensions to insult, or to revenge? What pride persuades you that you have a
right to punish, when you think I ought to pardon?

Don't, my Lord, give me prejudices for laws, nor usurpation as a title; Time
and possession may strengthen the power of injustice, but cannot make it lawful. In the difficult road we have travelled together, Heaven has placed us is the
same path; I have spirit to keep up to you, my Lord, and can allow no distinction
between creatures, who feel, think, and act, in the same manner.[58]

But I hate to declaim; and though your letter is very proper to animate me,
I will carry the subject no farther.[a] I will give you the account you have desired;
I even consent to make you the arbiter between Lord Ossory and me: Prepared,
however, to appeal from your judgment, if you condemn me after the facts I am
going to disclose.

The History of Lady Catesby, and Lord Ossory.

What I am going to confide to your Lordship, is interesting only to a friend. Wholly engrossed by my afflictions, I am, notwithstanding, fully sensible, they contain nothing extraordinary, but the manner in which I have felt them; but events appear to us in a very different light, from the difference of our characters: I am inconsolable under a misfortune, which would, perhaps, have been very light to another.[a]

Married at sixteen, and a widow at eighteen,[59] I returned to London, just at the time you set out for Vienna: nothing then promised me the considerable fortune I have since been mistress of. Without ambition, without fondness for splendor, I did not wish for that fortune! Alas! would my brother still enjoyed it! What riches can make me forget him! How willingly would I part with all this idle pomp to recover a friend so dear to me! You loved him, my Lord, and you know how justly I regret him. He left us to go into France, and I remained with my aunt, who had been a parent to us both. Lady Anne[60] her daughter, marrying Lord Osmond,[61] and my aunt giving up to them her house in Pall-Mall,[b] it was fixed, I should continue with Lady Osmond.

My Lord Catesby's extreme jealousy had accustomed me to retirement: I found little pleasure in the great world: Reading and musick employed all my time. The men thought me amiable; they told me so; but without being insensible to the pleasure of admiration, I was infinitely so to the cares of my lovers. I laughed at their transports; and ridiculing the follies of which love made them guilty, I fancied reason and pride would always secure me from its power.

Soon after my cousin's marriage, we left London for Hertfordshire.[62] Lord Ossory, and Mr. Ashby[63] returned, at that time, one of them from France, and the other from Italy:[64] As they were both friends to my Lord Osmond, they were invited to Hertford, they set out directly, and arrived together. I was with Lady Osmond, when my Lord presented them to her: The moment I cast my eyes on one of them, my taste was for ever fixed.

Lord Ossory professed himself an enemy to love: till I saw him, I was perfectly indifferent: this conformity of humours on which they sometimes rallied us, was the first bond of that friendship, which united us: He talked of love, but it was always to complain of its rigor; he seemed to know only its pains. My heart, which already sympathized with him, took a secret interest in his discourses; I repeated them to myself when alone, and supposing he regretted an unfaithful mistress, I partook of his chagrin: I was astonished how she could ever cease to love him, and it seemed to me, that a woman, who could betray or abandon him, must be born more perfidious than all others.

I past some time, without attending to the pleasure I felt in seeing Lord Ossory: I gave myself up to it without reflection; and only observed, that since his coming to Hertford, every thing was become more interesting to me.

Mr. Ashby declared himself my lover: You know his passions are lively, but of short duration; he addressed me with the most impatient ardor, but that ardor appeared to me importunate. Lord Osmond wished he might please me; he even gave him hopes, but I destroyed them the moment he spoke to me on the subject. Mr. Ashby grew insupportable to me; he became melancholy, jealous, impertinent; he quarrelled with me often, and passed whole days in hunting to avoid me. My Lord Ossory on these occasions, rallied me on his absence; told me, laughing, he saw I was afflicted at it, and offered himself to represent Mr. Ashby. He took his place near me, imitated his little cares; gathered flowers, and presented them to me with that timid countenance, that air of sadness, from which unhappy love cannot preserve itself, and which adds to the disgust of the beloved object. My Lord mixed so much grace with every thing he did, that this pleasantry, though repeated often, was always new and entertaining: it engaged us to seek each other; and when our conversation took a more serious turn, Lord Ossory lamented Mr. Ashby's unhappiness, and told me, he could not conceive any misfortune equal to that of loving me, and being displeasing to me. One morning when I had been walking a long time with Mr. Ashby, by one of his common caprices, he changed his humour on a sudden, and appeared infinitely gay, and lively: my Lord Ossory assumed a serious air; I saw a coldness in his looks; I was shocked at it; an unknown emotion took possession of my heart, and gave me inexpressible torment. I would have spoke to Lord Ossory, to ask the reason[a] of his sadness, but far from seizing those opportunities I gave him of approaching me, he did not even seem to give the least attention to my design. The hours past, and the day was at an end, without his having deigned to address to me[b] a single word. How long did that day appear! what despite did I feel against Lord Ossory! I resented his behaviour so much, that I thought I hated him. The moment I was alone, the tears gushed from my eyes, they removed the oppression of my heart, and gave me liberty to reflect on the secret cause of that sentiment, which made them flow.

Why torment myself because of my Lord Ossory's coldness? Why desire to speak to him? What had I to say to him? And why interest myself in the change of his temper? These questions which I put to myself, discovered to me at once the passion, to which I had given up my heart, without knowing it.

Shall I tell you more, my Lord? In confessing it, I had also the weakness to pardon myself this attachment. I found Lord Ossory so worthy to be beloved; the charms of his wit, the graces of his person, his air, his features, the nobleness of his sentiments, a thousand amiable qualities, the virtues he really possessed, those which my love added to them; every thing in him seemed proper to augment, and to justify my tenderness: I vowed never to discover my passion, but I vowed also to carry it to my grave.

I appeared in the morning with such an air of despondency, as made every body apprehensive for my health. Lord Ossory discovered so much inquietude, shewed himself so touched with my languor, that the lively interest he took in it, dispelled it in a moment; whilst I beheld him, whilst I listened to him, my gaiety returned, and brought back to my countenance that chearful lustre, which chagrin had banished thence. From that moment I carefully observed the progress of my conquest; my Lord shewed the warmest friendship for me, but he shewed no more than friendship.

The winter brought us back to town; I saw Lord Ossory seldomer; I became melancholy, thoughtful; I felt a disgust for all those amusements, which pleased me before I had given away my heart. Lady Henrietta was then at Venice with her father: Deprived of the only friend with whom I dared to trust my sorrows, I kept a perpetual guard on myself to conceal them: Sometimes I blushed at my love; I regretted my past tranquillity; I determined no longer to give way to my sentiments; I struggled with them; I examined my Lord with attention; I sought to find defects in him;[a] I wished it was possible he could displease me; but the more I saw, the more I heard of him, the more convinced I was that he was truly worthy of all the love I felt for him.

Mr. Ashby, whose levity was extreme, tired of my indifference, addressed his vows to Miss Germain; his infidelity made us friends: As his new mistress was often with me, he begged of me not to teach her to use him ill. My Lord Ossory had always a place in our conversation: We speak, without intending it, of the object, who is dear to us: His name is, without ceasing, on the borders of our lips; we would withold it, but it escapes us: We have pronounced it a hundred times, when we fancy we have not pronounced it once. Whether Mr. Ashby penetrated my secret thoughts, and wished to revenge himself, or whether he really believed what he asserted, he repeated to me continually that he should pity extremely that woman who attached herself to Lord Ossory: He painted him solid, amiable, generous; but insensible. He chagrined me by his discourse, yet I was never weary of listening to it: Lord Ossory was talked of, though to his disadvantage, and all conversation, of which Lord Ossory was the subject, had an attractive charm for me.

I passed part of the winter in all the pangs of suspense; my Lord's attention, his assiduity, redoubled; a thousand little cares which proceed from the heart alone, and which the heart alone knows how to set a just value on, all persuaded me that I was beloved; but he had never told me so: and that doubt inseparable from true passion, that fear which raises obstacles to our desires, and destroys our fondest hopes, made me always distrust those proofs that I thought he gave me of his tenderness. Whilst he was with me, the softest tranquillity reigned in my soul, my dearest wishes seemed fulfilled; when he was absent, I felt all my inquietudes revive.

We were one evening in Lady Osmond's closet; every body were at cards, except my Lord Ossory and myself; I was standing, leaning on Lady Dursley's[65] chair, and observing her play. She called my Lord Ossory to ask him a question; as he stooped down to speak to her, happening to move my hand, it fell by mere accident on my Lord's: I withdrew it hastily, but he, fixing on me the most passionate look, carried his to his mouth, and kissed that part of it which mine had touched. I was affected by this action, it softened me, it charmed me, and during the remainder of the evening, I could not keep myself from regarding him with a look of embarrasment, which told him too plainly what it endeavoured to conceal.

Pardon me, my Lord, if I am prolix in relating these little particulars: this inhuman passion has been so dear to me, all that relates to it is yet so recent in my memory, that it is impossible for me to speak on the subject without recalling every circumstance, that led me to give myself up to an inclination which has been the source of all my misfortunes.

Early in the spring we returned to Hertford, Lord Ossory begged to be of our party. I felt an extreme joy at it; I flattered myself it was on my account only; I was charmed that he preferred me to those amusements which publick places[66] offered him: Alas! I was but too grateful for so trifling a sacrifice! Less interrupted than in town, we passed whole hours in those beautiful gardens which Lord Osmond has adorned with every charm of art and nature.[67] My Lord improved me in the French language and I instructed him in the Spanish: our studies led us to reflexions, of which our sentiments were always the foundation. The secret of our souls seemed every moment ready to escape us; our eyes had already betrayed it, when one day, reading an affecting story of two tender lovers, who had been cruelly torn from each other, the book fell from our hands, our tears began to flow, and seized with I know not what kind of fear, our eyes were fixed ardently on each other. He put one of his arms round me, as if to detain me; I leaned towards him, and breaking silence at the same time, we exclaimed both together, Ah! how unhappy were these lovers![68]

A full confidence followed this accidental discovery of our tenderness: Lord Ossory confessed to me the passion with which he said, I had inspired him the first moment he beheld me. He told me the reasons which he had to resist the warm emotions of his heart, naturally inclined to love. You know he was engaged to Lady Charlotte Chester, when the old Marquis of Dorchester[69] offered himself, and was immediately accepted. Lady Charlotte preferred to an amiable lover, who adored her, and for whom she pretended an equal passion, a title, which she had then no hopes of with him, he having at that time two elder brothers. This ambitious woman disgusted Lord Ossory with all the sex, he believed them incapable of tenderness or of fidelity. He left London, and till he came to Hertford, preserved his fear of engaging in another attachment; but this fear was soon lost in the hope of finding in me a heart formed for his. He forgot the Marchioness, and thought of nothing but of delivering himself up to the love I inspired, which however he had the cruelty to conceal from me.[70]

With what fire did he paint to me, that love! How often did he swear that his happiness, that his life depended on my returning his passion! How melting were his looks! How ardent his expressions! His discourse, the very sound of his voice, penetrated my soul: His words are engraven there in characters never to be effaced.

Ah! my Lord! What a moment! The confession of a passion which one partakes, is like a sudden flash of light, which carries a new day into one's ideas. An unspeakable charm was diffused on every thing around me; every object became more smiling, more amiable in my eyes; all nature seemed more adorned and lovely. That garden, where I had just learned I was beloved, appeared to me the abode of some benevolent being, who had withdrawn the veil which had so long hid my happiness from me.

Seized with astonishment and joy, how could I hide those rapid emotions, emotions to which I had been till then[a] a stranger? And why should I have restrained them? I suffered him to see the pleasure his confession had carried into my soul; he enjoyed it, and augmented it by his transports, and by the gratitude with which he received the vows I made, never to cease loving him.

From that instant Lord Ossory has engrossed all the tenderness of my soul, and I have only breathed to love him.

'Twas about this time, the Duke of Suffolk came to Hertford: he passed six weeks there, and conceived that passion for me which he yet preserves. Why can I not reward him with a sentiment more tender than esteem? So constant an ardor ought to triumph over the remembrance of an ingrate. My Lord Duke offered me his hand, my refusal afflicted without offending him: he easily imagined that the rank of dutchess, with an immense fortune, offered by a nobleman, whose person was uncommonly agreeable, and whose character was high in the world's esteem, would not have been refused without a strong attachment for another. He explained himself to Lord Osmond, who assured him of the contrary; but without being able to convince him. I did not doubt but his suspicions fell on my Lord Ossory, and I believed it the more, because he never after pronounced his name before me, a piece of respect which I shall always acknowledge as an obligation.

We hid with care our secret correspondence, without any other reason than a little shame for having changed our resolutions: we saw each other continually, and at night wrote to each other[b] what we had not been able to say during the day. How dear is that time even yet to my remembrance! How happy did I live! What good is comparable to the sweetness of loving a man worthy of our most tender affection, who loves us, who tells us so, who repeats it every moment, and whose every wish is lost in ours. What pleasure to expect him, to see him appear, to lift up to him those eyes to which his presence gives new lustre, to read in his[c] that he thinks us lovely, and that we are so happy as to please him! How flattering to see oneself the object of all his cares, to imagine he feels all the transports he excites, that he enjoys all the pleasures that he gives!

Ah, my Lord, why do the levity, the inconstancy of our hearts, change into bitterness sentiments so soft and enchanting! From whence comes it, that of two persons who have equal power of procuring to each other, so true, so exalted a happiness, one should cease to feel it, and deliver up the other to eternal regret? Amiable sensibility! Dear and flattering present! No, it is not you who render us unhappy: our natural inquietude, our caprices, poison the gifts of Heaven, and we lavish away without possessing, the precious blessings which it bestows upon us.

Six months passed in this agreeable situation: towards the middle of autumn Lord Ossory was obliged to return to London, to be present at the marriage of Lord Newport[71] with Lady Mortimer. He shewed an extreme repugnance to leaving us, and quitted me with an unaffected and lively sorrow. He wrote to me two or three times a day; his letters breathed the soul of tenderness; he spoke only of the ardent desire he had to return, to see me again, and of the hopes he had of soon being united to me in those soft bonds, he came from seeing tied. My replies expressed the grief his absence gave me; and which nothing was able to dissipate. He returned, and the joy of seeing him again effaced the remembrance of those tedious hours I had passed without him.

The first transports of this joy being calmed, I fancied I perceived in his looks an unusual melancholy;[72] I asked the reason of it, with that tender interest which a heart truly enamoured cannot but take in the least inquietude of the beloved object. One day as I pressed him to trust me with his sorrows, I saw his eyes wet with tears: he endeavoured to hide them from me, and turning away his face, Ah! said he to me, with a voice broken and interrupted, I have a reproach to make myself, a reproach which your goodness renders every instant more lively! Do not insist on my explaining the reason of it; if I speak, you will love me less, you will perhaps no longer love me at all: I am not worthy of the heart you have given me; no man is worthy of it: How much is your soul above mine? How ought I to blush before you! Ah! Lady Catesby! Is this your lover! Is this the man beloved by you, who has prepared for himself eternal remorse? – No, I am no more that happy lover who once hoped to deserve you. This strange discourse pierced my heart with sorrow: I begged him to open his whole soul to me; he refused; I did not dare to press him for fear of adding to his affliction: Time seemed to soften it, and my curiosity subsided. His love was always the same, and his grief dissipating by little and little, I was not obstinate to discover his secret. Lord Ossory was so dear to me, I found such sweetness in sacrificing every thing to him! How could I renew a subject of conversation which might displease or afflict him?

We were to leave Hertford in a week; Lord Ossory had prevailed on me to consent to give him my hand a month after our return to London: I wished however to have waited my brother's return; whose last letters had assured me he intended to cross the seas in the beginning of winter. Lord Ossory might have expected a better match than I was at that time: however my fortune was sufficient to bear the additional expence which a wife would occasion: it put me in a condition to refuse the advantageous settlements he would have made: A plan of the marriage articles was sent to him; he took pleasure in examining them, in settling them with me: we were agreed on all points,[a] when one evening a messenger enquired for my Lord Ossory with an appearance of great mystery, and would deliver his pacquet into no hands but his own. He was at play, and left it to speak to this man, but instead of coming back, he sent to beg Lord Arthur would take his cards. At supper time one of his servants came to tell us he found himself a little indisposed, and was gone to bed.

Never did my heart feel any inquietude equal to what seized it at this message. I did not imagine my Lord was ill, but I was convinced he had received some ill news. I sent Betty several times to enquire after his health, and to find out how he was employed; she brought me word at first, that he was shut up in his apartment, and had commanded his servants not to enter. At length she learnt of his valet de chambre, that he wept bitterly, seemed in despair, and that he had never seen him in so shocking a state of mind.

What a night did I pass! My Lord Ossory was in the deepest affliction; he shut himself up; he wept; he had sorrows, and he did not seek me. Had he then grief he feared to trust me with! Did he doubt the interest I took in whatever concerned him? He had then secrets to me? I recalled to mind his discourse, and his embarrassment the day he returned to Hertford; I began to fear, without knowing what I feared. The idea only that he was in tears, made mine flow; I was not able to calm my troubled heart; and the morning surprised me in that painful suspense, which one is always eager to get rid of, but of which one often has occasion to lament the loss.

As soon as the hour allowed, I sent to know how my Lord did: they returned answer, that he was not in bed,[73] that he was dressed, and had sat down to write.[b] My Lord Arthur, his lady, and son,[74] were the only strangers remaining at Hertford: they left us that very day. To avoid appearing, I ordered them to say I was asleep, and went to walk by the side of the canal: I wandered a long time without perceiving the path that I had taken: as I was returning, I saw my Lord Ossory, who advanced towards me, but so feeble, so dejected, so changed, that it was easy to judge in beholding him, that some fatal, some unforeseen event, must have reduced him to that state. He joined me, bowed, without lifting up his eyes, took one of my hands, which he gently pressed between his, and led me to an arbor where we both seated ourselves, without speaking a word. I had not courage to ask him any questions; he attempted to speak, but his voice expired upon his lips: at last, falling at my knees, and hiding his face in my robe, he wept aloud, with all the marks of inexpressible affliction. His tears, and his melancholy silence, stabbed me to the heart; I pressed him tenderly to speak; I wept with him, his sorrow overwhelmed me; I conjured him to moderate it; to lodge it in my bosom: he seemed to yield to my intreaties, and raised his head. His eyes, bathed in tears, were fixed on mine, our tears were mingled; he appeared determined to explain himself; I again pressed him to it, when starting suddenly from me, he left me with the most precipitate haste. I called to him, but in vain; I would have followed him, but had not strength. All my fears, my alarms, were for him alone; I could not conceive what could afflict him to that excess, nor how it was possible he should find such difficulty in opening his soul to me. Going back to my apartment, they told me my Lord Ossory was gone: two hours after, they brought me a letter; it was from him: could I have imagined I should find there the following words?

'I leave you, Madam, and I leave you without the remotest hope ever to behold you again. How should I dare again to appear before you? I, who have betrayed you? Who, when arrived at the summit of my most ardent wishes, when beloved by you, have not been able to repress an unworthy inclination? Who have exposed myself to the loss of so precious a blessing – Ah! Madam! Detest, despise this monster, who has destroyed your happiness, and his own. So near being united to you! so charmed with my fate! so proud to reign in a heart like yours! When you had given me the preference. – Must I then! – Yes, the laws of honour command – How are you revenged! How am I punished! – I lose you! – Just God! I lose you![75] Yet of whom can I complain but of myself? – so dear as you were to my heart, so present to my remembrance, ought not your idea to have checked me? But was I then myself? – Alas! I shall see you no more; I shall be the object of your contempt, of your aversion – More unhappy still, a thousand times more unhappy if I am so, one moment, of your regret, of those tears which I have seen flow for an ingrate, for an inhuman wretch, forced to deprive himself for ever – Ah! pity me, Madam! I dare yet implore your compassion – Why can I not at least confess to you – But this horrible secret is not mine only.– I ought to respect – Who? – The author of my misery[76] – Is it then possible I am reduced to wish to be forgot by you? – Yet I cannot forget you! I shall always adore you; your image will be always present to me. Adieu! Madam! Adieu! May I not live long enough to hear what you think of an unhappy man who could never have deserved you!'

I remained like one inanimate: a blow so terrible, so little expected, so little deserved, almost annihilated my very being. Immoveable, and without raising my eyes from that fatal paper, it seemed to me in finishing it, that some invisible hand precipitated me into an abyss, and destroyed in me every principle of life. I remained till the next morning in a kind of stupidity, which suspended all the faculties of my soul. Too blest if that state had lasted, and if my reason had been lost with my happiness!

Lady Osmond was twelve miles off, with one of her relations: she received there the news of the duel[77] and death of my brother. When she returned, she consulted with her Lord the means of preparing me to bear this loss; being no stranger to the tender sensibility of my soul. They told her the way I was in; she asked if I had had letters from London, and finding I had received several, she concluded I was already informed of the fate of my brother. My faintings[a] succeeded each other[b] so rapidly, I was so incapable of listening to her, or of speaking, that my situation terrified her. It was not till the next evening, when I was come a little to myself, that I discovered by the consolation she endeavoured to give me, and by the details into which it led her, that my amiable brother was no more. I owed my life to this increase of affliction: my tears now opened themselves a passage, their abundance brought back to me the cruel power to reflect how wretched I was: it was with difficulty I hid one part of my sorrows, whilst I gave myself up, without constraint, to those for which I had no reason to blush.

I could not bring myself to return to London; I staid at Hertford, in spite of the entreaties of Lord and Lady Osmond, who loved me tenderly. I carried my mourning for my brother the same lengths I had done that for my Lord Catesby: I would see nobody: I found no pleasure but in abandoning myself to grief: I ran eagerly to every place where I had seen, where I had conversed with Lord Ossory; my cries, my groans pointed out those places where he had assured me of his love, of that love which no longer existed: I bathed with my tears his letters, his picture, a thousand trifles, that he had given me. Engrossed continually by his idea, I yet felt only the pain of being separated, for ever separated, from him: I regretted, without condemning him: I read every moment that fatal letter; I sought in vain to comprehend what he had wrote, and why he should abandon me: I pitied him, because he desired to be pitied: I neither believed him false nor perfidious; my heart always defended, always adored him. I had loved him without knowing whether he shared my tenderness;[c] and I loved him still, uncertain of the cause of his flight, without doubting the nobleness of his sentiments, and could not persuade myself he had deceived me.

I past part of the day in writing to him, without ever sending what I wrote: as soon as my letter was finished, an invincible repugnance prevented my sealing it: I read it over, I wept, I tore to pieces what I had been writing: an instant after, I began another, without being able to determine what step I should take. My head fatigued by a continual application to the same subject, by all the dark projects which sorrow gives birth to, lost by degrees the faculty of fixing on other objects. I thought no more of any thing but my brother and my Lord Ossory. Sometimes I fell into a sort of insensibility; every idea was then effaced from my mind: I returned to myself, only to feel my wretchedness with more force.

I invoked the soul of my brother; I called him to the succour of his unhappy sister; I begged of Heaven to take away my life; and I know not how my reason preserved itself in a state so near approaching to madness.

I expected my letters with impatience: I did not suppose I should receive one from Lord Ossory; yet, when I found none from him, amongst those they brought me, I felt the desire I had to see them vanish. I ran over Lady Osmond's, trembling, I feared to find there a name which yet I sought for with eagerness. Alas! it was there only to augment my sorrows: I learned that he was dangerously ill: I forgot every thing to think only of his present state. I wrote to one of my servants who was in London, to inform himself exactly of the course of my Lord Ossory's distemper, and to send me every day an express with the account. His illness was long, and whilst it lasted, I experienced that grief may be suspended by the fear of still greater affliction. But what a change did his recovery make in my situation! The first use my Lord Ossory made of his return to health, was to go to St. James's Church, where he was married to Miss Fanny[78] Montford. None of his friends were present at the ceremony; it was celebrated without pomp; and two hours[79] after he set out, with his bride, for the North of England.

How shall I picture to you, my Lord, the impression this news made on me? It seemed that all I loved was a second time torn from me: I had preserved, without perceiving it, a feeble hope; the instant that deprived me of it, opened again all my wounds: I knew my Lord Ossory was no longer mine; I repeated every moment of the day, that he never could be: but I had no idea of the pang which rent my heart, when I told myself he was another's.

His marriage explained to me neither his letter nor his conduct: why should honour engage him to espouse this lady, whom he then knew not, or knew but slightly? and how could honour impose on him a law for her, which was not more binding in regard to me? I lost myself in my reflexions; and whilst I sunk under the weight of my chagrins,[a] whilst a melancholy languor destroyed my health, faded my youth, and robbed me of repose, my Lord Ossory was content and tranquil: his wishes were fulfilled. I painted him to my imagination lost in the transports of a satisfied passion, as a lover who secludes himself from the world, to possess, without interruption, the object of his tenderness: I represented him to myself in the arms of his happy bride, forgetting me in the bosom of pleasures, banishing from his mind those weak remembrances of me, which might perhaps sometimes intrude upon his heart; but which a smile from her he loved, would efface. His taste, his inclination only could have determined him to this union; Miss Montford was of birth, but without fortune; and those who had seen her, assured me she was not handsome. I am ignorant by what charm she attracted him.

I will not attempt to express to you the torments of my heart: to judge of the cruel emotions by which I was agitated, it is necessary to have been in the same situation, and to have had the same degree of sensibility. Believe me, my Lord, those who have never felt the misery of being betrayed by those they loved, by those they loved with passion, can have but a faint idea of the sorrows which it is possible to experience in this life. The loss of a splendid fortune leaves us at least the advantage of shewing the greatness of our souls, either by that moderation which enables us calmly to bear this reverse, or by that noble firmness which raises us above fortune itself. That excess of vanity which reigns in the human heart, is often a powerful consolation under the greatest misfortunes. Happy those who can enjoy the secret pleasure of self-admiration! But what resource remains to her, who having fixed all her hopes of happiness on one only object, sees herself suddenly deprived of that object; and forced to accuse by her tears the very hand she would have chosen to wipe them off, had they flowed from any other cause? To be unhappy, and to be so made by those one loves, is a species of misery, not to be comprehended, but by such as have had the sad experience.

Lord Campley returned from Venice at the end of winter. Lady Henrietta obtained his permission to come down to Hertford; the pleasure of seeing her again, her softness, her friendship, the confession I made her of all my weaknesses gave a little ease to my heart. This amiable friend restored me insensibly to myself: I still felt my sorrows, but I became capable of concealing them, and of appearing once more in the world. Assured that my Lord Ossory was no longer in London, and that he had no intention of coming thither, I resolved to return: I abandoned that place where every object that presented itself to my eyes, nourished my affliction, and renewed my regrets.

You scarce knew me again; my condition moved your tender compassion. My features however, recovered their form, which they had lost by my extreme leanness: Time restored my bloom, but it could not restore either my gaity or my repose. I made a thousand efforts[b] to forget a perfidious traitor; sometimes I believed I loved no longer,[c] but I always remembered I had loved.[a] My Lord Ossory yet excited violent emotions in my soul; his distance scarce secured me against him: I carried an air of timidity into every place where it was possible I might meet him; every moment I fancied I saw him, that I heard his voice. My Lord Penshurst[80d] by a slight resemblance of him, caused an emotion which you yourself perceived. His very name was sufficient to make me tremble. I combatted the remains of this weakness; I fancied I was near triumphing over it, when his return revived in my heart all those sentiments, which time and his levity ought to have extinguished. Never was astonishment equal to mine, when I saw him enter at Lady Bellvile's;[81] his eyes instantly fixed themselves on me: I felt an agitation which made me afraid to stay, least I should betray myself.[82e] Whilst all the company, charmed to see him, ran eagerly to embrace him, and mixed with their compliments of condolance on the death of his wife, a thousand felicitations on his return,[f] Lady Henrietta had the goodness to[83] lead me out of the room: we went away together. You was a witness of my confusion; I in vain endeavoured to hide it: the strange perturbation of my senses discovered to you part of my secret. Lord Ossory was every day at my door; he found it shut to him alone; he interested one of my women, whom he knew,[a] in his favour; and prevailed on her to beg for him one moment's conversation with me. He wrote to me, he followed me every where; his obstinacy alarmed me; I felt that Lord Ossory could never be to me an indifferent person. Ashamed to find still this sensibility, I thought it my duty to fly from the danger of seeing him, of listening to him: Do you now, my Lord, think you ought to accuse me of *cruelty, of inflexibility, for having refused to receive Lord Ossory's visits, for sending back his letters without deigning to open them, for not desiring any explanation with him*? What regard do I owe him? What motive should engage me to hear him? Ah! What can he have to say to me, after having so long forgot me! He has too well informed me that he is able to live without me, to be happy without me! Ah! that he had been always so! Yes, that he had been always so, but far removed from me! If you know where he is, if you write to him,[84] beg him to renounce the project of appeasing me, of seeing me. Me, his friend? Ah! God![b] I cannot be so.

I am sorry Heaven has snatched from him her whom he loved, whom he preferred to me: But why should his loss be a reason for reproaching me?[85] Is it for me to console[c] him? Adieu, my Lord![86] keep my secret: Do justice to my sentiments; and if you wish I should believe the tender friendship you profess for me sincere, speak to me no more of Lord Ossory.

## LETTER XV.

Wednesday, Winchester.

I was not able to write to you yesterday. I was fatigued, I was even ill: I kept my chamber. This light indisposition gave great pleasure to Sir Harry;[d] he would stay with me; I knew not what to say to him; I desired him to sing; he has a clear, melodious, agreeable voice. Indeed, my dear Henrietta, it recalled to my memory those soft seducing sounds – And must I always think of him? – Won't you chide me? I abuse your complaisance; I say the same things incessantly; nothing can dissipate those ideas; I surprise myself sometimes in a humor for which I make myself a thousand reproaches. 'Tis said that solitude inclines us to misanthropy; I should imagine the great world infinitely more proper to produce that effect, if the natural indulgence of a good heart did not temper the bitterness of those reflexions which the understanding cannot help making.[87] In observing the inconsistencies, the absurdities and insignificance of so many persons amongst whom one must live; those who think themselves exempt from such follies, ought to regard themselves in the midst of these extravagants, as a healthy person environed with crowds of the sick. It would be unjust to bear them ill will for not enjoying as flourishing a state of health[a] as ourselves.

Last night every body assembled in my apartment: they rallied my Lord Clarendon on a passion which he has a long time preserved, though the object of his attachment little deserved such constancy. This passion has rendered him very unhappy during the last five years. What think you of this subject of pleasantry? Could you suppose, any one would find amusement in recalling to another's remembrance, the most painful moments of his life? Ah! What a manner of thinking must they have who can find pleasure in tearing open the wounds of a tender heart! My Lord Clarendon attended with complaisance to this cruel raillery: he shewed both sense and good-nature by the manner in which he bore it: but he cast down his eyes, he was embarrassed – Tell me, my dear, why we blush to have been deceived? We are then ashamed to have sincerity, and to suppose it in others. From whence comes it, that one feels humbled by being discovered to have a credulity, of which, if one examined the first principles, one ought rather to be proud? If it is by our own sentiments we judge those of others, distrust is not natural to a virtuous soul: Ah! Can those possibly suspect deceit, who feel themselves incapable of practising it!

I partook the pains of this poor nobleman: perhaps my concern proceeded less from a generous compassion, than from a lively retrospect to my own misfortunes: I will not however examine too narrowly, into the cause. I hate to seek for reasons[b] to weaken the idea I have of goodness: those moralists, who setting up for scrutinizers and judges of the soul, to vilify it, degrade its most exalted operations, only furnish me with conviction against themselves. Now we are on this subject, I thank you for the little book you have sent me. The author writes well, but does he think well? I would have people impelled to write by a more disinterested motive than that of displaying their wit. The Spectator[88] ought to be a model for those who study to penetrate the secrets of the human heart. Why employ those efforts to afflict us, which might as easily tender to us consolation? Would it not be better to elevate the soul than to abase it? It is from examples of goodness, of greatness, of generosity, that men aspire to be good, great, generous. Those who would render their knowledge useful, ought to assist us to profit of those seeds[c] of rectitude which nature has sown in our hearts. To rob us of the merit of owing to our efforts part of our good qualities, to attribute every laudable action to vanity or self-love, is to discourage us in the race of virtue. To talk to us only of our weaknesses, is like reminding an unhappy person, every moment, how much he is to be pitied: if we are unable to console him, ah! why thus inform him that he is miserable? To an evil which is incurable, lenitives alone – But, good God! Is it for me to reason, to criticise the polite Sir James Williams?[89] See the danger of reading;[90] I have almost wrote a book too. Adieu! I love you with all my heart.

## LETTER XVI.

Thursday, Winchester.

What a ridiculous, what an impertinent, what a vexatious adventure have I met with! Happily disengaged from Sir Harry,[a] who is twelve miles from hence, I intended to take advantage of his absence, to enjoy the pleasure of walking alone. As I crossed the walk I was in, to gain the park, I saw Sir James: he had followed me without letting me perceive it. This meeting extremely displeased me; I knew it was then impossible to avoid hearing him: determined to listen to him I had already meditated on my reply – But, my dear Henrietta could you believe it? Could you imagine the effect his discourse has produced in my heart, my weak unguarded heart? Sir James began, by telling me, *that the only motive of his journey to Winchester, was* – he hesitated – *to find* – to seize – *the opportunity* – which chance had now given *him*[b] – in short – *to render me a homage* – he again hesitated; but emboldened by my profound silence, he drew the most lively, the most animated picture of his ardor, of his sufferings, of his respect, of his passion – My God, of whatever he pleased, my dear, I gave him no interruption – Alas! I was too distant from him! – His confusion, his embarrasment, his expressions almost the same, the place, the hour, the season, the very day, so present to my memory; all recalled the idea of Lord Ossory. I seemed again to hear that voice so sweet, so adored, those flattering promises, those vows so cruelly betrayed: my head sunk on my bosom, forgetting Sir James, his confession, his love; forgetting prudence and myself. I gave a loose to my tears; I abandoned myself to a sorrow the marks of which I was unable either to restrain or to conceal. I know not what Sir James said, I know not what he thought of an emotion so extraordinary: I am ignorant how long this singular scene lasted. We heard my Lady Sunderland, she came towards us: Sir James struck into the wood, and your foolish friend crossed into a close walk, that she might not be seen, and hastened to write to you. – Surely, I have lost my reason – What can Sir James think? – I must see him again in an instant – that thought is insupportable.

## LETTER XVII.

Thursday, midnight.[91]

Sir James did not appear at dinner: he complained of the head-ach, and came down very late. He seemed melancholy, and I was embarrassed. I cannot express to you how much I fear an explanation. I will avoid it, if I can. Must my Lord Ossory then be always present to me? Can nothing efface the remembrance of that ingrate? Must he afflict me without ceasing! – What an idea must Sir James entertain of a woman, who weeps because an amiable man loves her tenderly! A man whose birth is equal to hers, whose fortune is very considerable – Oh, my dear Henrietta, I have a heart incomprehensible, feeble, and I think, contemptible. Those qualities, those virtues, which were the basis of our friendship, you alone possess; for me, I have no more than the appearance of them. A cruel passion, a constancy ill placed, have destroyed my natural disposition, and changed my character. I still retain the same principles, but I swerve from them: I act contrary to the clearest lights. I cannot rise above this vile half of myself, this feeble machine, to which the least impulse brings back the impression of its first tender emotions. Chide me harshly, I entreat you: I stand in need of your utmost severity.

But by what ill fate must Sir James and Sir Harry[a] persecute me? I can love nothing, I would not be beloved. The one is silent, pursues me every where, and is angry: the other speaks in a tone of voice, and with expressions that – Have men but one language? – Why has his made me call to remembrance? – Am I so much to blame, my dear? tell me – You are so kind to my faults, that my friendship for you forces me to reproach them doubly. If you find me ridiculous, yet do not love me less.

## LETTER XVIII.

Friday, Winchester.

You are afraid your letters are long, that they tire me: You, my dear Henrietta, to think you can tire me? Be assured, that, absent from you, my only amusement is to read those amiable letters. The sentiment which makes them dear to me, will never produce sorrow in my soul; my tears will never efface those beloved characters: I shall never remember with shame the pleasure I feel in reading them – Alas! who could have foretold me that those, from whence I once received so pure a joy, I should now not dare – When I received them, I was happy, so happy, that all those blessings, which others esteem, seemed to me nothing, to those I hoped to possess – What a change did a day, an hour, a moment, make in my fate! – That letter, that fatal inexplicable letter – The perfidious, to swear to me that he adored me, to explore my pity![92b] – Ah! my dear, I cannot forget him – No, I cannot! What I have wrote to my Lord Castle-Cary has given new life to that sincere, that ardent, tenderness, which nothing can ever destroy. I have struggled against the shame of yielding to the extreme weakness of my heart. My pride has supported me in this painful effort. I believed I might depend on my reason; I flattered myself – Vain hope! I can never cease to think of Lord Ossory. His absence makes me wretched: from whence comes this? Do I then think he ought to be sensible of mine? Can I suppose my disdain has not disengaged him? Was it to be followed that I fled? Have I the meanness to desire it? – Alas! I know not; but I did imagine he would have seen Lord Castle-Cary, that he would have endeavoured to see you – I am become fantastical, unjust: when he is mentioned to me, I am angry; when he is not, I am afflicted. In desiring to see me, he irritates me: he desists, his neglect displeases, it offends me. My God! is this your friend, is this a woman of sense, who is so inconsistent with herself? My good, my tender friend, love me for us both, for I sincerely hate myself.

## LETTER XIX.

Saturday, Winchester.

Sir James has wrote to me. His letter is tender; *he loves me, he will not tell me so. He does not dare to ask the subject of my tears; he shall never forget that moment. He sees that my heart is pierced with a grief which he respects.* He concludes with assuring me of his eternal love. – Eternal, my dear, they all promise an eternal love. The first proof Sir James will give me of his eternal love, and of his submission, is, to hide those sentiments, which he is sure of preserving for ever. I have answered him politely, and accepted his silence only. I am sorry to have inspired him with tenderness. If I cannot make him happy, I wish, at least, not to have made him miserable. He is amiable; he would have been agreeable to me, if any one could be so.

You are sure my Lord Ossory is not at Bath. They have not seen him at Hertford. Lady Osmond does not name him amongst those who are with her. She presses me to returnᵃ to Hertford! to see again those scenes! Ah! I will not go to Hertford.

Here is Sir Harry quickly returned, and returned the very same as when he left us. I received him very well; not well enough however, for he has a very discontented air – *Your Ladyship is writing* – a profound sigh, and the tiresome creature walks off – Ah no, he comes back, loaded with a basket of hyacinths and narcissusses,[93] with which he is going to ornament my closet. Whilst he is busy arranging them – *My Ladyship is writing* – to the great regret of Sir Harry. I feel that nothing can be more impolite, but if I was to shew the least gratitude for his little civilities, he would overwhelm me with them. 'Tis quite enough to bear all his ill humours in silence: he has so many with me, that I often examine myself to find if I have not done him some injury. That which makes his presence tedious, and his tenderness painful to me, is my thinking that in his heart he calls me ungrateful. In effect, why treat him ill? What have I to reproach him with? An embarrassment? A desire to be with me, which leads him to follow my steps, perhaps in spite of himself? An extreme submission! A passion to please me, which he scarce dares to let me see! – If you saw with what application he is employed in his work – poor Sir Harry – they say one is unjust when one loves: one is much more so when one does not. What right have I to be impolite to Sir Harry? Because he wearies me, must I afflict him? Ought I to abuse the power which his weakness gives me over him? Do we owe nothing to those we make suffer?[94] I will go talk to him – But what shall I say? – I will ask him for snuff,[95] what o'clock it is, what kind of weather; let fall my handkerchief to give him the pleasure of taking it up. One must be obliging.

Lord Castle-Cary begs my pardon: he finds I was in the right: but he cannot conceive what can have made such a change in my Lord Ossory's character: he should not have known him again by his strange conduct in regard to me. Adieu! my dear and tender friend.

# LETTER XX.

Sunday, Winchester.

Ah! Great God! What emotion! What surprise! Under a cover in an unknown hand, a letter from my Lord Ossory – Yes, from him – It is his hand – My God! It is from him! – From whence comes it? – Who brought it? – How! – Wherefore! – He write to me again! – To me? – What would he with me? – My hand trembles – My pen drops from my fingers – I must take breath. –

They cannot tell me from whence this letter comes. A man on horseback gave it to one of my servants, whom he enquired for – Can Lord Ossory be in this country?[96] – Behold me like a fool; like one distracted – Like – But to what can I be compared but to myself – I cannot write – My head is disordered – O, my dear, if you could see me – That letter – It distracts me.

Alas! What is become of that happy time, when the sight of that writing would have melted my heart with softness? At present, it terrifies me – It gives me disorder inexpressible – O, my dear Henrietta! Why am I not with you! Why cannot I repose in your bosom, the pangs I feel! They are so exquisite, they are of such a kind – I cannot describe them; but I sink under them.

What power has this man over me? I once believed he had that of making me happy: he has lost that, he has lost it voluntarily – Must he then still retain the cruel power of afflicting me? – I wish to hide myself, to forget myself, to lose my very being – This letter – I know not what to do. How unhappy am I! When time seemed to have weakened my tender sentiments, and diminished my chagrin, this ingrate returns to town, his caprice excites him to see me; and when, to avoid him, I leave all who are most dear to me, he torments me even here; he writes to me: he has the cruelty to write to me.

This cover! This artifice – When I send back the letter to London, how shall I convince him I have not read it? – He is not himself sincere enough to believe me on my word – So artful – But what can he write to me? – Dare he attempt to justify himself? How can he? – Ah! It is neither love nor friendship which prompts him to importune me; it is vanity. He cannot bear to see himself scorned: he writes to triumph over my resolutions; to prevail over my pride, over my resentment – After two years of forgetfulness, dare he flatter himself, that I yet think of him? – Is this weakness or curiosity? – Whence comes this desire of seeing me? – Yet what have I to fear? – Has he any reproaches to make me? – I will read his letter; I will answer it – But see – Lady Southampton! Alas! Why have not I a soul like hers! Adieu!

## LETTER XXI.

Sunday night.[97]

He complains of me, my dear Henrietta! He has the presumption to complain, to teach me lessons of generosity? The husband of Fanny Montford is astonished at my inconstancy! He expected from me other sentiments – And all this with a haughtiness – Read, read, I entreat you, the copy of his insolent letter – This unfaithful man has not the least idea of the sorrows he has inflicted on me – But is it possible for a man[a] to comprehend the miseries which he may cause?

To Lady Catesby.

To fly an unhappy man, to reject his submissions, to abandon him to his remorse, to despise his repentance, to reflect without pity on what he deserves to suffer; is the behaviour of a woman devoid of all sentiment, who thinking herself injured, gives herself up to all the fury of resentment,[98] and from whom indeed, one has no right to expect more softness or complacency.

But to open her heart to the generous emotions of pity, to compassionate the fate of him, who is the more to be lamented, because he has merited those miseries under which he groans; to forget, to pardon, to remit to him as a friend, part of his offences as a lover; to grant some indulgence to the penitence of a criminal; to hear him, at least, is what I expected from the noble, the enlightened soul of Lady Catesby.

But she is changed; she is no longer that faithful friend,[99] that tender mistress, whose love nothing could weaken. Her letters, the only consolation of my exile, the only balm of my afflicted soul; those letters, so dear, so often pressed fondly to my lips, so often bathed with my tears, those charming letters, all that now remains of my past happiness, they still tell me you have loved me; but your eyes have contradicted their pleasing assurances, and your departure has too well confirmed my misfortune, and convinced me of your hatred.

Ah! Lady Catesby! Lady Catesby![100] Is it then you, who treat me with this inhuman cruelty? You, who have a thousand times promised me your eternal esteem? How are you certain you are not unjust? You have received wrongs, I confess; but you are still ignorant of which kind they are:[b] Till now, I have not been at liberty to explain my conduct: Condescend only to hear me, Madam: in the name of all that is dear to you, do not refuse this concession to a man who adores you, who has never ceased to love, to admire, to regret you. In spite of the strongest appearances, believe me, he is not unworthy the favour he now presumes to ask.

Pardon the manner I have taken to engage you to read my letter. One of my servants waits your reply at the farm.

*That inhuman cruelty! How do you know you are not unjust*? Could you have imagined he would have dared to doubt, whether I have acted justly in regard to him? *Those letters bathed with his tears* – From whence are those tears? From what cause – Ah! Let them still flow! Let him weep! He has betrayed that *tender mistress*, who preferred him to all mankind; who lived for no other purpose than to love him; whose ardent vows to Heaven had only for their object the happiness of this cruel – Ah! Let him weep – How ought he to reproach himself? – That *faithful friend* may abandon him without being *inhuman* or *unjust* – Insolent supplicator! *He does not believe himself unworthy the favour he asks* – Examine well the style of his letter – Shall I reply to it? – I know not – What can I say to him? – But I feel myself disordered – I cannot go on – My dear, my amiable friend, why did I leave you, and at a time when I had such need of your counsels? My Lord Ossory was the cause – Alas! Have I ever known an affliction of which he was not the source?

## LETTER XXII.

Monday, Winchester.

I am yet in suspence what I ought to do: the oftener I read Lord Ossory's letter, the more am I enraged against him. Because I am capable of a just resentment, my soul is no longer *the same, he once knew it*: a mean condescension would, in his opinion, become me better than what he is pleased to call, an *inhuman cruelty*.

O, my dear Henrietta, these men regard us merely as beings placed in the universe for their amusement; to trifle with, in that species of infancy, to which they are reduced by those impetuous passions,[a] which they reserve to themselves the infamous liberty of avowing with confidence, and submitting to without shame. They have left to that sex they presume to despise as weak and irresolute, the difficult task of resisting the softer impulses of the heart, of conquering Nature herself. Slaves to their senses alone, when they appear to be so to our charms; it is for themselves they pursue, for themselves they address us: they consider only the pleasures[b] we are capable of bestowing: they withhold their esteem from the object of their pretended adorations; and if they find in us strength of mind, and dignity of sentiments, we are *inhuman creatures*: we pass the limits their tyranny has prescribed to us, and became *unjust*ᵃ without knowing it.

I am piqued – I will answer him – I will wait however till the bitterness which I cannot hide, is a little moderated – I will not see him – I will never see him – I will endeavour not to write with severity, that I may remit to Lord Ossory, who ought to be indifferent to me, part of the offences of a lover, whom it is my duty to hate. – No, there is not an expression in his letter which does not wound my very soul – *I know not of what kind are those wrongs* – How can he say this? Has he not betrayed me, quitted, abandoned me? Has he not destroyed my dearest hopes? Has he not deprived me – Alas! of himself, of the only object of my tender attachment! Has he not done me all the injury that was in his power? And is it possible I can *pardon* him? Why had I not resolution to tear his letter the moment I saw the hand? Why, must he – This ungrateful man has made it his whole happiness to trouble, to destroy mine.

## LETTER XXIII.[101]

Monday, past midnight.[102]

Would you believe it, my dear Henrietta, I cannot write to Lord Ossory? I have twenty times begun a very short letter, without being able to finish it. Every thing which I would wish not to say, offers itself readily to my mind;ᵇ Reproaches flow spontaneously from my pen: I study to seem indifferent, and my sensibility breaks out in spite of me: no expression, either of coldness or moderation, pleases me: My heart, carried away by a rapid emotion, pants to explain itself without disguise. I must wait a little.

Two o'clock.[103]

I shall never be able to write this answer: I write, I erase;[104] After all, why do I torment myself?[105] Is it necessary I should write to him? Perhaps it is, for he may interpret my silence a consent to see himᶜ – If he should come hither – So near as he may be – He has no estate in this country – Is it chance, or the desire to find me which brings him? Do not my dear, ridicule my anxiety; do not say, I love him – Alas! how is it possible I can still love him? It is not love which thus takes up all my thoughts – It is – I know not what it is; but I am most unhappy. I am retiring to bed; but without hope of finding rest. Pity your tenderest friend, pity her, without examining too deeply into the cause of her sorrows: we have often agreed in pronouncing it cruelty, to refuse compassion to those miseries, which may to us appear light and trifling: it is not the species of suffering, but the sensibility of the sufferer, which ought to excite our pity: Alas! I am then very worthy of yours.

# LETTER XXIV.

Tuesday, Winchester.

I enclose a copy of my answer. I never knew before the difficulty of writing, when one wishes to use a language foreign to the heart: it is an oppressive burthen, from which I am at last relieved. Could you believe, that, during the hour which has past since my letter was dispatched, I have twenty times wished it were possible to recall it? I am afraid it is too disobliging – That it may afflict him. I have read his again with attention: it appears to me in a new light: those very expressions that excited my anger, now move my tenderest compassion: how affecting is that passage where he speaks of my letters! *He pressed them to his lips, they were his only consolation* – But what were then his sorrows? *His exile*! – If he had loved me – Ah! how could he have wedded another, if his heart – I can comprehend nothing – He says he is unhappy – I would not think he is indeed so – Alas! if he had suffered as I have done – had tasted that bitter cup, had felt such unutterable anguish! – how should I pity him! How easily would my pride yield to the sweetness of consoling him, of restoring joy to his soul! My tears begin to flow; they will not be restrained,[106] I cannot support the idea of his grief, of those never-ceasing sorrows of which he speaks. Though reflection ought to convince me they have never in reality existed, they present themselves every moment to my imagination; and though reason rejects the pleasing delusion, my heart too easily gives it admittance.[107]

To Lord Ossory.

I neither expected your complaints, my Lord, nor the request which accompanies them: the time in which an explanation of your conduct was interesting to me, has long been past: if it sometimes finds a place in my thoughts, it is like the remembrance of a painful dream, which the morning dissipates, and of which one only retains a melancholy and confused idea. It is of little consequence to me to know the motives which engaged you to restore me to reason[108] and myself; it is sufficient for me, that you did so. I do not think I depart at all from my character, in refusing to see you, in refusing it in the most determined manner. I can never regard you as a friend, to whom I am obliged[a] to remit such offences as are neither pardonable in a friend nor a lover. Ought he, who could abandon me so long to the uncertain conjectures of my own tortured mind, to the suspicions which I could not but entertain of his tenderness, and his probity, to be astonished at my indifference? Has he a right to reproach me? Why should I seek to know the circumstances of my wrongs, when I cannot doubt of the facts? I know enough to make me perfectly careless as to those particulars, I may yet be ignorant of: I expect from the complaisance I have forced myself to show in writing to you, a favour which I have a right to demand. Give me back, my Lord, those letters, the style of which recals to your memory, those sentiments which I blush ever to have felt, and do not complain of a heart which has been noble enough, never to complain of yours.

Don't you find, my dear Henrietta, a species of falshood in this manner of writing? It is indeed, what I ought to think, but it is not what I do think. That haughty indifference is not in my heart; I am sorry I have sent this letter – Why should I dissemble? Would it not have been better to have spoke sincerely, to have confessed the real situation of my soul in regard to him? To have said, *I perhaps love you still, but I no longer esteem you: I renounce you; the constancy of my sentiments is no proof that I believe you worthy of my attachment: it is in my natural character; the indelible features of which have engraven on my soul a weakness, which once was dear to me, and of which I still love the remembrance: it does not depend on you, but on the lively impressions which my heart has received. Like one who beholds his own image with complacency, and takes delight in contemplating the object, without thinking of the glass which presents it to view, so I please myself with recalling the idea of my love, without thinking with the least degree of pleasure of my unworthy lover.*[109]

This had been more noble, more open and generous, I wish I had done it. I hate dissimulation, I hate even the appearance of it. But the letter is gone – I have long lost the habit of being pleased with myself; Regret seems attached to every step I take. Of all those good qualities, I once fancied myself mistress of,[a] there only remains the knowledge of my faults: and of all those blessings[b] I once promised myself, your friendship is the only true and real one I possess.

## LETTER XXV.

Wednesday, Winchester.

Certainly, my dear, my head is a little disordered. I am unquiet, agitated: I count the hours, the moments; Time seems to me uncommonly long. I expect, without knowing what I expect. The least noise sets me a trembling; if my door opens, my heart beats. Every time my servants pass in or out of my apartment, I look at them with eyes which seem to require something of them: I hear a tedious repetition of, *what would my Lady have*? – Ah! Good God! Your Lady knows not what she would have – Can you divine, my dearest Henrietta, the cause of all this emotion? O how low, how mean, how shameful is it! – It is the expectation of an answer – No, I cannot suffer myself to betray such weakness.

I wish to leave this place, to fly from so dangerous a neighbourhood: yet if my Lord Ossory is determined to see me, to speak to me, where can I be secure against this obstinate resolution? He will find a way to satisfy it; he may obtain from chance, perhaps from my weakness, the conversation he so pressingly demands: are men ever weary of any pursuit in which their caprice engages them? They are never humbled by our repulses; this is one of the advantages they reserve to themselves. Has a woman the misfortune to love, to love too tenderly? Does she grow weary of her lover? What reproaches, what persecutions is she not obliged to suffer? She may banish him; but he returns, he seeks her every where, he pursues her; he complains, threatens, beseeches, sighs, abandons himself to his passion; being heard, is a consolation he will not refuse himself. He is very little anxious, whether this conduct gives uneasiness or disgust: his soul is not delicate enough to be wounded by the idea of becoming importunate. Attentive to himself only, nothing can make him renounce a good of which he flatters himself with the possession; and often, by the force of obstinacy, he obtains, if not the heart, at least the person, the strongest object of his attachment. He, when he finds his chain heavy, breaks it, and abandons us without pity: he sees not our tears, he hears not our complaints. Our native softness, a decent pride, force us to hide our sorrows – Ah! how is it possible we can be so weak to give up our hearts! Love is to us the source of so much wretchedness – A reflexion strikes me, my dear; it is, that I must certainly weary you: I tell you my thoughts as they rise, and Heaven knows they contain nothing amusing – O, how displeased am I with myself, how little pleased with others! – There is Sir Harry who has the vapours, and swoons away like a woman.[110] He was with me this morning; his vertigos seized him; I knew not what to do to bring him to himself. I could find nothing but a bottle of perfumed water; I threw it all on his face: his sister cried out, I should poison him – I hope he will come here no more;[111] at least, that he will find some other place to faint in. Adieu![112]

## LETTER XXVI.

Thursday, Winchester.[113]

Nothing yet from my Lord Ossory. Not answer me! It becomes him well to behave with haughtiness – He is displeased, perhaps – Was my letter so cruel? – The vain creature cannot support the style of indifference from a woman who once expressed such tenderness for him; that of hatred would have offended him less – Ah! if I was to write to him at present – But no more, let us not think of him.

I have received two letters from my Lord Castle-Cary; he complains of you. I will tell him, he is in the wrong; but to you, I must say, he has reason for his complaints. You laugh at his jealousy: you are to blame: if you had ever felt its horrors,[a] you would not allow yourself to imbitter his torments by these pleasantries. With a tender and generous nature, is it possible you can ridicule an involuntary emotion, which affects the soul with such exquisite sorrow? It is a folly, you say, and an extravagance: it may be so, but it is a folly which wounds one to desperation. It is in the anguish of a man who adores her, that Lady Henrietta finds amusement: *he ought to be sure of your tenderness, to know you, to believe*[114] *you*. Does love then listen to reason? By reflecting on my own sentiments, I have perhaps, acquired some little knowledge of the human heart. She, my dear, who can laugh at the inquietude, at the sorrow of a man who is attached to her, either no longer loves him, or deceived herself when she imagined she ever loved him.

The anguish of a lover cannot be indifferent to a mistress, who returns his passion; she is afflicted, because he is sad; she weeps, because his tears flow: she seeks to calm, to dissipate, the chagrins which she partakes – Ah! how can one give those pains, and render them yet more bitter by railleries, by a gaiety, that – Fie, Henrietta! Fie! You have retarded my Lord Castle-Cary's happiness: soften at least this tedious time of expectation, by a complaisance which you owe to the sincerity and warmth of his affection. I love him; you know it: and your faults may fall a little upon me. He writes me letters of four pages, all filled with your cruelties: you are angry with him, and he is wretched. Pardon him for your friend's sake.[a] He does not wish to hide you from the world; he desires to have you admired: appear,[115] show yourself, go every where, he consents to it: be lovely in the eyes of all mankind; but do not value yourself on being so, in any eyes but his. Adieu! he desires me to chide you; I do chide you; but I do not love you the less.

## LETTER XXVII.[b]

Friday, Winchester.

My Lord Ossory's letter has touched you: you think my answer too *haughty; you do not approve this excess of severity* – Go on, my dear, add to my uneasiness. I admire with what ease we adapt every thing to our own present sentiments: you had just forgiven my Lord Castle-Cary when you sat down to write. Softened by the pleasures of a tender reconciliation, you think I ought to pardon also; that it is cruelty not to pardon. You entreat me, you conjure me to hear my Lord Ossory. If I was inclined to give you that proof of complaisance, is it in my power? – How can I listen to him! He no longer desires to be heard – You pity him! Can you then believe, that after his desertion of me, after his marriage, and two years of forgetfulness, my indifference has power to afflict him! – He wished only to try me: his vanity persuaded him, I still loved him; that his least concessions would destroy my resolutions. Without doubt, his offering to justify himself, was sufficient to efface the remembrance of his perfidy, of a treachery of the blackest kind;[c] I ought to have flown to receive the heart he deigned to restore to me: so valuable a blessing merited my eager acceptance;[d] My gratitude, perhaps – Insupportable insolence[e] of men! Intolerable pride! – I ought, however, to thank my Lord Ossory; his last caprice has been of more service to me than time or reason; it has destroyed the remains of that inclination, over which I feared I could never have triumphed: I could not till now, think of this ingrate without tenderness; at present I could behold him, without the least emotion; I am tranquill:[116] I no longer fear his sight, his importunities: is not this the very point I have so ardently wished to arrive at? – With what cruelty has he sought to disturb my peace of mind,[a] to rekindle that love which he was never worthy to inspire me with? From whence comes it then, that I ever loved him with such fondness? I have been looking at his picture this morning; I held it above an hour in my hand; I contemplated it without being affected: I am even astonished at my former attachment. Why has that image alone had power over my heart? What is there in him so seducing? What delusion lent such charms to that countenance? Where are those graces which I admired in those features? – O, my dear Henrietta! our prepossession makes all the merit of the objet we prefer to others: it adorns the idol of our hearts; it gives him every day some new ornament. By degrees, the splendor, in which we have clothed him, dazzles ourselves, imposes on us, seduces us; and we foolishly adore the creature of our own imagination. This portrait, once so dear, is that of a deceiver: Alas! I long regarded it as the representation of a being almost celestial! – I cannot see him! – I hate him – I hate myself – But I love you always.

## LETTER XXVIII.

Saturday, Winchester.

You die with desire, that Sir Harry should declare himself. Behold him declared, proposed, and rejected! My Lady Wilton painted to me in the strongest colours, her brother's love, his respect, the silence he had imposed on himself for fear of displeasing me; and passing from his praises to mine, she expressed the most obliging desire of acquiring in me a sister as well as a friend. You will judge of my embarrassment, my dear, and of the polite evasions it forced me to make use of. I urged my disgust almost invincible to marriage, from the little happiness I had found in that state; my insensibility to love; the habit of a liberty which I could not lose without regret. Indeed, I do not make that use of my freedom, which attaches most widows of my age to the state; but it gives me the same species of pleasure which a miser feels in calculating his riches: he enjoys the blessings which he knows he can procure, and possesses, in imagination, all those which the extent of his fortune makes attainable. One man only, said I to her, could have determined me to sacrifice this precious liberty: no other will ever have the same ascendant over my soul. Lady Wilton is satisfied with the reasons I have alledged; but for Sir Harry, to whom she has communicated my sentiments, he is very far from approving them. There is no living with him any longer; he does not speak to me, does not look at me; contradicts every body; scolds other people's servants, drives away his own, breaks every thing he touches, throws down all he finds in his way: goes like an idiot across the parterres, and coming back, in a reverie, strikes his head against the gate which is shut, astonished to find himself stoped – But how unjust is this sex! Is their humour a law? At what is Sir Harry angry? Has he a right to expect his will should determine mine? I have loved one creature of his species – Ah! that is sufficient – But I have a letter from you – Alas! of what do you inform me! That Lady Egberth[117] has quitted the court, has resigned her place – How I pity her! How her misfortune touches me? She is given up to retirement, to devotion, and it is my Lord Westbury's[118] death which has caused this great change: a very extraordinary one without doubt: no body had more reason to be attached to the world than this lady – Ah! my dear! To lose a man she loved so sincerely; that she had so long loved; to have surmounted so many obstacles; to be on the point of espousing him, and to see him snatched from her in a day, in a moment, by an accident – I cannot restrain my tears at this melancholy event. But what madness is it in men of rank to run the hazard in these races, of losing without honour, a life dear to their country, and which they ought only to expose for it? Are they not responsible to their friends,[119] their relations who love them? Was he not so to a mistress, who is plunged by the loss of him into sorrow and despair? Poor Lady Egberth! Her situation, and the reflexions it has engaged you to make, have melted my heart. Adieu!

## LETTER XXIX.

Sunday, Winchester.

Ah! How shall I tell you! How express to you! – Have I strength to write? – Alas! how could I complain of him! – Henrietta! My dear Henrietta! He is ill, dangerously ill – Lord Ossory is dying! My God! He is dying – See the billet which I have just received.

To Lady Catesby.

I have now but a few moments to live; the countenances of those about me, and the resistance they make to my will, assure me of it. It is with difficulty I obtain permission to write – Alas! why have I so much desired it! – What have I to say to you? You will hear with pleasure, that the object of your contempt, of your aversion, has finished his wretched days – Ah! Lady Catesby![120] What cruelty! – But is this a time to complain of it! Pardon at least, the memory of an unhappy lover; I have never deceived you: I have loved you always. Those letters which you have demanded of me with an inflexibility, of which I thought your heart incapable, shall be faithfully restored to you after my death. Do not, Madam, deprive me of them whilst I yet breathe.

After *his death* – *I shall hear with pleasure* – Can he believe this, can he imagine it? – Ah! Inhuman! There remained only this blow – Ill! dying perhaps – Alas! where is he? With whom? In what hands! – Has he advice? – Is there any near him? – O, this anguish is insupportable.

The person who brought this fatal billet, returned without stopping, without waiting a moment, without speaking a single word. How shall I find out[a] – Abandoned to my fears, to the most lively inquietude – Ah! Pity me! My heart is torn in pieces. A feeble hope dawns upon my mind: I have sent to the house where one of Lord Ossory's servants passed two or three days. They assure me, that servant came from Sir Charles Halifax's,[121] who has lately bought an estate four[122] miles from hence. I have dispatched away John, with all possible haste, to inform himself if my Lord Ossory is there, with orders to stay wherever he finds him, and send me messengers continually to let me know the state in which he is. In this sad suspense, my eyes and hands are raised to Heaven: Lady Egberth is ever present to my idea: I fear – All-powerful God! May my ardent prayer reach thy awful throne! May it suspend thy decree! Vouchsafe at least to change the object! If the end of one of us, must be the terrible warning voice to bring back to thee the erring heart of the other,[b] Ah! let it be me! Let my death rekindle in his soul, that love which is due to thee alone! O, my dear Henrietta! if he dies, you have no longer a friend.

## LETTER XXX.

Tuesday, Winchester.

He is a little better; but his fever is constant and violent; happily, the most dangerous symptoms have left him these two days. He has yet moments of delirium, in which he is very restless. Alas! he is not out of danger! I did not write to you yesterday; I can now scarce hold my pen; I am not myself; I have not tasted food. Shut up in my chamber, I admit no body; it is impossible for me either to listen to[c] or to answer any one. They directed me very well: my Lord Ossory is at Sir Charles Halifax's, in the midst of as good assistance as London itself could have procured him. By a happy chance, Dr. Harrison is in the country; he is with him. John has wrote me word, that when he arrived, he found the whole family in tears. Alas! I believe him. Who can know my Lord Ossory, and not feel for him? How is it possible to avoid loving him? So noble in his manners, so gentle, so benevolent; the good qualities of his soul are painted on his countenance; he conquers all hearts: I never heard him mentioned, without an encomium following his name. What man ever more amiably joined true dignity with good nature, with that familiarity which is not afraid to condescend, and which impresses more deeply that respect, it seems to resign all claim to? Who but must lament that a being so worthy to exist, is going perhaps to perish! – I expect with fear, with impatience – But some body enquires for my woman[123] – Ah! what happiness! –*A tranquil night, five hours sleep, no delirium, the fever considerably abated:* Dr. Harrison *will answer for his life, and even for his quick recovery.* O, my tender, my sincere friend! Give me joy! I bless God whose goodness has restored him to me – Tears of pleasure fill my eyes – Ah! may he live! May he be happy! May every blessing he desires be his portion! Amiable and dear Ossory, thou accusest me of cruelty! That thou couldst read my heart, and hear the vows it offers up for thee! How cruel are the forms which keep me here! Why is it not allowed me to fly to thee! To partake, to soften all thy pains! to bathe thy face with those tears, which are drawn from me by that eternal fondness which attaches me to thee! Ah! rekindle all thy hopes! She, whom thou lovest, is not *cruel,* she is not *inhuman*; she will pardon thee, see thee, love thee – Ah! my God! Whither does this too lively emotion[a] carry me! – O, my good, my indulgent friend! Pardon my foolish wandering – I am not myself – My soul is hurried along – But I feel myself burning – Disordered – I cannot hold up my head; my eyes are heavy – Alas! what is it that makes me thus? – Adieu! he will live, my dear! My prayers are granted.

## LETTER XXXI.

Saturday, Winchester.

I have passed three days without writing to you, my dear, and I am afraid my silence has made you uneasy. I have had a sore throat, a fever, and my pulse very irregular: they bled me in spite of myself. Sir Harry would not lose this opportunity of showing his officious zeal: he has taken possession of my apartment; he does all the honours of it: this man is really good; he is unhappy: he sometimes makes me pity him; but oftener wearies me with his assiduity: I have a heart too full of sensibility not to compassionate his love, though too much prepossessed to return it.

John is come back: Lord Ossory is upon the recovery, and they hope his health will soon be quite re-established: I feel at present another kind of inquietude from the indiscretion of my messenger – But here is Abraham, my Lord's valet de chambre – My God, what can he want with me? How my heart flutters! – So alarmed at one of his servants! What should I then be, if my Lord himself – what contradictions reign in my weak heart! A few days since I wished ardently to see him, and now the name only of his servant disorders me – He brings me a letter – Poor Abraham! He is so overjoyed to see me again, he cannot speak to me – But let me read his letter – It is with difficulty he has wrote it – He has been very ill – See, my dear, what he says.

To Lady Catesby.

Have you then deigned, Madam, to interest yourself in my life? This goodness touches me to the soul. But do I owe it to your compassion alone, or to the feeble remains of that tender friendship – Alas! I scarce dare flatter myself you preserve the slightest remembrance of it. – How sweet would it be to me to think it not intirely extinguished; to think it still possible the ardor of my heart might rekindle it in yours! But you will not hear me. Receive, Madam, my respectful acknowledgments: without examining into the nature of that sentiment which has inspired you with so generous a concern for my danger, I ought to think myself blest in having excited it.

You see he is no stranger to the anxiety I have been in for his life. It is to John, my impertinent servant, I am obliged for these perplexing[124] acknowledgments. But I am forced to bid you adieu: they wait for my letter: I would not leave you a day longer in uncertainty of what had caused my silence? I must write an answer for Abraham to take. Ah! my dear, of what importance is that answer!

## LETTER XXXII.

Sunday, Winchester.

See, my dear Henrietta, into what an embarrassment I am thrown by my vivacity, by the precipitation with which I sent away John, without giving him orders to conceal himself, without commanding him not to mention my name! The imprudent creature thought he could not execute his commission, better than by going directly to Sir Charles Halifax's, enquiring for Abraham, telling him he came from me, and desiring permission to place himself in Lord Ossory's antichamber. My Lord,[125] charmed to hear one of my servants was so near him, and that he came by my orders, insisted on seeing him: Mr. John, as he told me himself, received this command to enter, with great pleasure: he answered all my Lord's questions with great exactness: assured him, *his Lady was more dead than alive when she sent him; that she had a great deal of friendship for his Lordship, and was scarce satisfied with three expresses a day, which he had the honour to send her.*

If you had seen with what satisfaction this idiot gave me an account of his commission, how he applauded himself on the wonders he had done! After all, I ought only to complain of my own want of foresight. I sent back Abraham yesterday without any answer: I excused myself on account of the present weakness of my head. Alas! it is not that I most fear: the weakness of my heart is what restrains me[126] – Abraham again – Another letter – I need not take the pains to copy this: it is almost exactly the same with the last; except the addition of much inquietude on account of my indisposition, which no longer exists. *See me, Madam, hear me* – Always the same. I must answer it; but what difficulty do I find in writing to him! His zealous messenger tells Betty he must not return without a letter. In proportion as my fears for his life vanish, my anger resumes its empire[a] over my soul. I am sorry Lord Ossory can no longer doubt that friendship, of which he artfully pretends to be so uncertain: by this pretence, he humours my vanity; his address does not escape me. O, these men! these men! Observe how they make their advantage of every thing! When all means of subduing our resolves seem to fail, an unforeseen incident, chance, *a fit of sickness*, brings them to the point they had in view. We refuse to see, to listen to them; we fancy all at an end, but their resources are never exhausted. When the discarded lover knows not how to proceed otherwise, he has a fever, my dear; he has but a moment to live; he fills our imagination with terror; he represents himself in a light, which cannot fail of softening us; he places before our eyes the alarming idea of his death, of the dissolution of that enchanting form which first seduced our unguarded hearts; and the most malignant fever is not what kills him, no, *'tis our cruelty*? Lord Ossory has forgot to say that – but Abraham waits – I never thought I had so little understanding; I am quite at a loss what to say – O, that abominable John! Why did he not conceal himself! But why do I talk thus idly! – Is not he who writes to me, the same Lord Ossory, who has caused me such exquisite afflictions, who abandoned me at Hertford, who married Fanny Montford? Are these injuries lessened? No; but *he has been sick*. I will write to him – I have wrote – I shall not send you a copy of my answer; it is very short, very studied, and very bad. Adieu! my dear Henrietta! My tenderness for you is always the same.

## LETTER XXXIII.

Monday, Winchester.

I come from taking a walk on the banks of a rivulet, which bathes the walls of a pavilion, where I often go[b] to see them fish. As it was very early, I amused myself with observing across the river, some young country girls, who were going with baskets of flowers and fruits, to the neighbouring town. They sung, they laughed in their boat; they presented the very image of joy; their habits were neat, their baskets prettily arranged. They wore large straw hats, under which, one is apt to fancy every face handsome; they were really very agreeable. As the boat went off, one better made than the rest, arrived; she appeared very melancholy, and without showing any regret, because they had not stayed for her, she set down her basket upon a heap of gravel, and began to walk backwards and forwards by the river side. I bid Betty call her; she came to us; I purchased all her nosegays, and asked her, why she did not sing like the others? My question moved her; she endeavoured to restrain her tears, and told me with a most charming sincerity, that *she was ready to break her heart; that Moses, one of my Lord Wilton's tenants, had made her die with grief, she and another: and that the remembrance of that other made her shed a great many tears.* The poor child interested me, I would know all, and here you have the history of my little gardener. It is, that Moses – Pray attend, my dear – Moses is a wicked miser; he had agreed, that Tommy his grandson should marry Sally,[127] who loves *Tommy as she loves her eyes.* The wedding day was fixed, the clothes were bought, the relations invited, the fiddles bespoke; and behold, a letter which came from Oxford, has induced Moses to change his mind. Tommy's sister is dead, and has left him some money, and the *vile Moses*, will not now accept Sally for his grandaughter; at least, not unless her fortune is encreased in proportion to Tommy's inheritance. Sally's mother, who is very proud, has broke off the match: and as she is pretty high spirited, she will twist Sally's neck off, if she loves the grandson of that Jew[128] Moses; and poor Sally must have her *neck twisted off*, for she will always love him; and honest Tommy *will break his heart too*, rather than renounce Sally.

Between the happiness, and the misery, of these simple and tender lovers, an hundred and fifty guineas was an insurmountable barrier: I have removed it, my dear: the Jew Moses, the proud gardener, honest Tommy, and pretty Sally, are all agreed again. This moment is one of those in which I have felt the advantage of being rich: the day after tomorrow, I am to marry my amiable villager, and I intend to marry her with splendor. I give a grand supper, an illumination, fire-works, and musick on the water; which will be followed by a masquerade, at which every body will be welcome. My Lord Wilton has lent me the pavilion on the river; it is large, finely ornamented, and very proper for my design. The ladies are all enchanted with this feast: Sir Harry, in spite of his ill humour, is my steward; he receives my orders with as much gravity, as if he was taking out a patent to be prime minister. Lady Wilton, and Sir James, are to do the honours of the masquerade; Lady Sunderland of the supper; as to me, I shall be employed in observing whether they acquit themselves well of the commissions I have entrusted them with. I am gay, my dear, I begin to resume my taste for amusements; I will not examine the cause of this alteration; I should find it perhaps – Do not fancy, however, that Sally's marriage is a pretence for celebrating the recovery of *poor Lord Ossory* – Is it not thus you call him? – John, however, does not know; my secret is safe; Adieu! my dear Henrietta! I wish I could see you dance at this ball.

## LETTER XXXIV.

Tuesday, Winchester.

Another letter! – A very exact and a very dangerous correspondence: I have every moment occasion to remind myself that Lord Ossory has betrayed me. In spite of this remembrance, how shall I resist the tender emotions of my heart?

They persuade me to listen to him. But what can he say? His reiterated offers to justify himself, astonish, and offend me. Ah! how is it possible! He married; he has even a daughter by this marriage – They say she is called *Juliet* – Insolent! To give my name to the daughter of his wife! Lady Arthur, aunt to the late Lady Ossory, has been here eight days; she talks continually of the graces and beauty of this little Juliet: I never met with so impertinent a creature: but I will give you my Lord's letter.

To Lady Catesby.

Alas! Madam! On what do you congratulate me? Of what value to me is the life which you refuse to make happy? From you these cold civilities! Ah! you could not afflict me more sensibly than by this insulting politeness; it is always attended by indifference. It is your pity, your tender pity, which is necessary to my peace; it is the condescension of one day, one hour, that I entreat of you. Will you not hear me? Am I condemned without hope of pardon? Will you refuse me a favour which is granted to the vilest criminals? We have at least been *friends* – Do you then no longer remember you have given me a still softer name? Our mutual love, your promises, your tender vows, are they all effaced? Recall Hertford to your remembrance, my dear, my adorable Juliet. – It is a man once honoured with your tenderness, who begs of you, upon his knees, one moment's conversation. By all that has power to move you, I conjure you not to reject my prayer! Do not continue to afflict an unhappy man, whose fate is in your hands. No; I will not give up, but with my life, the hope of obtaining your generous forgiveness. I have a secret which I cannot reveal but to yourself: give me one day, Madam; in the name of Heaven be not inexorable.

His *dear*, his *adorable Juliet*; familiar enough, upon my word: and you see with what obstinacy he resolves to be heard. Ah! That sickness! In what has it engaged me? See him! The very idea of an interview makes me tremble. But this audacity of determining to see me! – How strangely resolute! Ought he not to fly my very looks? With what face can he appear before me? Have not I a right to load him with reproaches? – Yet he is not afraid to see me! – Whence comes it then, that I am in dread of him? I, who can lift my eyes up[a] to him with that noble confidence, which is the offspring of integrity and innocence? He bids me remember *Hertford*! Alas! if he had seen me after his departure, would he have dared to bid me remember it? He knows the wrongs he has done me; but how far is he from imagining how exquisitely I have felt them! Can he ever excuse that cruel desertion? Ah! Why did he ever feign a passion for me? Why does he yet feign it? I had prepared myself with pleasure for the entertainment I am to give! This letter comes to disturb my joy, to embarrass me, to revive the memory of those hours – Ah! nothing has had power to efface it – You will perhaps laugh at my chagrins; you tell me I *ought to have seen him,*[b] *to have heard him, that all should be forgot*. You, who have never had any thing to pardon[a] but the slightest faults, a few emotions of jealousy, of impatience, of ill humour perhaps, you think one may resolve in a moment; that it is easy to determine – I cannot comprehend that hope of pardon. My design is not to afflict him: I would see him, if I thought I could bear his presence: I would hear him, if it was possible to excuse – But I will write to him this moment.

To Lord Ossory.

Wherefore, my Lord, should I not have forgot long since, an attachment I have found such reason to regret?[129] What should engage me to cherish the memory of the most unfaithful of men? Have you not already made it your request, I would *forget you*? How can you without confusion, endeavour to recall that time, and those scenes, to my remembrance, which I cannot think of without hating you? What right have you now to ask my friendship, after having made so cruel a return to that I was once weak enough to feel for you? If your levity has restored me to myself, you ought only to blame your own heart. I am ignorant what new caprice makes you assert that your happiness depends on the conversation you ask of me; but I cannot prevail on myself to grant it. So long accustomed to think I should never see you again, it is impossible for me to support even the idea of your presence. If you have any secrets it is necessary you should communicate to me, I consent to your writing them: you may depend on my secrecy, and on my punctuality, in returning immediately whatever you please to write. To receive your letters, my Lord, is the only complaisance I can force myself to shew you.

I am sorry I have sent this letter: they say that in lovers' quarrels, reproaches are the preliminaries of peace. Adieu! my amiable Henrietta! Believe, I love you always.

## LETTER XXXV.

> Wednesday – no – Thursday.
> Six in the morning.

O my dearest Henrietta! How shall I express to you the tumult, the emotion of my heart! I have seen him – He has spoke to me – It was himself – He was at the masquerade – Yes, he – My Lord Ossory – Ah! tell me no more of seeing him, of hearing him – I am now certain I am unable to bear the presence of that – I know not what name to give him. Could any thing be more daring, or more imprudent? To expose me thus – I think I hate him – I wish, notwithstanding, I had possessed more power over myself – I wish I had heard him. What is then this unknown emotion which drags me with irresistible force, and compels me to act contrary to my will? I must go from hence; I must return to London – It is not from obstinacy, but from necessity, from weakness, I fly Lord Ossory. I must resolve to avoid him, since I am not able to see him with any degree of tranquility.

The day was already far advanced, when fatigued with dancing, and weary of the ball, I went to take the air on the terrace, which joins to the pavilion. A mask in a black domino,[130] who had followed me above an hour, came and seated himself by my side. In a place so spacious, and where it was apparent I sought only solitude, I thought it a little extraordinary he should chuse the very seat on which I had placed myself, merely to be troublesome; but judge of my surprise, when seizing one of my hands, and pressing it between his, he said, in a faltering and passionate tone, *does Lady Catesby then still delight in making others happy? I was told that species of pleasure had no longer any charms for her.* The sound of that known voice penetrated the inmost recesses of my soul: I knew him instantly: Ah! what other man would have presumed to take such a liberty, to address me in such a style – I would have fled from him; he seized my robe, and held me in my place. At the same instant, hastily throwing off his mask, the hood of his domino fell off – Ah! my dear Henrietta! How lovely did he appear! The disorder of his hair gave a new grace to his features; an air passionate, animated – How different was the effect which the sight of that amiable countenance had on me, from what might have been expected! I lost, that moment, the faculties of sight and hearing: a mortal coldness seized me. I am ignorant what Lord Ossory said to me, or how he assembled the company about me: but when my senses returned, I found myself surrounded by an infinite number of persons, amongst whom my eyes in vain sought for Lord Ossory: I perceived him at last at the farther end of the terrace,[a] from whence, as soon as he saw me perfectly recovered, he retired with precipitation. The ball is at an end, and I am now writing to you in bed, full of reflexion, of uneasiness. I know not how to act. Adieu.[131]

## LETTER XXXVI.

Friday, Winchester.

I have received such pressing invitations from Lord Osmond, my cousin and his Lordship continue to entreat me with such earnestness to come to Hertford, that I cannot long resist their importunities. I know not why, but I feel my repugnance to return thither greatly abated. I have mentioned my design here, and if I was vain, should value myself highly on the unwillingness which every body expresses[b] to part with me. Sir James goes away at the same time: as to poor Sir Harry, his sorrow is inexpressible; it gives me extreme pain: I hope my absence will be of service to him: they tell us, my dear, absence is a salutary remedy for love; a violent one however, which the patient takes with disgust, and which does not succeed with all constitutions. I am coming nearer to you, my amiable friend: what pleasure do I find in that thought! After staying some time at Hertford, I shall return to London, and we will go together to my pretty house at Hampstead[132] – Here is Abraham – What a packet he brings me! all in my Lord's hand – Permit me, my dear, to leave you – I burn to read it – What is it he can say to me? You shall know as soon as I have read the packet over.

To Lady Catesby.

The adventure of the ball has too well convinced me, Madam, how vain it is to hope from chance, or my own address, the happiness of a conversation with you. The horror my presence gave you, the condition in which I saw you, and the grief I felt at being the cause, have determined me to give up all thoughts of approaching you without your positive command. I consent to commit to writing what I intended to have related to you on Wednesday, if you had been able to have favoured me with a hearing. You engage to keep my secret; I know you too well to have the least doubt of your discretion: however, as it may be painful to you to conceal from Lady Henrietta, a story in which you are so much interested, I dispence with your promise of secrecy in favour of this lady: whoever is dear to you, acquires by that claim, a right over my heart: to me, it is impossible your friend can be indifferent. Ah! Lady Catesby! if, after reading these papers, you are not inclined to pardon me, you never loved him, whose passion for you cannot end but with his life.

## HISTORY OF LORD OSSORY.

When Lady Charlot Chester had given that preference to the Marquess of Dorchester, which I flattered myself my assiduity, and the sincerity of my attachment, had given me a better right to expect, I determined to avoid her, and went into France with that design. I was sensibly affected by her perfidy; it prejudiced me unjustly against the whole sex; I judged of all, by the only one with whom I had had any connexion; and was strongly persuaded that interest and vanity were the only passions of which they were susceptible. I armed myself against them, with the knowledge I fancied I had of their souls, and employed my experience with success to defend me against the power of their charms.

I was represented at court, and wherever I appeared, as a savage, who to that ferocity attributed to his nation, joined an obstinate aversion to the established manners and customs of the world. My gravity appeared ridiculous, especially at a time of life when the wild and irregular sallies of youth, for which youth is an excuse, are not unbecoming. I know not how far the French carry their indulgence on this head; but here I have seen too many, who not knowing when to drop this excuse, have not been able, in their more advanced age, to forget the follies of their youth.

Six months after my departure from London, my eldest brother was killed in a sea engagement, and my second died in Scotland, of a fall from his horse in hunting. My fortune was now become equal to Lord Dorchester's, and I fancied Lady Dorchester might possibly repent having been so precipitate in fixing her choice: the regret I flattered myself she would feel, was the only real advantage I then hoped for, in inheriting the estates and titles of my ancestors.

My abode in France did not remove the impressions I carried thither: I thought the women charming, but the idea of Lady Charlot, and the remembrance of her inconstancy, defended me from love. I returned to London, cured of my passion, but not of my resentment at having been abandoned. The sight of Lady Dorchester chagrined me, and gave me a disgust to London: I resolved therefore to quit it once more, and was preparing for a second tour to Italy, when Osmond, hearing of my return, pressed me to make him a visit at Hertford: I accepted his invitation, intending to stay a few days only; but I found in your eyes, attractions strong enough to fix me in my native country, and reconcile me in that amiable sex,[a] of which Lady Catesby is the brightest ornament. You inspired me with sentiments before unknown to me; Sentiments which convinced me I had never loved Lady Charlot, and that wounded vanity may excite in our souls those regrets, which seem to take their source only from betrayed or neglected love.

Ashby importuned you with his addresses; his example intimidated me: the aversion his tenderness gave you to him, determined me to spare no pains to conceal mine. Listened to, preferred as a friend, I dreaded appearing as a lover. I found it so sweet to be honoured with your confidence, to make one in all your amusements, to behold you every moment without wearying you, or inspiring you with constraint; that I had not courage to risk losing all these advantages, by making a declaration of my passion. Sometimes I fancied you saw what passed in my soul: I one day forgot I had no right to appear jealous; my anger and ill humour became visible to every body: my sorrow affected you; it affected you too nearly – What pleasure do I feel in recollecting those first moments[b] of my happiness! Those blissful hours, when without being yourself perhaps conscious of it, you partook of all the soft emotions of my soul! They are past, those transporting moments, and Lady Catesby remembers them no more.

With what pain did I conceal from you sentiments so tender and animated! How did the remembrance of Lady Charlot intimidate me! I no longer regarded her inconstancy in the same light; since I had loved you, I excused her levity; and concluded, I possessed none of those attractions which give birth to love,[c] and render it lasting. I at length presumed to confess my passion; my vows were heard, you yielded to give me your hand:[d] every thing conspired to promise happiness to my future days. In the intoxication of my joy, too ready to flatter myself, I added to my account of present pleasure, the supreme felicity which was so soon to be my portion, when I received an invitation to be present at the marriage of Lord Newport. I know not whether a foreboding of my misfortune encreased my regret at parting from you, but I left Hertford overwhelmed with sorrow.[133] Before I enter into the humiliating detail of the fatal adventure which separated us, permit me to implore your indulgence – But how can I hope to soften you, if I am no longer dear to you; if my very sight alarms you; if that heart, once so sensible to my least inquietude, is now for ever barred against me? What repeated vows do you betray, if the care of my happiness no longer interests you! Cannot the remembrance of a passion so dear to us both, of those pure and exquisite pleasures it once bestowed, rekindle in your bosom a spark of that fire which my seeming infidelity has extinguished? Ah! Madam! let love again spread a veil before your eyes,[134] to hide from you my fault, and only permit you to see my repentance.

I was returning to Hertford, with all the haste and impatience of a lover, eager to behold again the object of all his wishes, when on the road,[135] I happened to meet with Montford, Bennet, Anderson,[136] Lindsey, and several others, who had been my acquaintance at the university; except Montford, who was my particular friend, I had scarce seen any of them since I left the college: they had stopped Abraham, who was a little before me, and when I came to the post-house, where they waited for me, they insisted on stopping me also. They were returning from hunting, and were going to sup with Montford, whose mother had a house in the neighbourhood. It was impossible to resist their entreaties, or, to speak with more propriety, their importunities: they obliged me to accept an invitation which promised little amusement to a man of my temper, and robbed me of the pleasure of arriving soon enough that night at Hertford, to see you even for a moment. These hours were stolen from love; I lost them with inexpressible regret, and made the sacrifice with an extreme repugnance. Montford's mother was gone, that very morning, to London, whither she was called by unforeseen business: thus our supper became one of those noisy and libertine parties, from whence order and politeness are banished; which sometimes end in ridiculous wagers, and often, even in breaking to pieces[a] every moveable in the way, and cutting each other's throats[b] amidst the ruins. Disgust seized me during the first course; it encreased every moment: The insupportable mirth of my companions, in which I could not share; the confused noise of their voices, all speaking at the same time; and the unbounded freedom of their conversation, made me curse a thousand times the hour in which I was so unfortunate to meet them. The coolness I preserved in the midst of these madmen, added to the distaste they inspired me with. I perceived it; and willing to remove some part of the horror I felt at my situation, I fancied the only means would be to lose, like the rest, a portion of my reason: I could not now reach Hertford early enough to see you; I resolved therefore to do as others did, and endeavour to partake of their foolish and contemptible gaiety: My project succeeded; I drank freely,[137] and began soon to find my old companions a little more supportable.

The conversation turned on a variety of subjects, none of which were pursued very far: It fell at last on women; they talked with more vivacity than decency: Some praised them in the strongest terms, others spoke of them with the most illiberal contempt. Lindsey, naturally tender and polite, defended them with warmth: He brought the whole company over to his opinion, that the sweetness of being beloved by one, infinitely surpassed the malignant pleasure of slandering them all. We now vyed with each other in extolling these charming beings, on whom Heaven has bestowed the power of rendering us happy. One spoke of their beauty, the charms of which have such an empire over our hearts; another extolled their wit, still more enchanting, the fineness of their taste, and the delicacy of their sentiments. Montford alone insisted that an uncultivated understanding, and ingenuous modesty, infinitely exceeded that knowledge and those accomplishments, on which women of condition value themselves, and that the most simple were the most amiable: the point was warmly disputed; he persisted; and to prove the truth of what he advanced, sent orders to his sister's governess to join the company, with her lovely charge. A man must have been as little capable of reflexion as he then was, to think of exposing a sister to the impropriety of appearing in the midst of ten or twelve young libertines, flushed with wine,[138] and little in a condition to recollect what they owed to her rank, her sex, and blooming season of life.[a] Whilst we waited in expectation of her entrance, Montford informed us, that she came only the preceding day from the school,[139] in which she had been educated; he expressed the most lively friendship for her, and assured us no body could be more simple, or more amiable. The young lady came, to confirm by her presence, the praises her brother had lavished on her ingenuous simplicity: her air expressed her character; soft, modest, unaffected: a noble form, graceful in all its motions,[b] compensated for the want of perfect symmetry: she had all those charms which accompany the first bloom of youth; and her features without being regularly beautiful, were all together infinitely attractive.[140] She placed herself by her brother, and in obedience to his repeated commands, pledged his friends in those healths which they all at once eagerly proposed to her. Her presence having reanimated their joy, it was happy for her that her extreme simplicity made her ignorant of the transports she excited, and of the expressions in which they magnified her charms. Bennet took charge of the governess, and soon rendered her incapable of attending to the care of her lovely pupil. Miss Montford,[141] weary of a kind of conversation to which she was not accustomed, insisted on leave to retire: she obtained it, though with difficulty; and quitted us with much greater pleasure than she had felt at coming amongst us. Some moments after, distracted with noise, and fainting with excessive heat, I rose up to go into the air, of which I had never more occasion: I walked through the hall, and found myself in a passage, in which there was no light: I observed one at some distance, and directing my steps that way, traversed a long gallery of pictures,[142] at the end of which, I came to a large closet, where I perceived a woman alone: I had not time to distinguish who she was; rising up hastily, she threw down a little table, on which stood a candle, which went out in the fall. By the sound of her voice, and her questions, I knew it to be Miss Montford: I told her who I was, and begged the favour of her to direct me to the garden, where I was going to walk for the air: she told me she would ring immediately for a light; but in the profound darkness we were in, it was impossible to find the string of the bell, the apartment being almost as new[a] to her as to myself. She strove however to recollect where the chimney was placed, and we both took a great deal of pains[b] to find it. My embarrassment, and the ill success of our searches, appeared ridiculous to her; she laughed so heartily at our distress, that her gaiety excited mine. The young lady was not much more herself than I was; she called, but in vain; the servants were at too great a distance to hear us: as we walked at random, we struck our heads against each other; Miss Montford redoubled her laughter, ridiculed my uneasiness, and by a thousand childish pleasantries, forced me to laugh also. Determined both of us however to put an end to this scene, we agreed to give up all hopes of making ourselves heard, and to endeavour to find a door into another gallery, which led to the garden.[143] Miss Montford took me by the hand, and going from one chair to another, found the place where she was sitting when I entered the closet: she told me the door was then directly opposite to us; she advanced, and I followed her: unhappily she entangled herself in the table she had before thrown down, and fell with violence to the ground; her fall occasioned mine; I was alarmed for her, but her repeated bursts of laughter, soon convinced me she was not hurt. The excess of her mirth had an extraordinary effect on me: it inspired me with a presumption fatal to us both: the intoxication of my reason communicated itself to my heart: abandoned to my senses, I forgot my love, my probity, the laws of honour which had always been sacred to me, the sister of my friend: a woman whom I ought to have respected, appeared to me at that instant, only as a female delivered up to my wishes, to that gross passion which has its source in instinct alone. Hurried away by an impetuous emotion, I had the cruelty to take advantage of the disorder and simplicity of a young imprudent, whose artless innocence alone occasioned her error.

Scarce was this moment of madness passed when reason resuming all its rights, I saw my fault in its full extent: the unhappy victim of my crime[144] pierced the air with her cries; she groaned, she wept, and by her just anguish encreased mine, already too great for expression. The moon just then began to rise, and her dawning light enabled me to find that door, the search of which had been attended with consequences so fatal: confused, ashamed, in all the wildness of despair, I thought of nothing but flight: I went out of that closet, which inspired me with horror, and passing from the garden into the court, where my servants waited, I stept hastily into my chaise, and took the road to Hertford, pierced with the most poignant sorrow, which my reflexions rendered every moment more insupportable.

How severely was it renewed at the sight of you! With what goodness did your generous heart interest itself in my affliction! What tender questions! How did they stab my soul with remorse! How did I abhor myself when I reflected I had betrayed you? The pleasure, however, of seeing you, of being continually near you, of thinking I was dear to you; the idea of my approaching happiness; an invincible charm attached to your looks, to your conversation, all together alleviated my sorrow. I was beginning to consider my unhappy adventure as a weakness, of which the remembrance might in time be lost, when its dreadful consequences brought it back to my memory with redoubled force, and obliged me to submit to the just punishment of my imprudence! Ah! what a punishment! If you have loved me, if you have deigned to regret me, judge of my sufferings by your own! Judge of my tortures in forcing myself from you! From you, whom I adored, whom I must always adore, in whatever manner you may treat me! You may possibly remember, Madam, that a messenger enquired for me, the evening before I left Hertford: he brought me a letter; it was from Miss Montford, and expressed in the following terms.

To Lord Ossory.

The unhappy sister of your friend, the wretched Fanny Montford, is lost, dishonoured by the indiscretion of her brother, by yours, my Lord, and still more by her own. She tells you this, without knowing what she has to hope from this step: She has nothing to expect from you; you promised nothing: what right then can she pretend? And yet, if you abandon her, have you nothing to reproach yourself with? I ardently entreat your answer: if it does not soften the horrors of my situation, I will not wait till my shame becomes publick: I have already resolved on the only means by which I can escape infamy: I will bury with me this dreadful secret, and nobody shall ever reproach you with the misfortune or the death of
    Fanny Montford.

Paint to yourself Madam, my condition after reading this letter: think in what reflexions I passed that night, the last of my stay at Hertford. I formed a thousand projects; my reason destroyed them, as fast as they presented themselves to my imagination: I thought sometimes of going to Montford, of confessing my crime,[145] and of giving up to his sister half my estate; all, if she required it. Alas! of what value was wealth, if deprived of you! But how could I have the confidence to propose to my friend a reparation, which, in a parallel case, I would not myself have accepted? After having injured him, ought I to insult the misery I had caused? To risk becoming the murderer of him whose sister I had dishonoured, in violation of all the sacred laws of hospitality and friendship?[146] The little innocent too, Madam, who owed to me its being, was I allowed to place it in the rank of those born to wretchedness, to deliver it up to baseness and contempt? Would it not bring into the world a right to accuse me, to abhor the author of its existence? The conclusion of the letter froze my veins with terror and apprehension. In the midst of agitations not to be described, of regret which tore my inmost soul; wholly engrossed by my love for you, wild with despair at losing the object of all my tender hopes; I resolved to listen only to the voice of honour, and to give up the dearest interests of my heart to the person whose situation demanded this cruel sacrifice.

What struggles had I with myself! How much did this painful effort cost me! It was you whom I abandoned! It was you whom I must renounce! I went to seek you, determined to repose my sorrows in your faithful bosom, to confide to you my crime,[147] and my designs; to implore your advice, your tender commiseration; but my purpose vanished at your sight. How was it possible I could make you such a confession! I found myself unable to begin the shocking recital; I had not even courage to give you a letter I had wrote in the first tumult of my grief: I left you; I bid adieu to Hertford; and quitted you in the melancholy persuasion I should never see you again. I left my letter with Abraham, whom I ordered to deliver it to you when I was gone; and joining the messenger, who waited for me at the post-house, I took the road to Middlesex, and went directly to Lady Montford's.

The violence of those different emotions with which I was agitated, and the efforts I made to hide my sorrow, threw me into a burning fever; I was in a kind of delirium, and scarce knew even myself. As soon as I arrived, I enquired for Montford; as he was in town, they introduced me to his mother: after some moments of indifferent conversation, I mentioned her daughter, and finding she had no particular view for her, I demanded her in marriage. My offer was received with no less joy than surprise: Lady Montford could not hope so advantageous a match for her daughter: though of a family which might entitle her to a rank equal to what I offered to raise her to, yet her moderate fortune seemed to forbid such a hope: her mother conducted me to her apartment, and introduced me as a lover who was soon to become her husband. Miss Montford's face was spread with blushes at seeing me, she cast down her eyes, and regarded me with a melancholy and timid countenance. As is customary on these occasions, we were left together; shame and remorse[148] threw me at her feet, gratitude made her fall at mine: neither of us possessed the power of voice; sighs and tears were the only expressions of our hearts. I fixed a day with Lady Montford for signing the marriage articles, and pretending pressing and indispensable business, parted in haste for London.

I reached my house in an agony, not to be conceived: I was pierced to the soul with my own sorrow, and yet more with that which I imagined you would feel. As I entered my closet, a drawing done by your hand, struck my sight; I could no longer resist the violent emotions of my heart: I gave myself up to rage, and uttered exclamations, which drew all my servants around me: a kind of frenzy deprived me of my senses: during a long time, I knew nothing that happened to me; I was insensible of my illness, and of my danger. My spirits, enfeebled by the violence of my transports, and by the medicines which were given me, had reduced me to the weakness of infancy. Montford never quitted me; what he had been told of my intentions in regard to his sister, redoubled his attachment, and rendered his cares more tender, and more attentive: he applauded himself on the caprice which inclined him to make her appear at that supper; he fancied she had then inspired me with love, and this belief filled him with transport: his discourses on this subject, gave a new poignancy to my sorrows. I recovered at length, and married Miss Montford. What difficulty had I to restrain my tears at the foot of that altar, where it was supposed I had received from the hands of Heaven, the only companion who could make my life happy! After having thus torn me from her who only has that power, indulgent Heaven is willing to restore her to me: but she is changed; she is become haughty,[a] inhuman, unrelenting; she will not pardon me.

I left London for Derbyshire,[149] whither I conducted a wife, young, soft, tender, grateful, perhaps amiable; but she was not Lady Catesby; she was not the dear object my heart had made choice of; whom I must always love, but to whom I could now only dedicate sighs, tears, and a fruitless and unprofitable regret.

Lady Ossory was delivered of a daughter; the sight of her gave me the first emotion of joy, which I had felt since I left you. Amiable little innocence![b] How often have I bathed her with my tears, whilst I applauded myself on having at least fulfilled my duty towards her. Ah! what tenderness would she not owe her father, if she knew at what a price he had given her a right to call him by that name!

I passed whole days in the woods to avoid Lady Ossory; I feared her presence; her amiable attention to please, was irksome to me: I had all the regard for her which friendship demanded, but none of the tender solicitudes of love: I owed her both notwithstanding; but how could I give to her a heart you had already entire possession of?[c] Conscious I ought to make amends by my generosity for the coldness of my sentiments, and ever ready to procure for her pleasures[d] which I was incapable of partaking,[e] I gave her balls and entertainments, I loaded her with presents; she disposed as she pleased of my fortune; it was all lavished on her, even to profusion; she seemed satisfied, and I believed her happy; time discovered to me she was no more so than myself.

Sometimes I had an inclination to write to you, to open my whole soul, and inform you of my reasons[a] for a marriage which must have surprised you so greatly. But it was my wife, the mother of my lovely infant, whose weakness I must have disclosed. Ah! how could I confess to you there had been a moment of my life in which I had forgot I loved you? In which I had failed in that probity, on which the esteem you had honoured me with was founded! Lord Preston,[150] my friend from my infancy, was alone entrusted with the secret of my passion for you; he knew it even before yourself: to him I addressed myself to make enquiries about you. I heard from him that you continued at Hertford, where you were plunged in grief for the death of your brother – Ah! Pardon to a despairing passion, the strange contrariety of its wishes! What would I not have given to have rendered you happy, to have restored tranquillity to your soul? And yet I felt a secret pleasure in thinking you were at Hertford, that you were there alone, that you were afflicted; that it was possible I might have a right to some part of those precious tears; that amidst the sorrows due to the loss of a beloved brother, a sigh might sometimes escape towards a lover who adored you. Your return to London, gave me the most lively inquietudes:[b] you received the Duke of Suffolk's visits; jealous, unjust, I trembled lest he should obtain a blessing to which it was no longer in my power to pretend.

I received every week a circumstantial detail of all your actions: the kind of indirect correspondence I seemed by this means to keep up with you, was the only pleasure for which I had now the least relish. How did these details touch my heart! How did they augment my esteem, and my attachment! What woman at your age ever conducted herself with so much prudence! Or ever blended so engagingly the most austere wisdom, with the most amiable vivacity, and exactest knowledge of the world! What other ever possessed in the same degree those soft, those gentle virtues, which give such charms to social life! That polite and indulgent condescension to others, which renders that superiority beloved in you, which you are yourself afraid to display in half its lustre! – Ah! Lady Catesby! Is it to excite the unmeaning admiration only that Heaven has showered on you its most precious gifts? There has been a time in which you thought you had received them for no other purpose than to make me happy.

After a year's stay in Derbyshire, Lady Ossory was attacked by an indisposition which seemed to threaten a consumption; immediate assistance a little re-established her health; but in the beginning of the winter she fell again into a languor which made every one apprehensive for her life. Her danger, her amiable resignation,[151] and engaging sweetness, during the course of her distemper, affecting me infinitely, I became assiduous about her. When I reflected on my conduct towards her, I was afraid I had given her cause to be unhappy; I redoubled my cares and my attention, to efface the impression which my indifference might possibly have made on her mind: I never left her chamber; I gave her all her medicines with my own hand. I felt in those moments all the force of the bond which united us; I had not fulfilled its duties, and I reproached myself bitterly for my neglect.

I supported her one day to gain a little gallery, in which she had an inclination to attempt walking: her weakness forced her to be in a manner carried in my arms: after going a few steps, she turned back into the chamber, seated herself, and still leaning upon me, perceived that I pressed her gently to my bosom: she seemed surprised, regarded me attentively, and seeing in my eyes all the marks of the most affectionate and tender compassion, she took one of my hands, and bathing it with her tears,[a] *I am very unhappy*, said she, *to cause you so much uneasiness, but I was destined to afflict you:*[152] *the state I am in, would raise a flattering hope in a heart less generous than yours: my death will break those bonds which constrain you; that chain under which you have so long groaned, and the weight of which you have been scarce able to bear. A strong attachment had prepossessed your soul; I have no right to complain of it; my gratitude is, and ought to be, the greater: but pardon, my Lord, pardon these tears; it is the first time I have dared to shed them before you: I have concealed my poignant sorrows in my own breast: your goodness, the tender pity I see this moment in your eyes, my approaching dissolution, have drawn from me the confession of a sentiment which it has not been in your power to return. So much respect, so many benefits heaped on me, to make amends for that love which you have refused me, whilst they made me admire still more the husband I adored, have, without ceasing, embittered the regret of not possessing the power to please him. I wish*, continued she, *that the person[b] whose idea has shut your heart against me, may preserve for you a tenderness worthy of your constancy. I imagined I ought to hide from you my tender attachment, to spare you the proofs of it; the dread of being importunate, forced me to stifle even the strong emotions of my gratitude; suffer them to break forth in these last moments. You have sacrificed to the honour of an unfortunate creature, a good which was dear to you: may it be restored to you when she is no more! And may my ardent prayers[c] draw down upon you all the blessings of that Heaven which hears me, which calls me hence, and where I hope soon to be employed in watching over the happiness of my generous benefactor; of him who made so godlike an effort, that he might not abandon me to that shame, from which death itself would not have secured me. Love my daughter; love her, my Lord, and forget the miseries her unhappy mother has brought upon you.* Lady Ossory might have spoken for ever without fear of interruption: every word she pronounced, was a dagger that stabbed me to the heart. I had neglected her, it was now too late to repair by a behaviour more tender, that long indifference of which she had had but too much sensibility.[d] Ah! Madam! how terrible is it[e] to have done a wrong, and how severely would the injured know themselves revenged, if they could comprehend the bitter effects of remorse in a feeling and virtuous heart! I sent to London for Doctor Lewin, and Doctor Harrison;[153] I called in all in whose skill it was possible she could have the least confidence. It is not to you, Madam, that I am afraid to confess the ardent desire

I had of saving her: but neither her youth, nor the assistance of art, could recover her from a state already desperate: she expired in my arms; and in spite of the assurances they gave me of the nature of her distemper, a distemper born with her, and which the delicacy of her constitution could not long have resisted, I regarded myself with abhorrence as one of the causes of her death: I recollected incessantly what she had said to me; I could not console myself for not having had power enough over my soul, to dissemble at least, and conceal from her that another possessed my heart. But when one has lost all hope of being happy one self, is it possible to be always attentive to the happiness of another?

As soon as this melancholy scene was a little effaced from my memory, I reflected with transport that you were still free: I flattered myself a passion once so tender, was not entirely extinguished; that you preserved the remembrance of it; that my presence, and the sincere recital of my unhappy adventure, might yet be able to revive it. The knowledge of your character helped to deceive me: I will confess my crime,[154] said I, she will hear me, she will pity, will forgive me – How cruelly have you destroyed the sweet illusion!

As I quitted London only to spare you the displeasure of meeting a woman bearing the name which you had condescended to make choice of, in determining to change your own, I returned thither three months after the death of Lady Ossory. With what ardor did I approach the place inhabited by you! What a lively desire had I to see you, to speak to you, to hear the pleasing sound of that lov'd voice! – I arrived; I ran to seek you; as I passed by Lady Bellville's[155] door, I observed some servants in your livery; I was told you were there: My impatience made me overlook the indiscretion of the step I was taking: I went in; I saw you; you knew me again: What anger was on your countenance, what disdain in your eyes! You seized a pretence for putting an end to your visit; you retired; and I remained there; immoveable, pierced with grief; and self-convicted that I merited those marks of a contempt which I found it impossible to support. I called in vain at your door; I wrote to you in vain; My letters constantly refused, my efforts to see you rendered fruitless by your precautions; all my attempts unattended with success, threw me into a despair[a] of appeasing your resentment. I only obtained the compassion of your woman, who had very little influence over you. Castle-Cary did not dare to interest himself openly for me, through fear of displeasing Lady Henrietta. At length, you filled up the measure of your cruelty; you left London, and it was not long before I followed you. Halifax came to purchase an estate here; I accompanied him; I wrote to you: With what haughtiness did you receive this proof of my tenderness! You answered me only to deliver yourself from my importunities; with a pride, an inflexibility, to which your heart is naturally a stranger, and in which I discovered nothing of the gentle, the amiable soul of Lady Catesby. After leaving me three days in the most painful suspence, 't was to demand your letters you wrote to me – Your letters! – Ah! never ask them of me – I can never consent to restore them – I fancied you softened: the goodness, which interested you for my life, appeared to me a return of that tender inclination, which once attached you to me: I flattered myself that friendship at least would plead in my favour. But I was deceived; you no longer loved me; my presence filled you with horror; it deprived you almost of life: the sight of a lover once prefered, once tenderly beloved, spread over your cheeks the paleness of death. It is then true[a] that I have lost all hope of softening your heart? Can nothing rekindle that tender flame? – But you have reason for this cruelty, Madam; I ought only to complain of myself. I should be happy indeed, if I could complain of you – With what pleasure should I then have pardoned – Ah! Lady Catesby! If you ever deign to think of a man whom you believe faithless and ungrateful, what advantages have you over him! You may hate, despise, him whom you overwhelm with affliction; whilst he cannot but esteem, revere, adore her who renders him the most unhappy of mankind.

Poor Lady Ossory! How her story touches me! Can I refuse my tears to her deplorable destiny? What strength of mind! To adore her husband, yet conceal her love from him, on the noble principles of tender respect and gratitude! Why did he not love her? Why did he not make her happy! She was worthy of his attachment. Why did he avoid her? Why afflict a heart so full of sensibility? Had she not a right to his tenderness? What cruelty to deprive her of it? I am shocked at the inhumanity of his behaviour, and cannot approve that unsocial chagrin, of which he made her the victim. Unfortunate Miss Montford! She who banished you the heart of your husband,[b] ardently wishes to recall you to life, to see you possessed of a heart which ought to have been yours: She would not disturb your happiness – Alas! my dear Henrietta! What a difference? I have wept, but Lady Ossory has died – I reproach myself for having hated her: I was very unjust, very inhuman: it was her part to have detested me. I am sensibly affected at her death. Since he gives me permission, I will send you the packet. I know not yet what to think – Ah! that amiable Miss Montford! How melancholy has been her fate! She whom I thought so happy!

## LETTER XXXVII.

Saturday, Winchester.

Lord Ossory had reason to say, the species of his offence was unknown to me. How could I have imagined? – What a strange adventure! – That closet – That fatal darkness – His daring presumption – He calls it a misfortune – *I forgot my love*, says he – Yes, these men are extremely inclined to be forgetful: it is however possible their hearts and their senses may act independantly of each other: they tell us so at least, and by these pretended distinctions reserve the liberty of being excited by love, seduced by pleasure, or hurried away by instinct. But observe, my dear, they will not admit us to avail ourselves of the poor excuse they so confidently plead in regard to themselves: those emotions, though divided in them, are united in us. This is certainly acknowledging a great superiority in our manner of thinking; but at the same time reducing us to a terrible uncertainty, as to the nature of those sentiments which lead them to seek our favour: how is it possible we can ever distinguish by which of these impressions they are actuated, the effects being so similar, and the cause so hidden?[156]

However, my dear Henrietta, this perfidious, this ungrateful, this treacherous lover, has only been inconstant – Scarce even that – His head disordered – His reason distracted – Ah! what a distraction! How many tears has it cost me! Is it possible I can forgive it? But why did Lord Ossory leave me two years in ignorance of this fatal secret? He has given a reason[a] – What has he suffered! What probity, what generosity in such a sacrifice! He speaks of his daughter: *amiable little innocent*! says he – I am pleased to see this tenderness in his nature – Poor babe! I believe, my dear, I shall love her too –[157]Ah! if he had told me this at Hertford, what tears would he have spared us both! I should have put myself in his place: it would have been infinitely less painful to me to have yielded him up, than to see myself abandoned: I should have found consolation in the share I should then have had in the nobleness of his behaviour: I should have lamented him without doubt, but my sorrows would have lost much of their poignancy. I should not have hated, have despised him: on the contrary, he would have preserved all my esteem. Friendship would have joined us in those refined, those tender bonds, so dear to virtuous hearts. He would not have buried himself in the North of England to avoid me; we should have continued to see each other: I should have loved Lady Ossory: what right should I then have had to complain? Why might not this amiable woman have been my companion, my friend? She would perhaps have been still living. I should not have had to reproach myself with having been the innocent cause of her afflictions. But to what purpose, are all these suppositions, with which I tire you? *Lady Ossory is dead*. Her husband has been culpable: is he yet so? This is the point which embarrasses me. The reason of his concealing the secret is very trifling: so little confidence in me – But it was his wife – I know not what to resolve.

## LETTER XXXVIII.

Sunday, Winchester.

I shall leave this place on Tuesday for Hertford: Abraham is here; his Lord has sent him to enquire after me: I believe, however, he is less anxious about my health, than my answer. The affecting death of Lady Ossory damped the first transports of my joy; the soft impression of pity is yet strong; but my heart speaks, and will be heard in its turn. Is it possible even you, my dear Henrietta, can conceive the happiness I feel at this moment? Lord Ossory is not unworthy my tenderness: how sweet is it to grant to his merit, what I feared I should have yielded only to my prepossession in his favour! He has not acted inconsistently with those distinguished qualities, which first gave him possession of my soul: the lover who is soon to appear again in my presence, is estimable, sincere, generous – Ah! all is pardoned, all is forgot! I will not make him purchase by submission, by anxiety, by suspence, a favour he so earnestly entreats: an immediate reconciliation shall be the reward of his confidence – How happy is it that he has thus opened all his heart to me![158] I will write to him instantly: why should I defer a moment the pleasure it is in my power to give him! The following is a copy of my letter.

To Lord Ossory.

You suppose me changed, my Lord, but I am still the same. Sensible to your confidence, I think I ought to be no less so to your friendship. I am going to Lord Osmond's: if you come to Hertford, I shall receive Lord Ossory with that lively pleasure which it is natural to feel at the sight of a friend whom one has long imagined lost for ever.

In inviting him to Hertford, in telling him I shall see him with pleasure, have I not said every thing? It is with difficulty I conceal the pleasing emotions of my heart: my joy sparkles in my eyes: every body says I am grown handsomer within these two days. O, my dear friend, how I wish to see you!

But I have many farewels to take; many parting tears to shed. Poor Sir Harry! He really deserves pity: I have opened my heart to him; he knows my attachment: I thought I owed something to the violent passion he has for me: this confidence, convincing him of my esteem, has calmed his sorrow a little. *He will be my friend*, he says, *the knowledge of my happiness shall console him* – His behaviour affects me. Adieu! my dear Henrietta! I expect your congratulations to meet me at Hertford: I shall be there on Thursday, perhaps on Wednesday: you may imagine I am very impatient to get thither.

## LETTER XXXIX.[159]
### Lord Ossory to Lady Henrietta.

Monday, Hertford.

You write, lovely Henrietta, to Lady Catesby: your hand, your arms, were known, but to whom were they to give your letter? Is there such a person in the world as Lady Catesby? If there is, it is not however at Hertford[a] you must seek her. If, instead of that friend so deservedly dear to you, your heart will admit a new object of its esteem, Lady Ossory is ready to answer your tender congratulations: she has opened your letter with a freedom which will perhaps surprise you; but what rights has not this charming woman, this Juliet? – She is mine, for ever mine: no longer Lady Catesby, she is my wife, my friend, my mistress; the good genius who has restored to me all those blessings, of which I have been so long deprived. Permit me, Madam, to thank you for the generous warmth, with which you have always interceded with your lovely friend for my pardon: she has condescended to grant it, and has shown in this act of goodness, all the nobleness of sentiment of which you know her capable. Yesterday was the day for ever happy –

### Lady Ossory.

This impertinent creature! He will leave me nothing to say to you.[160] O, my dear Henrietta! They were all united against me: I was only invited hither to be drawn into a snare:[161] my cousin managed the conspiracy; they did not give me time to breathe. A repenting lover at my feet, relations so dear to me, soliciting for him, a tender heart, the minister present – Upon my word they married me so hastily, I do not believe the marriage is valid.[162] Lady Osmond is so urgent – so very absolute –

### Lady Osmond.

I come just in time to vindicate myself, a *snare*, a *conspiracy*, *a marriage which is not valid*? What would you think of me, my dear Henrietta, if you were less acquainted with my sentiments in regard to our fair friend? Yes, my dear, I have married her to the most amiable nobleman in England. The marriage is valid I assure you: none of the parties concerned have the least desire to break it. Juliet has certainly great reason to complain of me: her happiness has always been one of my most ardent wishes: I believe it now perfect,[a] and I expect your compliments on this occasion.

### Lady Ossory.

You are expected here with impatience – No feasts, no balls, without my dear Henrietta; I should have said, no happiness, if the person whose eyes follow my pen, was not already a little jealous of my tender friendship.

### THE END.

# THE

# PERUVIAN LETTERS,[1]

Translated from the French.[2]

With
An additional original volume.

By

R. Roberts,[3]

Translator of Select Tales from

Marmontel,

Author of Sermons by a Lady,

And Translator of the History of

France, from the Abbé Millot.[4]

London:
Printed for T. Cadell, in the Strand,
MDCCLXXIV.

# PREFACE[5]

Having already three times offered my works to the Public,[6] and met with a favourable reception, I have ventured to prefix my name to this.

I read the first volume of the Peruvian Letters many years since,[7] and found an elegant simplicity, in the manner in which the story was told, in the language in which it was originally written, that I much admired, and could not help thinking the Peruvian character pleasingly delineated. I was not indeed altogether satisfied with the conclusion, being desirous the Indian Princess should become a convert to Christianity, through conviction; and that so generous a friend as Deterville might be as happy as his virtues deserved. This thought determined me to add a second volume.

I was, I must confess, a little afraid of engaging in the novel kind of writing,[8] being fearful of deviating in the least from that strict delicacy which ought to be always observed by a woman's pen. I hope I have written nothing which can at all hurt the young female mind;[9] but if I have in any degree been beneficial to it, that thought will be among those which will afford me comfort in that dread hour when all the transitory pleasures of this life shall be able to give none,[10] by the reflection of not having lived in vain.

The first sheets from the press of this little work were corrected by Dr. Hawkesworth; but since I have been deprived of so able a person,[11] that task has been performed by myself. Indeed it was not entirely finished at his death, and the last letters have been written under that dejection of spirit, for the irreparable loss of so dear and valuable a friend, as is not to be conceived by those minds who are happy enough not to be so much inclined to attachment, nor so fatally susceptible of grief.

This book, begun under his auspices, I dedicate to his revered memory, not only as a monument of my strong affection, but a testimony of my eternal gratitude for innumerable obligations received from him; to whom, while life remains, I must ever pay the tributary tear.

THE AUTHOR

# LETTERS WRITTEN BY A PERUVIAN PRINCESS.[12]

## LETTER I.

Aza! my dear Aza! the cries of the tender Zilia,[13] like the morning vapour, are dissipated[14] before they arrive in thy presence: Vainly I call thee to my aid; vainly I expect from thy love a redemption from my slavery.[15] Alas! perhaps the misfortunes which are yet unknown to me, are the most terrible! perhaps your ills are greater even than mine.

The city of the Sun, given up to the fury of a barbarous nation, ought to fill my eyes with tears; but my grief, my fears, my despair, are only for you.

Dear soul of my life, what did you in that frightful tumult? was your courage only useless to you, or was it worse? was it fatal! cruel alternative! dreadful inquietude! O! my dear Aza, may you yet be preserved in safety, and may I sink, if it is necessary, under the evils that overwhelm me.

Since the terrible moment, (which should have been snatch'd out of the chain of time, and replunged into the everlasting abyss) since the moment of horror wherein these impious savages forced me away from the worship of the Sun, from myself, from your love; detained in close captivity, deprived of all communication, ignorant of the language of these fierce men, I feel only the effects of misery, without being able to discover the cause of it. Plunged in the darkest obscurity, my days resemble the most horrid nights.

Far from being affected with my complaints, my ravishers do not seem moved even with my tears, equally deaf to my language, and to the cries of my despair.[16]

What people are there so savage as to be unmoved at the signs of woe? What dreary desert could produce human beings insensible to the voice of groaning Nature? Oh! the barbarians, cruel masters of the thunder,* and of the power to extract it;[17] cruelty is the only guide of their actions. Aza, how wilt thou escape their fury? where are you? in what situation? if my life is dear to you, find means to let me know your own destiny.

---

\*    Alluding to the cannon.

Alas! what a change is there in mine! Whence can it be, that days in themselves so like each other, should, with respect to me, have such a dreadful difference? Time continues his circuit, darkness succeeds light, nothing in nature appears out of sorts; yet I, but now supremely blessed! I am fallen into the horrors of despair; nor was there an interval to prepare me for this dreadful change.

You know, Oh! delight of my heart, that on that sad day, that day for ever horrid, the triumph of our union was to have shone forth. Scarce did it begin to dawn, when impatient to execute a design which my tenderness had inspired me with in the night, I ran to my Quipos,*[18] and taking advantage of the silence which then reigned in the Temple, began my knotting, in hopes, that, by their assistance, I might render immortal, the history of our loves and our happiness.

As I proceeded in my work, it appeared to me less difficult: The innumerable threads, by degrees, grew under my fingers a faithful painting of our actions and our sentiments; as it has been hitherto the conveyer of our thoughts during our long absence from each other. Entirely taken up with my employment, I forgot how time passed, when a confused noise awakened me, and set me in a tremor. I thought the happy moment was arrived, and that the hundred gates† were opening to give a free passage to the Sun of my days; I hid my Quipos under my robe, and ran with precipitation to meet you.

But how dreadful a spectacle presented itself to my eyes! The horrid remembrance will never be erased from my mind.

The pavement of the temple was stained with blood; the image of the Sun trodden under foot; our affrighted virgins flying before a troop of furious soldiers, who massacred every one who opposed their passage; our Mamas‡ expiring under their wounds, their garments still burning with the fire of the thunder; the groans of fear, the cries of rage,[19] spreading dread and horror on every side, brought me at last to a sense of my misery.[20]

Having recovered my senses, I found, that by a natural, and almost involuntary motion, I was got behind the altar, and embraced it. While I saw the barbarians pass by, I was afraid to give passage to my panting breath, for fear it should cost me my life. I remarked, however, that their cruelty abated at the sight of the splendid ornaments which adorned the Temple; and that they seized those with whose lustre they were most struck; plucking off the plates of gold which lined the walls. I then judged that the robbing us of those was the motive of their barbarity, and that to avoid death, my only way was to conceal myself

---

*      A great number of strings of different colours, which the Indians make use of, for want of writing, in reckoning the pay of their troops, and the number of their people.
    Some authors say, that they likewise use them to transmit to posterity the memorable actions of their Incas.

†      In the Temple of the Sun, were a hundred gates, which the Inca only had power to have opened.

‡      A kind of governants over the Virgins of the Sun.

from their sight. I designed to have got out of the Temple, to have been conducted to your Palace, to have demanded of the Capa-Inca* assistance, and an asylum for me and my companions; but no sooner did I attempt to stir, but I was seized. Oh! my dear Aza, how did I then tremble![21] these impious men dared to lay hands on a daughter of the Sun.[22]

Torn from the sacred abode; dragged with infamy out of the Temple; my eyes for the first time beheld the threshold of that celestial gate, which I ought not to have passed but with the ensigns of royalty.† Instead of the flowers which the virgins should have strewed beneath my feet, my path was covered with blood and carnage. Instead of the honours of a throne which I was to have shared with you, I found myself a slave under tyrannical laws. Shut up in a dark prison, the place that I occupy in the universe, is bounded by the extent of my being. A matt, bathed with my tears, receives my body, worn out with the distress of my mind; but, dear support of my life, how light will all these evils appear to me, if I can but be assured that you still live.

In the midst of this horrid desolation, I know not by what fortunate chance I have preserved my Quipos. They are still in my possession, my dear Aza; and I look on them as the treasure of my heart; as they are capable of expressing both your love and mine: The same knots which shall convey to you the news of my existence, changing their form under your hands, will inform me of your destiny.[23] Alas! by what means shall I convey them to you? and by what address can they be restored to me? at present I know not; but the same understanding which taught us to use them, will, I hope,[24] assist us with means to deceive our tyrants. Whoever the faithful Chaqui‡ may be, who shall bring you this precious deposit, I shall envy his happiness. He will see you, my dear Aza, and I would give all the days allotted me by the Sun to enjoy that pleasure one moment.

## LETTER II.

May the tree of virtue, my dear Aza, for ever spread his shadow over the pious citizen[25] who received from my window the mysterious tissue of my thoughts, and delivered it into your hands. May Pacha-Camac§ [26] lengthen his days, as a reward for his merit in conveying to me heavenly pleasures with your answer.

The treasures of love are open to me; and I draw from them a joy that delights my soul. While I unravel the secrets of your heart, my own bathes itself in a sea

---

* The general name of the reigning Incas.
† The virgins consecrated to the Sun, enter the Temple almost as soon as born, and never come out till the day of their marriage.
‡ Messenger.
§ The Creator God more powerful than the Sun.

of perfumes. You live, and the chains that were to unite us are not broken; such a degree of happiness was the object of my desires, but what I did not dare to hope.

Whilst I abandoned all thoughts for myself, my fears for you distracted me. But you restore me to myself again. I drink large draughts of the sweet satisfaction of pleasing you, of being praised by you, of being approved by him I love. But, dear Aza, while I enjoy these delights, I do not forget that I owe to you all that I am. As the rose draws its brilliant colours from the rays of the sun, so the charms which please you in my spirit and sentiments, are borrowed from your luminous genius; nothing is mine but my tenderness.

If you had been a common man, I had remained in that ignorance to which my sex is condemned; but you, disdaining to be the slave of custom, broke through the barrier, in order to make me worthy of yourself. You did not suffer a being like your own, to be confined to the humble advantage of only giving life to your posterity: It was your pleasure that our divine Amutas* should adorn my understanding by their sublime intelligence. But oh! light of my life, could I have resolved to give up my tranquil ignorance, and engage in the painful employment of study, had it not been for the desire of pleasing you? but for a desire to merit your esteem, your confidence, your respect, by qualities which strengthen love, and which love renders pleasing, I had been only the object of your eyes, and as such, absence would have already effaced me out of your remembrance.

But alas! if you still continue to love me, why am I a slave? When I cast a look on the walls of my prison, all hope[27] disappears, horror seizes me, and my fears are renewed. They have left you at liberty, yet you come not to my aid: You have been informed of my distress, and yet it still continues. No, my dear Aza, among those savage people, whom you call Spaniards, you are not so free as you imagine. I discern as many marks of slavery in the honours which they pay to you, as I do in my own captivity. Your goodness of heart seduces you; you believe the promises which those barbarians make you by their interpreters, because your own word is inviolable; but I, who understand not their language, and whom they think not worth deceiving, I see their actions.

Your subjects take them for gods, and on that account join their party. Oh! my dear Aza, how wretched are the people whose opinions are determined by fear! free yourself from your error, and suspect the forced goodness of these foreigners. Fly from your empire, since the Inca Viracocha† has prophesied its destruction.

Redeem your life and liberty at the price of power, grandeur and riches; the gifts of nature only will then be yours, and with those we shall live unmolested. Rich in the possession of each other's heart, great only by our virtues, powerful

---

\*    Indian Philosophers.
†    Viracocha was looked upon as a God, and the Indians firmly believe, that, at his death, he predicted that the Spaniards should dethrone one of his descendants.

only by our moderation, we shall in a cottage enjoy the view of the heavens, the prospect of the earth, and our own mutual tenderness.

You will be more a king in reigning over a soul like mine, than in the shew of the affection of a people without number; my submission to your will, shall make you enjoy without tyranny, the undisputed right of commanding. While I obey you, I will make your empire resound with my joyous songs; your diadem* shall be always the work of my hands, and nothing of royalty shall be wanting to you, except its fatigues and cares.

How often, dear soul of my life, have you complained of the duties of your rank? How have the ceremonies which accompanied your visits, made you envy the lot of your subjects? Your wish was to live for me only: Are you now afraid to lose those clogs of which you so often complained? Am I no longer that Zilia, whom you preferred to empire? I cannot bear the thought; my heart is still the same, and why should I imagine there is any change in yours?

I love the same Aza, who possessed my heart from the first moment I ever saw him; he is still before me; continually do my thoughts recall that happy day, when your father and my sovereign lord gave you, for the first time, a share of that power before reserved for him only, of entering the inner part of the Temple.† My mind still presents to me the pleasing appearance of our Virgins, who, there assembled, receive new charms from the admirable order that reigns among them: So in a garden, we see the arrangement of the finest flowers, add a brilliancy to their beauty.

You appeared in the midst of us like a rising sun, whose tender light prepares the serenity of a fair day. The fire of your eyes covered our cheeks with the blushes of modesty, and our looks were detained captive in sweet confusion: At the same time, there appeared in your countenance a brilliant joy; for never before had you seen so many beauties together. The Capa-Inca was the only man we had till then beheld; silence and astonishment reigned among us. I know not what were my companions' thoughts; but what my own heart felt is not to be expressed: For the first time, the united sense of trouble, uneasiness, and pleasure, were mixed within it. Confused with the agitation of my soul, I was going to fly from your sight; but you turned your steps toward me, and respect kept me standing. Oh! my dear Aza, the memory of this first moment of my happiness will be ever dear to me. The sound of your voice, like the melodious chanting of our hymns, conveyed into my soul that soft tremor, that holy respect, which the presence of the Divinity inspires.

Trembling, affrighted, I had lost even the use of speech; but emboldened at last by the softness of your words, I dared to lift up my looks towards you, and

---

\*    The diadem of the Incas was a kind of fringe wrought by the Virgins of the Sun.

†    The reigning Inca only has a right to enter the Temple of the Sun.

meet yours. No; death itself shall never efface from my mind the tender feelings of our souls at this moment, and how instantaneously they were blended together.

If we could have any doubt of our original, my dear Aza, this gleam of light would have destroyed our uncertainty. What principle, but that of fire, could have transmitted betwixt us[28] the lively intelligence of hearts, which was communicated, spread, and felt, with such strange rapidity.

I knew not enough of the effects of love, not to be deceived by it. With an imagination full of the sublime theology of our Caciputas,* [29] I looked upon the fire which animated me as a divine motion; I thought the Sun had manifested his will to me by you his instrument, that he chose me for his selected spouse, and I sighed in rapture – – but after your departure, examining my heart, I found it filled by your image.

What a change, my dear Aza, did the sight of you make in me! All objects seemed new to me, and I thought I now saw my fellow virgins for the first time. How much did their beauty brighten in my eyes! I could not bear the sight of them, but retiring, gave way to the anxiety of my soul, when one of them came to waken me out of my revery, by giving me fresh uneasiness: She informed me, that being your nearest relation, I was destined to be your wife, as soon as my age would permit that union.

I was ignorant of the laws of your empire,† but after I had beheld you, my heart was too well instructed not to feel an idea of happiness in the thoughts of being united to you. Far, however, from knowing the whole extent of this union, and accustomed to the sacred name of Spouse of the Sun, my hopes were bounded to the seeing you daily, adoring you, and offering my vows to you, as to a Divinity.[30]

You, my amiable Aza, you filled up the measure of my delight, by informing me that the august rank of your wife, would associate me to your heart, to your throne, your glory, and your virtues: That I should continually enjoy those precious conversations, those conversations so short in proportion to our desires, which would adorn my mind with the perfection of your soul, and add to my own happiness the delicious hope of being hereafter a happiness to you.

Oh! my dear Aza, how flattering to my heart was that impatience of yours, so often expressed on account of my youth, which retarded our union! How long did the course of two years appear to you, and yet how short was their duration! Alas! the happy moment was arrived! What fatality changed it to misery? What God was it who could punish innocence and virtue in this manner? Or what infernal power separated us from each other? Horror seizes me – my heart is torn – – my tears bedew my work. Aza! my dear Aza!

---

\*     Priests of the Sun.

†     The laws of the Indians oblige the Incas to marry their sisters, and when they had none, to take the first princess of the blood of the Incas, that was a Virgin of the Sun.

# LETTER III.

It is you, dear light of my soul, it is you who call me back to life. Would I preserve it, if I was not sure that death, by the same stroke, would cut short your days with mine? The moment was arrived that the divine flame, with which the Sun animates our being, seemed going to expire. Laborious Nature was just preparing to give another form to that portion of matter which belonged to her in me. I was dying; you was losing for ever half of yourself, when my love restored my life, which I now dedicate to you. But how can I inform you of the many wonders that have happened to me? How shall I recollect ideas that were all confusion, even when I received them, and which the time that is since past, renders still less intelligible.

Scarcely, my dear Aza, had I entrusted our faithful Chaqui, with the last tissue of my thoughts, when I was surprised by an uncommon noise in our habitation; about midnight two of my ravishers hurried me out of my gloomy retreat, with as much violence as they had employed in snatching me from the Temple of the Sun.

Though the night was very dark, they made me travel so far, that sinking with the fatigue, they were obliged to carry me into a house, which I could perceive, notwithstanding the darkness, it was exceedingly difficult to get at.

I was thrust into a place more streight and inconvenient than even my prison had been. Oh! my dear Aza, could I persuade you what I do not myself comprehend, if you were not assured that a lye never sullied the lips of a child of the Sun.*[31]

This house, which I judge to be large,[32] by the number of people it seems to contain, is not fixed to the ground, but being in a manner suspended, kept in a continual balancing motion.

Oh! light of my mind, Ticai-Viracocha[33] should have filled my soul like yours, with his divine knowlege, to have made me capable of comprehending this prodigy. All I know of it is, that this dwelling was not built by a being friendly to mankind; for a very short time after I had entered it, the constant motion, joined to a disagreeable smell, made me so extremely sick, that I am surprized I did not die of my disorder; but that was only the beginning of my evils.

Some days passed,[34] and all was tolerably easy; when one morning I was awakened out of my sleep by a noise more frightful than that of Yalpa. Our habitation sustained such shocks, as we suppose the earth will feel when the moon, by her fall, shall reduce this universe to dust.† The cries of numerous voices, joined to this wild uproar, rendered it still more dreadful. My senses, seized with horror,[35]

---

\*    It passes for certain, that no Peruvian ever told a lye.

†    The Indians believe that the end of the world will be brought about by the fall of the moon upon the earth.

filled my soul with nothing but the idea of destruction, not of myself only, but the whole creation:[36] I trembled for your life; my dread increased by degrees, to the utmost excess, when I saw a company of furious men, covered with blood, rush into my chamber. The dreadful spectacle was too much for my senses to bear; they forsook me for a time, and I am still ignorant of the consequences of this direful event. But as soon as I was recovered, I found myself in a handsome bed, surrounded by several savages, who, by their aspect,[37] I knew were not the cruel Spaniards.

Imagine to yourself my surprise, when I found myself in a strange dwelling, among new faces, without being in the least able to comprehend how this change was brought about? I shut my eyes, the better to recollect myself, and if possible, find out if I was still in this world, or whether my soul had not quitted my body to pass into unknown regions.*[38]

I confess to you, dear idol of my heart, that tired of a hateful being, disheartened by suffering torments of every kind, pressed down under the weight of my horrid destiny, I looked with indifference at the approaching end of my life, which I thought I beheld not far off:[39] I obstinately refused all sustenance that was offered me, and in a few days was on the verge of the fatal term, which I saw without regret.

The decay of my strength had an effect upon my understanding. My weakened mind received no images but such as resembled those of a slight design traced by a trembling hand: the objects which had most affected me, excited in me only that vague sensation which we feel when we indulge a shadowy reverie. This state, my dear Aza, is not so uneasy as it appears at a distance. It terrifies us because we think of it with all our powers about us; but when it arrives, infeebled by the gradations of pain which conduct us to it, the decisive moment appears only as the moment of repose. A natural propensity, which carries us towards futurity; even that futurity which will never exist for us, reanimated my soul, and transported it into your palace. I thought I arrived there at the moment when you had received the news of my death. I represented to myself your pale disfigured image,[40] such as the lily appears when scorched by the burning rays of the sun.[41] Is then the tenderest love sometimes cruel? I rejoiced at your sad looks, and excited them by sorrowful Adieus. I found a sweetness, which arose to pleasure, in diffusing an uneasiness[42] over your future days; yet the same love which made me thus barbarous, wounded my heart, by sharing with you your miseries. At last, awakened as from a deep sleep, startled at the sight of your agonies, trembling for your life, I called for help, and again beheld the light.

---

*    The Indians believe that the soul, after death, goes into unknown places, to be there recompensed or punished, according to its deserts.

Shall I again see you, you the dear arbiter of my existence! Alas! who can assure me of it! I know not where I am, perhaps it is far distant from you! but should we be separated by the vast immense inhabited by the children of the Sun, the light cloud of my thoughts shall hover for ever about thee.

## LETTER IV.

However great the love of life, my dear Aza, pain diminishes, despair extinguishes it. The indifference with which Nature seems to hold our being, by abandoning us to that despair, shocks us at first, and afterwards, the impossibility of working out our own deliverance is such an humiliating circumstance, that it leads us to despise ourselves.

I live no longer in, or for myself; every breath which I take is a sacrifice which I make to love, and every day becomes more painful. If time brings some solace to the ills that consume me, far from clearing my fate, it seems only to render it more obscure. All that surrounds me is unknown, all is new, all engages my curiosity, and nothing satisfies it. In vain I endeavour to understand, or to be understood, both are equally impossible to me.

Tired with so many fruitless endeavours, I thought to dry up the source of them, by depriving my eyes of the impressions they received from external objects. I persisted, for some time, in keeping them shut; but the voluntary darkness to which I condemned myself, only served to preserve my modesty from being continually offended by the presence of these strange men, whose kindnesses are so many torments.[43] My soul, shut up in myself, was not the less agitated: thus my inquietudes were not the less sharp; and the desire to express them was still more violent. On the other side, the impossibility of making myself understood, spread an anguish over my senses, which was not less insupportable than the pain which an apparent reality would cause. How dreadful is this situation?

Alas! I thought I had begun to understand some words of the savage Spaniards; I found a resemblance to our august language in them. I flattered myself, that in a little time, I should be able to explain myself, so as to make myself understood. But I was far from finding the same advantage among my new tyrants; they expressed themselves in so rapid a manner, that I could not so much as distinguish the inflexions of their voices. From every circumstance that I am able to judge by, they appear of a different nation, and their manners and characters so unlike, that I cannot help thinking that Pachacamac[44] has distributed to them in great disproportion the elements of which he formed human kind. The solemn fierceness of the first, shews that they are formed of the hardest materials;[45] but these seem to have slipt out of the hands of the Creator before he had collected sufficient matter[46] for their formation. The scornful look, the gloomy fixed aspect of the Spaniards, are strong indications that they can be calmly cruel; which the barbarity of their actions has too sadly proved. The smiling countenance, the

complacent looks, and a quickness in every thing they do, which seems to proceed from a desire of serving, and which appear in every thing these men do,
prepossess me in their favour; yet I cannot help seeing contradictions in their
conduct, which holds my judgment in suspence.

Two of these savages seldom quit my bed-side; one, who by his dignified air,
I guess to be the Cacique,* shews me a great deal of respect;[47] the other gives me
that assistance which my disorder requires, but his goodness is severe, his assis-
tances are cruel, and his familiarity imperious.

The moment that I recovered from my fit, and found myself in their power,
he who takes upon him the cure of my disorder, (and whom I have well observed)
more bold than the rest, would take me by the hand, which I drew away with
inexpressible confusion. He seemed surprised at my resistance, and without any
respect to my modesty, immediately caught hold of it again. Feeble, dying, and
speaking only such words as were not understood; how could I prevent him?
He held it, my dear Aza, as long as he thought proper, and since that time I am
obliged to give it him myself several times every day, in order to avoid such disputes, as always turn to my disadvantage.

This kind of ceremony†[48] seems to be a superstition of these people; they
imagine they find something there which indicates the nature of a distemper;
but it must undoubtedly be their own nation that feel the effects of it, for I
perceive none; but suffer continually by an inward fire, that consumes me, and
leaves me scarcely strength sufficient to knot my Quipos. Yet in this occupation
I employ all the time which my weakness will permit; the knots which strike my
senses seem to give more reality to my thoughts: The kind of resemblance which
I imagine they have with words, causes an illusion which deceives my pain: I
think I speak to you, tell you of my love, assure you of my vows and my tenderness. The sweet delusion is the support of my life. If my illness obliges me to leave
off my work, I sigh for your absence. Given up thus entirely to my tenderness,
there is not one of my moments which does not belong to you.

Alas! what other use can I make of them? Oh! my dear Aza! if you were not
the lord of my soul; if the chains of love did not bind me inseparably to you;
plunged in the darkest abyss, could I turn away my thoughts from the light of
my life? you are the sun of my days; you enlighten them; you prolong them; and
they are yours. I receive comfort from you, and bear to live. What will you do for
me? you love me, and that is my reward.

---

\*      Cacique is a kind of governor of a province.
†      The Indians have no knowlege of physic.

# LETTER V.

Alas! what have I suffered, my dear Aza, since I consecrated to you my last knot? The loss of my Quipos was still wanting to complete my wretchedness; but when my officious persecutors perceived that work increased my disorder, they suffered me not to use it.

At last, they have restored to me the treasure of my tenderness; but I purchased it with my tears.[49] Only this expression of my sentiments had I remaining, the sorrowful painting of my grief to you; and could I lose it and not despair?

My strange destiny has snatched from me even the relief which the unhappy find in speaking of their miseries; we are apt to think there is pity when they[50] are heard, and from a participation of sorrow there arises some comfort: But I cannot make myself understood, and am surrounded with nothing but expressions of gaiety.

I cannot even enjoy that new kind of entertainment[51] to which the inability of communicating my thoughts reduces me. Surrounded by people, whose attentive looks disturb the solicitude of my soul, I almost forgot the fairest present which Nature has made us; the power of rendering our ideas impenetrable, without the concurrence of our will. I am sometimes afraid that these curious savages discover the disadvantageous reflections with which I am inspired, by the oddness of their behaviour.

One moment destroys the opinion which another had given me of their character; for if I were to judge by the frequent opposition of their wills to mine, I should certainly conclude that they look on me as their slave, and their power would appear tyrannical.

Not to reckon upon infinite numbers of other contradictions, they refuse me, my dear Aza, even the necessary food for the sustenance of life, and the liberty of chusing what place I would lie in. They keep me, by a kind of violence, in the bed, which is become insupportable to me.

On the other side, if I reflect on the extreme concern they have shewn for the preservation of my life, and the respect with which the services they render me are accompanied; I am almost tempted to believe that they take me for a species superior to human kind.

Not one of them appears before me without bending his body more or less, as we do in worshipping the Sun. The Cacique seems to imitate the ceremonial of the Incas, in the days of Ramai.* [52] He kneels down very near my bedside, and continues a considerable time in that uneasy posture; sometimes he is silent, and with his eyes cast down, seems lost in thought, while in his countenance appears

---

\*　　The Ramai was the principal feast of the Sun, when the Incas and Indians adored him on their knees.

that respectful confusion which the great Name* [53] inspires us with when spoken aloud. If he finds an opportunity of taking hold of my hand, he puts it to his lips, with the same veneration that we have for the sacred Diadem.† [54]

Sometimes he utters a great number of words, which are not at all like the common language of his nation; the sound of them is soft, distinct, and harmonious:[55] He accompanies them with that air of concern, which is the forerunner of tears; those sighs which express the necessities of the soul, the most plaintive action, and every thing that usually expresses the desire of attaining favours.

Alas! my dear Aza, if he rightly knew me, if he was not deceived with regard to what I am, what good could he hope to receive from me!

Must they not be an idolatrous nation? I have not seen any adoration paid by them to the Sun: Perhaps women are the objects of their worship. Before the great Mancocapac‡ [56] brought down the earth, at the will of the Sun, our ancestors deified whatever struck them with dread or pleasure: Perhaps these savages feel the same sentiments for women.[57]

But if they adored me, would they add to my other misfortunes the dreadful constraint in which they keep me? No, they would endeavour to please me; they would obey the expressions of my will: I should be free and released from this odious habitation: I should go in search of the master of my soul, one of whose looks would erase from my memory all my past misfortunes.[58]

## LETTER VI.

What a dreadful surprise, my dear Aza! how are our evils increased! how deplorable is our situation! our misfortunes are without remedy: I have only to let you know them, and die.

At last they permitted me to rise, and I hastily availed myself of that liberty. I ran to a small window, which I opened with all the precipitation which my curiosity inspired. What did I see? dear love of my life, I cannot find expressions to paint the excess of my astonishment and the mortal despair that seized me, when I discovered nothing around us but that terrible element, the sight of which[59] makes me tremble.

My first glance but too well informed me what occasioned the troublesome motion of our dwelling. I am in one of those floating-houses which the Spaniards made use of to arrive at our unhappy country, and of which a very imperfect description had been given me.

---

*    The great Name was Pachacamac, which they spoke but seldom, and always with great signs of veneration.
†    They kiss the Diadem of Mancocapac, in the same manner that the Roman catholics kiss the relics of their saints.
‡    The first legislator of the Indians. See the History of the Incas.

Conceive, my dear Aza, what sad ideas entered my soul, with this fatal knowledge. I am certain they are bearing me from you: I breathe no more the same air, nor do I inhabit the same element. You will for ever be ignorant where I am, whether I love you, whether I exist; even the loss of my being will not appear an event considerable enough to be carried to you. Dear arbiter of my days, what value can my future life[60] be of to you? Permit me then to render to the divinity an existence which I can no more enjoy, and which I can no longer support:[61] My eyes will never behold you again, and they shall cease to see any other object.[62]

In losing what I love, the world is lost to me; it is now nothing but a vast desert, which I make echo with my cries. Hear them, dear source of my tenderness, feel for me, and suffer me to die. What illusion deceives me, my dear Aza![63] it is not you that calls me to live, it is my fearful nature, which shuddering with horror, lends this voice,[64] more powerful than its own, to retard a period[65] which to us is always formidable – – but it is over, the readiest means shall deliver me from my miseries.[66]

Let the sea for ever swallow up in its waves my unhappy tenderness, my life, and my despair.

Receive, my unfortunate Aza, receive the last sentiments of a heart, which never admitted any image but yours; which was willing to live for you alone, and dies filled with your love. I love you; I will own it, I feel it, and I breathe it for the last time.

## LETTER VII.

Aza, all is not lost: I breathe, and you still reign over one heart. The vigilance of those who watched me disappointed my fatal design, and I have only the shame left of having attempted it. It would be too long too inform you of the circumstances of an enterprize destroyed as soon as projected. Should I have dared ever to have lifted up my eyes to you, if you had been a witness of my passion?

My reason, subjected to despair, was no longer of service to me: My life seemed of no value: I had forgot your love.

How shocking is a cool temper after the violence of passion! in what different lights do we see the same objects! in the horrors of despair fierceness is taken for courage, and the fear of suffering for firmness of mind. Let a look,[67] a surprize, call us back to ourselves, and we find that weakness only was the principle of our heroism; that repentance is the fruit of it, and contempt[68] the reward.

The knowlege of my faults is the severest punishment I can receive. Abandoned to the bitterness of repentance, hid beneath the veil of shame, I hold myself at a distance, and fear that my body occupies too much space: I would hide it from the light; my tears flow plentifully; my grief is calm, not a sigh escapes, tho' I am quite given up to melancholy. Can I do too much to expiate my crime? it was against you.

In vain, for these two days, these benevolent savages have endeavoured to make me share in the joy that transports them. I cannot at all conceive what can be the cause of this joy; but if I did know it, I should not think myself worthy to share in it.[69] Their dances, their exclamations,[70] a red liquor like Mays,* [71] of which they drink plentifully; their eagerness to behold the Sun, wherever they can perceive him, would convince me that their rejoicings were in honour of that Divine Luminary, if the behaviour of the Cacique was conformable to that of the rest.

But instead of taking part in the public joy, since the fault I committed, he interests himself only in my sorrow. His zeal is more respectful, his cares are more assiduous, and his attention is more exact.

He understood, that the continual presence of the savages of his train about me, was an addition to my affliction; he has delivered me from them, and I see now scarcely any but himself.[72]

Would you believe it, my dear Aza? there are some moments in which I feel a kind of pleasure in these mute dialogues; the fire of his eyes recals to my mind the image of that which I have seen in yours; the similitude is such, that it seduces my heart. Ah me! why is this illusion transient, and the regrets which follow it so durable, that they will end only with my life, since I live only for you.

## LETTER VIII.

When one object alone fills all our thoughts,[73] we interest ourselves no farther in events than as we find them relate to our own case. If you was not the only mover of my soul, could I have passed, as I have just done, from the most shocking despair, to the most flattering hope? The Cacique had several times, in vain, attempted to allure me to that window which I cannot now behold without shuddering; at last, yielding to repeated solicitations, I ventured to approach it. Ah! my dear Aza, how well was I rewarded for my complaisance!

By an incomprehensible miracle, in making me look through a kind of hollow cane, he shewed me lands so distant, that without the help of this wonderful machine, my eye could never have reached it.

At the same time, (by signs which are now grown familiar to me) he gave me to understand that we were going to that place, and that the sight of it was the sole cause of those rejoicings which appeared to me, to have been occasioned by a sacrifice to the Sun.

---

\*      Mays is a liquor which the Indians make a very strong and salutary drink of, which they offer to the Sun on festival days, and get drunk with after the sacrifice is over. See hist. of the Incas, vol. ii.

I was soon sensible of the benefit of this discovery: Hope, like a ray of light, glanced over my heart.[74]

I am certainly going to this land which they have shewn me, and which plainly appears a part of your empire, since the Sun there sheds his beneficent rays.* I am no longer enslaved by the cruel Spaniards; who then can prevent my returning under your government?

Yes, my dear Aza, I go to be reunited to what I love; my love, my reason, my wishes, all assure me of it. I fly into your arms; a torrent of joy overflows my soul; the past is vanished, my miseries are at an end, and indeed forgotten; futurity alone employs my mind, and fills my soul with good.[75]

Aza, my dear hope, I have not lost you; I shall see your face, your robes, your shadow: I shall love you, and tell you so myself: What torments are too much to suffer for such a happiness?

## LETTER IX.

How long are the days, my dear Aza, when one reckons their passage! time, like space, is known only by its limits. Our hopes seem to me the hopes of time; if they quit us without being distinctly marked,[76] we perceive no more of their duration, than of the air which fills the vast expanse.

Ever since the sad moment of our separation, my heart and mind worn by misfortune, have been sunk by that total absence, that oblivion which is horrid to nature, the image of nothing:[77] The day[78] had passed away without my knowing it; for I had not one hope to fix my attention: But that pleasing sensation now marks every moment; their duration appears to me infinite, and what appears most wonderful, in recovering the tranquility of my mind, I recover at the same time a quickness of thought.

Since my soul has been capable of joy, an infinity of objects present themselves, and employ it even to fatigue: Scenes of pleasure and happiness succeed each other alternately; fresh ideas are easily received, and some are imprinted without my seeking for them, and even before I am sensible of them.

Within these two days, I understand several words of the Cacique's language, which I was before utterly ignorant of. But they are only terms applicable to objects, not expressive of my thoughts, nor sufficient to make me understand those of others: They give me some intelligence however, which conduces to my satisfaction.[79]

I know that the name of the Cacique is Deterville; that of the floating-house, a ship; and the country we are going to, is called France.

---

* The Indians are ignorant of our hemisphere, and believe that the Sun only enlightens the land of his children.

When I first heard the name I was alarmed, as not remembering to have heard any province of your kingdom so called; but reflecting on the infinite number of countries under your dominion, the names of which I have forgotten, my fears disappeared. Indeed, how could it long subsist with that solid confidence which the view of the Sun continually gives me! No, my dear Aza, that divine luminary enlightens none but his children: It would be criminal in me to doubt this. I am returning to your empire; I am on the point of meeting you; I rush forward to my happiness.

Amidst the transports of my joy, gratitude prepares me a delightful banquet: You will load the benevolent Cacique[80] who shall restore us to each other with honour and riches: He shall carry into his own country the remembrance of Zilia; the reward of his virtue shall make him still more virtuous, and his happiness shall be your glory.

Nothing, my dear Aza, can equal the kindness he shews me. Far from treating me as his slave, he seems to be mine. He is now as complaisant to me as he was contradictory during my illness. My person, my uneasiness, my amusements, seem to engage all his care, and make up his whole employment. I admit his services with a less degree of confusion, since time and observation[81] have informed me that I was mistaken in supposing his actions to be idolatry.

He does indeed continue to shew me the same marks of respect which I took for worship; but the tone, the air, and manner with which he expresses them, convince me that it is only the custom[82] of his country.

For example,[83] he sometimes makes me pronounce very distinctly some words in his language, and he cannot be ignorant that deities do not speak. When I repeat after him, "Yes, I love you," or "I promise to be yours," joy expands over his countenance, he kisses my hands with transport, and with an air of gaiety, quite opposite to that gravity which always accompanies acts of devotion.

But though I am quite easy on this head, I am not so with regard to the country from whence he comes. His language and apparel are so different from ours, that they sometimes shock my confidence; uneasy reflections overshadow my dearest hopes; I pass alternately from fear to joy, and from joy to uneasiness.

Fatigued with the confusion of my thoughts, sick of the uncertainty which torments me, I had resolved to think no more on the subject; but what can suspend the motions of a soul deprived of all communication with others, that acts only on itself, and is excited to reflection by such important concerns?[84] I know that the loss of one sense may be the cause that we are sometimes deceived; but I cannot help being surprised, that with all mine about me, I am only dragged on from error to error. The intelligence of tongues is that of the soul:[85] Oh! my dear Aza, how many sad truths appear through my misfortunes! But let me banish these grievous reflections; we touch the land: The light of my days shall in a moment dissipate the darkness which surrounds me.

# LETTER X.

At length I am arrived at this port,[86] the object of my desires; but, my dear Aza, I see nothing yet that gives me the happiness I had hoped for. Every object strikes, surprises, astonishes, and leaves only a vague impression behind, and stupid perplexity, which I cannot throw off.[87] My errors destroy my judgement; I remain uncertain, and almost doubt of every thing I see.

Scarcely were we got out of the floating-house, but we entered a town built by the sea-side. The people, who followed us in crouds, appeared to be of the same nation as the Cacique, and the houses did not at all resemble those of the cities of the Sun; but if they of the Sun are more splendid, by the richness of their ornaments, those are to be preferred on account of the curiosities with which they are filled.

Upon entering the room assigned me by Deterville, my heart bounded; for I saw fronting the door, a young person dressed like a Virgin of the Sun, and ran to her with open arms: But how great was my surprise[88] to find nothing but an impenetrable resistance, where I saw a human figure move in a very extended space!

Astonishment held me immoveable, with my eyes fixed upon this object, when Deterville made me observe his own figure on the side of that which thus engaged my attention: I touched him, I spoke to him, and saw him at the same time very near and very far from me.

These are things[89] which confound reason and blind judgment. What ought we to think of the inhabitants of this country? Should we fear, or should we love them? I will not take upon me to come to any determination upon this subject.

The Cacique made me understand, that the figure which I beheld was my own! But what information does that give me? Does it make it the less wonderful? or am I the less mortified to find nothing but error and ignorance in my mind? I am concerned to confess, my dear Aza, that the persons who have the least knowlege in this country, are much wiser than all our Amutas.

The Cacique has given me a young and very sprightly China;* and it is with great pleasure I see myself once more served by my own sex.[90] Many other women wait upon me; but I had rather they would not, for their presence terrifies me. It is easy to be seen, by their manner of looking on me, that they have never been at Cuzco.† [91] However, as my mind is continually bewildered amidst doubt and uncertainty, I can form no judgment of any thing. My heart, alone unshaken, desires, expects, hopes for one only happiness, without which every thing else is pain and vexation.

---

\*    Maid servant, or chamber-maid.

†    The capital of Peru.

## LETTER XI.

Though I have endeavoured all in my power to gain some information with regard to my present situation, I know no more than I did three days before. All that I have been able to understand is, that the other savages of this country are, in appearance, equally good and humane as the Cacique. They sing and dance, as if they had lands to cultivate every day.* If I was to judge from the contrariety of their customs to those of our nation, I should not have the smallest hope; but I remember, that your august father subjected to his dominions, provinces very remote, the people of which were entirely different from ours: Why may not this be one of those provinces? The Sun deigns to enlighten it, and his beams appear to me brighter[92] than I ever saw them. This gives me confidence, and I am only uneasy in thinking how long it must be before I can be fully informed of what regards our mutual interest; for, my dear Aza, I am very sure that the knowlege of the language of the country will be sufficient to inform me of the truth, and dispel my disquietude.

I miss no opportunity of learning it, and make use of all the moments that Deterville leaves me at liberty to take the instructions of my China. They are not indeed of much service to me; for, as I cannot make her understand my thoughts, we can hold no conversation, and I only learn the names of such objects as strike the sight. The signs of the Cacique are rather more useful to me; custom has made it a kind of language betwixt us, which at least serves to express our desires. He yesterday conducted me into a house, where, without this knowlege, I should have behaved very ill.

We entered into a large and more sumptuous apartment than that which I inhabit, where a great many people were assembled. The general astonishment expressed at my appearance displeased me; and the excessive laughter which some young women endeavoured to stifle, but which burst out again when they cast their eyes on me, gave me such sensations, as I should have taken for shame, had I been conscious of any fault; but feeling nothing but a repugnance to stay in such company, I was going away, when I was detained by a sign from Deterville.

I found that it would have been committing a fault to have left them, and I was careful not to incur that blame that was thrown on me undeservedly. As I fixed my attention, during my stay, upon those women, I found out that the singularity of my dress occasioned the surprise of some, and the laughter of others. I pitied their weakness, and endeavoured to convince them, by my countenance, that my soul did not so much differ from theirs, as my habit did from that with which they were adorned.

A young man, who I should have taken for a Curaca,† [93] if he had not been dressed in black, came, and taking me by the hand with an air of affability, led

---

\*    The lands in Peru are cultivated in common, and the days they are about this work are always festivals.

†    The Curacas were petty sovereigns of a country, who had the privilege of wearing the same dress as the Incas.

me to a woman, whom, by her exalted mien, I took for the Pallas* of the country. At the same time speaking several words to her, which I remembered, by having heard Deterville repeat the same a thousand times. What a beauty! What fine eyes! "She has the grace and the shape of a nymph," says another man.

Except the women, who said nothing, they all repeated almost the same words: I do not yet know their meaning; but surely they must express agreeable ideas, for the countenance is always smiling when they are pronounced.

The Cacique seems to be extremely well satisfied with what they say. He keeps close to me; or if he steps a little from me to speak to any one, his eyes are never off me, and he explains to me by signs what I am to do. For my part I observe him very attentively, as I would not offend against the customs of a nation, which knows so little of ours.

I am afraid, my dear Aza, I can hardly make you understand how extraordinary their manners[94] are to me. They have so quick a vivacity, that words are not sufficient to express their thoughts; but they speak as much by the motion of the body as the sound of the voice. Their continual gestures have fully convinced me of how little importance that behaviour of the Cacique was, which once gave me so much uneasiness, and upon which I formed so many false conjectures.

He yesterday kissed the hands of the Pallas, and all the other women; nay, what I never saw before, he even kissed their cheeks. The men came to embrace him; some took him by the hand, others pulled him by the cloaths, all with an air of sprightliness of which we have no idea.

If we are to judge of their minds by the liveliness of their motions, I am sure that our measured expressions, and the sublime comparisons which so naturally convey our tender sentiments and affectionate feelings, would to them appear ridiculous. They would call our serious modest air, stupidity; and the gravity of our gait, meer stiffness. Would you believe it, my dear Aza?[95] If you were here, I could be pleased to live among them. A certain affability, which is diffused over all they do, renders them amiable; and if my soul was more at ease, I should find a pleasure in the various objects that successively pass before my eyes; but as they have nothing to do with you, novelty loses its charm. For you alone are my good and my pleasure.

## LETTER XII.

It is long, my dear Aza, since I have been able to give up a moment to my favourite occupation, and I have a great many extraordinary things to tell you, which makes me catch this short leisure to begin my detail.[96]

The day after I had visited the palace,[97] Deterville caused a very fine habit, of the fashion of his country, to be brought to me. After my little China had put it on according to her fancy, she led me to that ingenious piece of mechanism which doubles objects. Though I was now habituated to the effects, yet I could

---

\* A general name of the Indian Princesses.

not help being surprised at seeing my figure stand as if I was over-against myself. My new accoutrements did not displease me. Perhaps I should have regretted leaving off my old, if they had not continually exposed me to be stared at.[98]

The Cacique came into my chamber just as the girl was adding some ornaments to my dress. He stopt at the door, and gazed at me some time[99] without speaking. So deep was his reverie, that he stepp'd aside to let the China go out, and put himself into her place without being sensible of it. His eyes fixed upon me; he examined all my person with so serious an attention that I was a little confused, tho' I knew not his reason.

However, to shew my gratitude for his new benefactions, I offered him my hand, and not being able to express my sentiments, I thought I could say nothing more agreeable to him than some of those words which he amused himself with teaching me to repeat: I endeavoured even to give them the same tone that he did in pronunciation.

The effect they produced startled me;[100] his eyes sparkled, his cheeks reddened, he approached me trembling, and seemed to have a mind to snatch me in his arms; then stopping suddenly, he pressed my hand, and pronounced in a passionate tone – "No, respect her virtue" – [101] and many other words which I understood no better than these. Then throwing himself upon a seat on the other side of the room, he leaned his head upon his hand, and sat moping with all the tokens of afflicting pain.

I was alarmed at his condition, not doubting but I had occasioned him some uneasiness: I drew near him to signify my repentance, but he gently pushed me away without looking at me, and I did not dare say any thing more. I was in the utmost confusion, when the servants came in to bring us victuals; he then rose, and we ate together in our usual manner, and his grief seemed to have no other consequence than a slight melancholy; yet he was not less kind and good to me, which did not a little surprise me.

I did not dare to lift up my eyes to him, or make use of the signs which commonly served us instead of conversation; but our meal was at a time so different from our usual hour of repast, that I could not help expressing my wonder at it. All that I could understand of his answer was, that we were soon to change our habitation. The Cacique, after going in and out several times, came and took me by the hand. I suffered him to lead me, still reflecting on what had passed, and considering whether the change of our place was not the consequence of it.

Scarce was I got without the outer door of the house, before he helped me up a pretty high step, and I advanced into a chamber so low, that one could not stand upright in it;[102] but there was room enough for the Cacique, the China, and myself, all to sit at ease. This little apartment is elegantly furnished; has a window on each side, which gives sufficient light; but it is not spacious enough to walk in.

While I was considering it with surprise, and endeavouring to find out what could be Deterville's reason for shutting us up so close, (Oh! my dear Aza, how familiar are prodigies in this country!) I felt this machine, or hut, I know not what name to give it, move and change its place. This motion made me think of the floating-house. The Cacique saw I was frightened; and as he is attentive to my smallest uneasiness, dispersed it by making me look out of one of the windows. I saw, with extreme surprise, that this machine suspended pretty near the earth, moved by a secret power which I did not comprehend.

Deterville then shewed me that several Hamas,* of a species unknown to us, went before, and drew us after them. Oh! light of my days! these people must have a genius more than human, that enables them to invent things so useful and so singular; but there must also be in this nation some great defects that moderate its power, otherwise it would certainly be mistress of the whole world.

For four days we were shut up in this wonderful machine, leaving it only at night to take our rest in the first house we came to; and then I always quitted it with regret. I confess, my dear Aza, that, notwithstanding my tender solicitude, I have tasted pleasures during this journey that were before unknown to me. Shut up in the Temple from my earliest infancy, I was unacquainted with the beauties of the universe, and every thing I behold ravishes and enchants me.

The extended fields, which are continually changed and renewed, hurry the attentive mind more rapidly than we pass over them; the eyes, without being weary, rove[103] at once over an infinite variety of delightful objects. There seems to be no other bound to the sight, than that of the world itself; this[104] flatters us, gives us a satisfactory idea of our own grandeur, and seems to bring us nearer to the Creator of these wonders.

At the conclusion of a fine day, the heavens present to us a spectacle not less admirable than that of the earth. Transparent clouds assembled round the sun, tinctured with the most lively colours, shew us mountains of shade and light in every part, and the majestic order[105] attracts our admiration till we forget ourselves.

The Cacique had the good-nature to let me every day step out of the rolling hut, in order to contemplate, at leisure, the wonders which he saw me admire.

How delicious are the woods, my dear Aza! if the beauties of heaven and earth carry us out of ourselves, by an involuntary transport, those of the forest bring us back again by an inconceivable bias,[106] the secret of which Nature only can unfold. When we enter these delightful places, an universal charm confounds the use of our senses. We think we see the cooling breeze before we feel it. The different shades in the colour of leaves, soften the light that penetrates them, and seems to strike the feeling as soon as the sight. An agreeable odour[107] leaves it difficult for us to discern whether it affects the taste or the smell. Even the

---

\* A general name for beasts.

air, without being perceived, conveys to our essence an ætherial pleasure, which seems to give us another sense, though it does not mark the organ of it.

Oh! my dear Aza! how would your presence embellish those pure delights! how much have I wished to share them with you, the witness of my tender thoughts! I should have made you find, in the sentiments of my heart, charms more powerful than the universal beauties of Nature can bestow.

## LETTER XIII.

At length, my dear Aza, I am arrived at a city called Paris: Our journey is at an end, but I fear my troubles are not so.

More attentive than ever, since my arrival, to all that passes, my discoveries produce only uneasiness, and presage nothing but misfortunes. I find your idea the least of my curious desires,[108] but cannot meet with it in any of the objects I see.

As well as I can judge by the time we spent in passing through this city, and the great number of inhabitants which fill the streets, it contains more people than could be got together in two or three of our countries.

I reflect on the wonders that have been told me of Quito,[109] and endeavour to find here some resemblance of the picture which I drew to myself[110] of that great city; but, alas! how different? This place is composed of bridges, rivers, trees, fields; it seems to be a world, rather than a particular seat of habitation. It would be in vain to attempt to give you any just notion of the height of the houses. They are so prodigiously elevated, that it is easier to believe Nature produced them as they are, than to imagine men could ever build them.

In this place the family of the Cacique resides. Their house is almost as magnificent as that of the Sun: The furniture, and some parts of the walls, are of gold, and the rest is adorned with a various mixture of the finest colours, which prettily enough represent the beauties of Nature.

At my arrival, Deterville gave me to understand that he was conducting me to his mother's apartment. We found her reclined upon a bed of almost the same form as that of the Incas, and of the same metal:* After having held out her hand to the Cacique, who kissed it, bowing almost to the ground, she embraced him, but in so cold and constrained a manner, that, if I had not been previously informed, I should never have seen the mother in her caresses.

After a few moments conversation, the Cacique gave me a sign to draw near her. She looked on me with a disdainful countenance, and without answering what her son said, continued gravely to turn round her finger a thread which hung to a small piece of gold.

---

*     The beds, chairs, and tables of the Incas were of massy gold.

Deterville left us to go up to a large stately man, who advanced some steps towards him: He embraced both him and another woman, who was employed in the same manner as the Pallas.

As soon as the Cacique appeared in the chamber, a young maiden, about my age, ran to us, and followed him with a timid eagerness that seemed remarkable. Joy shone upon her countenance, yet not sufficient to banish the traces of melancholy that seemed to be seated there. Deterville embraced her last, but with so natural a tenderness as touched my heart. Alas! my dear Aza, what would our transports be, if, after such a succession of misfortunes, Fate should again restore us to each other?

During this time I stood near the Pallas, who I was afraid either to leave, or look up to, so great was my awe.[111] Some severe glances, which she threw from time to time upon me, added to my confusion, and put me under a restraint that affected my very thoughts.

But the young damsel whom I before mentioned, as soon as she had quitted Deterville, guessing at my disorder, came to me, took me by the hand, and led me to a window, where we both sat down. Though I did not understand any thing she said, yet her eyes, full of goodness, spoke to me the universal language of benevolent hearts; they inspired me with a confidence and friendship which I would gladly have expressed, but not being able to utter the feelings of my soul, I pronounced all that I knew of her language.

She smiled several times, looking on Deterville with the most complacent softness. I was enjoying this conversation, when the Pallas spoke some words aloud, looking sternly[112] on my new friend, who immediately changed countenance, and thrust away my hand, which she before held in hers, taking no further notice of me. Some time after, an old woman, of a morose appearance, entered the room, went up towards the Pallas, then came to me, took me by the arm, and led me to a chamber at the top of the house, leaving me there alone.

Though this moment could not be looked on as the most unhappy of my life, yet, my dear Aza, I could not help feeling the most poignant grief. I expected to have found at the conclusion of my journey some relief from my fatigues, and that in the Cacique's family, I should have met with the same kindness as from him: But the cold reception of the Pallas, the sudden change of behaviour in the damsel, the rudeness of this woman, in forcing me from a place where I had rather have staid; the inattention of Deterville, who did not oppose the violence shewn me; in a word, all aggravations that could increase the pains of an unfortunate girl, presented themselves at once in their most lively colours! I thought myself abandoned by the whole world, and was bitterly lamenting my fatal destiny, when I beheld my China coming in. Her presence seemed to me an essential good[113]: I ran to her, embracing her with tears, and was still more melted at seeing her touched with my affliction. When a mind is reduced to pity itself,[114] the compassion of another is truly valuable. This young woman's affections softened my anguish: I related to her[115] my sorrows, as if she could understand me: I asked a thousand questions, as if it had been in her power to answer them. Her tears spoke to my heart, and though mine continually flowed, yet they were more supportable than before.

I comforted myself with the thoughts[116] that I should see Deterville at the hour of refreshment; but they brought me up victuals, and I saw him not. Since I have lost you, dear idol of my heart, this Cacique is the only human creature that has shewn me an uninterrupted course of goodness; so that the custom of seeing him became natural to me. His absence redoubled my affliction. After vainly expecting him for a length of time, I laid me down, but sleep had not closed my eyes,[117] before I saw him enter my chamber, followed by the young woman whose sudden coldness had so sensibly afflicted me.

She threw herself upon my bed, and by many caresses, seemed desirous to repair the ill treatment she had given me.

The Cacique sat down by my bed-side, and seemed to receive an equal pleasure in seeing me again, as I did in perceiving I was not abandoned. They talked to each other with their eyes fixed on me, and gave me every mark of the most tender affection.

I perceived that their conversation insensibly grew serious. Though I was ignorant of their meaning, it was easy for me to judge that they had a perfect confidence and friendship in each other. I was careful not to interrupt them; but as soon as they returned to my bed-side, I endeavoured to gain from the Cacique, some light with regard to those particulars which had appeared to me the most extraordinary since my arrival.

All I could understand from his answers was, that the name of the young woman present was Celina; that she was his sister; that the large man whom I had seen in the chamber of the Palace[118] was his elder brother, and the other young woman that brother's wife.

I felt myself more inclined to love Celina, when I understood she was the Cacique's sister; and the company of both was so agreeable, that it grew daylight, and I did not perceive it, before they left me.

After their departure, I spent the remainder of the time designed for repose, in conversing with you. This is my happiness, my sole delight; it is to you alone, dear arbiter of my thoughts, that I unbosom my mind; you shall ever be the only depositary of my secrets, my love, my tenderest feelings.

## LETTER XIV.

If I did not continue,[119] my dear Aza, to rob my sleep of the time I give to you, I should no more enjoy those delightful moments, in which I live for you alone. They have made me resume my virgin habits, and oblige me to remain all day in a room full of strangers, who are changed for others every instant, without seeming to lessen their number.

This unwilling dissipation, in spite of myself, often separates me from my sad thoughts;[120] but if, for some moments, I lose that lively remembrance which unites us to each other, I soon find you again in the advantageous comparisons I make betwixt you and whatever surrounds me.

In the various countries which I have passed through, I have seen no savages so proudly familiar as these: Particularly, the women seem to have a kind of scornful civility, which disgusts me, and would perhaps give me as much contempt for them, as they shew for others, if I knew them better.

One of them was the cause of an affront that I received yesterday, which still vexes me. At a time when the assembly was most numerous, this woman, who had been speaking to several people without perceiving me; whether it was by chance, or that somebody pointed me out to her, I know not; but casting her eyes on me, she burst into a loud laugh, quitted her place, came to me, made me rise, and after having turned me backwards and forwards as often as she chose, and examined every part of my dress with the most exact attention, she beckoned a young man to draw near, and pointed out to him every part of my figure. Tho' I seemed displeased with the liberty which both of them took, yet, as the richness of the woman's dress made me take her for a Pallas, and the magnificence of the young man, who was covered with gold, made me look on him as an Anqui,* I did not dare to shew my displeasure: But this rash savage, encouraged by the familiarity of the Pallas, and perhaps by my submission, had the audacity to put his hand upon my neck; I pushed it away with a surprise and indignation, that shewed I understood propriety of behaviour better than he did.

Hearing me cry out, Deterville came up to me, and spoke a few words to the young savage, who, clapping one hand upon his shoulder, set up such a laugh as quite distorted his figure.

The Cacique disengaged himself, and, reddening with anger, spoke to him in so cold a manner, that the young man's gaiety immediately disappeared, and he seemed to have nothing to say for himself, but retired without coming near us again.

Oh! my dear Aza, what a reverence do the light manners[121] of this country make me have for those of the children of the Sun! and how does the insolence

---

*    A prince of the blood: There must be leave from the Inca, for a Peruvian to wear gold on his apparel, and the Inca gives this permission to none but princes of the blood-royal.

of this young Anqui bring back to my mind your tender respect, your modest reserve, and the decent charms that reigned in all our conversation! I took notice of it the first moment I beheld you, dear delight of my soul, and I shall remember it as long as I live. In you alone is united all the perfection which Nature sheds upon mankind, and my heart has collected all the sentiments of tenderness and admiration, that will attach me to you while breath remains.

## LETTER XV.

The more I see of[122] the Cacique and his sister, my dear Aza, the more difficulty I have in persuading myself that they are of this nation; they are the only people who seem to know what virtue is, and pay that respect which is due to it.

The simplicity of manners, the innate goodness, and the modest gaiety of Celina, would make one think she had been bred up among our virgins. While the honesty and serious tenderness of her brother, would persuade me that he was born of the blood of the Incas. They both treat me with the same humanity that we should shew to them, if by misfortunes of the same kind they had been cast among us.

I have no doubt but the Cacique is a good tributary.* He never enters my apartment but he makes me a present of some of the surprising things with which this country abounds. Sometimes they are pieces of that machine which doubles objects, inclosed in small frames of curious workmanship. At other times, he brings me little stones of astonishing lustre, with which it is here the custom to adorn almost every part of the body. They hang them to their ears, fasten them on the stomach, the neck, and the shoes, all which has a very agreeable effect.

But what I am most pleased with, are little utensils of a very hard metal, and most astonishing use. Some are employed in the works which Celina teaches me; others designed for cutting, serve to divide all sorts of stuffs, of which we make as many bits as we please, without trouble, and it is really very amusing.

I have an infinity of other curiosities still more extraordinary; which not being used among us, I can find no words in our tongue to give you any idea of them.

I keep all these presents carefully for you, my dear Aza; not only for the pleasure which your attention in examining them will give me, but because they are undoubtedly your right. If the Cacique was not subject to your dominion, would he pay me a tribute which he must know is only due to one of your supreme rank? The respect which he has always shewn me, made me at first imagine that my birth was not entirely unknown to him; and the presents which he now

---

* The Caciques and Curacas were obliged to furnish the dress and provisions of the Inca and the Queen; and never came into the presence of either without offering them some tribute of the curiosities of the province they commanded.

bestows on me, confirm me in the opinion that he looks on me as one destined to be your wife, since he treats me[123] with all the respect due to a Mama Oella.*

This conviction calms my mind, and makes me easy. I imagine that the only thing wanting is the power of expressing my thoughts in his language, in order to be informed what the Cacique's reasons are for detaining me, and to determine him to deliver me into your hands; but during this interval, how much do I suffer!

The temper of Madame (so they call Deterville's mother) is not near so amiable as that of her children. Far from treating me with any degree of kindness, she expresses, on all occasions, a coldness and contempt which mortifies me, though I am obliged to submit to it, without being able to discover the cause: I am the more surprised at this, as, through a contradiction of temper, which I cannot account for, she seems to chuse[124] I should be always with her.

This gives me insupportable uneasiness; for it is impossible not to feel the greatest constraint in her presence, and it is only by stealth that Celina and her brother dare give me any marks of their friendship. Even they themselves speak with great reserve before her, which makes them delight in spending part of the night in my chamber, and this is the only time that we enjoy, in peace, the pleasure of seeing each other. Though I cannot share in their conversation, yet is their presence always pleasing to me: And it is not for want of desire in them to make one happy, that I am not so. Alas! my dear Aza, they are unacquainted with my inmost thoughts, and know not that life, removed from you, is hateful to me, and that I do not indeed look upon myself to be existing, except when the remembrance of you and my own tenderness take up all my thoughts.

## LETTER XVI.

My Quipos are almost exhausted, my dear Aza; they appear so few that I am almost afraid to use them: When I sit down to knot, the fear of their being at an end stops me; so weak am I,[125] as if I could increase by sparing them. In losing them I shall lose the sole pleasure of my life, the support of my being; nothing will then alleviate the uneasiness of your absence, but I shall sink under my distress.

I tasted a most refined pleasure in preserving, by their means, the memory of every secret motion of my heart, which by them offered its homage to thee. My design was to have set down in my remembrance the principal customs of this singular nation, in order to amuse your leisure hours in future happy times. Alas! I have little hopes now left of ever executing my project.

If I at present find so great a difficulty in putting my thoughts in order, how shall I hereafter call them together without any foreign assistance? It is true, they offer me one, but the execution of it is so difficult, that I think it impossible.

---

* This is a name the Queens take, when they ascend the throne.

The Cacique has brought me one of his country savages, who daily gives me lessons in his tongue, and teaches me the method of giving a kind of assistance to thought; which is done by drawing small figures, that they call Letters, with a feather, upon a thin substance[126] called Paper. To these figures they give names; and those names put together represent the sound of words. But these names and sounds seem so similar to each other, that, if I do in a length of time succeed in learning them, I am sure it will cost me an infinity of labour. This poor savage takes an incredible deal of pains to teach me, and I take still more to learn; yet my progress is so slow, that I would give up the design, if I knew of any other method by which I could be informed of your fate and my own.

There is no other, my dear Aza; therefore my whole delight is now this new and singular study. I would chuse to be left for ever at it; all that interrupts displeases me, and the necessity which I am obliged to submit to, of being continually in Madame's apartment, gives me exquisite torture.

At first, indeed, by gratifying the curiosity of others,[127] I satisfied my own; but that satisfaction is soon at an end, when the eyes only can be amused. There is a sameness in all the women; their manners are alike, and I think even their words are the same. Appearances are more varied among the men; some of them seem to have the faculty of thinking; but in general, I suspect this nation to be different from what it appears; for affectation seems to be its ruling character.

If the earnest demonstrations of zeal, which here grace the most trifling duties of society, were natural, these people, my dear Aza, must certainly have their hearts filled with more humanity and goodness than ours; and how can we believe that to be possible?

If they had as much serenity of mind as always appears upon their countenances; if that propensity to be pleased, which I remark in all their actions, was sincere, would they chuse for their entertainments such amusements as I have been a spectator of?

They took me the other evening to a place where was represented, much in the same manner as is in your Palace, the actions of men who are no more;* with this difference only, that instead of reviving, as we do, the memory of the most wise and virtuous, only fools and madmen[128] seem to be represented here. Those who personate them rave and storm as if they were distracted; and I saw one of them carry his fury to so high a pitch, as even to kill himself. The fine women, whom they seem to persecute, weep incessantly, and shew such marks of despair, that the words they make use of are unnecessary to display the excess of their grief.

Is it not strange, my dear Aza, that a people, whose external appearance is so humane, should be pleased at seeing represented such misfortunes and crimes

---

*     The Incas have a kind of commedies, the subjects of which are taken from the brightest actions of their predecessors.

as either overwhelm with distress, or degrade to the lowest degree, creatures like themselves?[129]

But perhaps it is necessary here to represent vice with all its horrors, in order to make virtue amiable. This thought forces itself upon my mind, and if it is really a just one, how much shall I pity this nation? Our more favoured country,[130] adores goodness for its own charms; we require only models of virtue to make us virtuous; as nothing more is requisite than loving you, in order to be lovely.

## LETTER XVII.

I know not what to think of the genius of this nation, my dear Aza; it runs through all extremes so rapidly, that it requires a greater capacity than I am mistress of, to be able to judge of its character.

I have been spectator of a sight entirely opposite to what I saw before. That, dreadful and cruel, made my reason rebel, and humbled humanity. This, pleasing and agreeable, imitates Nature, and does honour to good sense. It consisted of many more men and women than the last did: This likewise represented some actions of human life; but whether it was an expression of pain or pleasure, joy or sorrow, the whole was done by songs and dances.

The intelligence of sounds, my dear Aza, must be universal; for I was as much affected by the different passions which were represented, as if they had been expressed in our own language. This seems to me very natural.

Human speech is doubtless of man's invention, for it differs according to the difference of nations. Nature, more powerful, and more attentive to the necessities and pleasures of her creatures, has given them general means of expressing them, which are perfectly imitated by the songs I heard.

If it is a true observation, that poignant sounds better express occasion for assistance in violent fear, or acute pain, than words which are only understood in one part of the world, and of no signification in another; is it less certain, that tender sighs strike our hearts with a more tender compassion than words, the odd arrangement of which sometimes produces just a contrary effect?

Do not brisk lively sounds naturally excite in our souls that gaiety, which a diverting story or a joke, properly introduced, can but imperfectly raise?

Are the expressions of any language so forcible, as to be able to give the genuine pleasure which the natural sports of animals excite? Dancing seems to imitate Nature, and inspires the same kind of feelings.

In short, my dear Aza, every thing in this last scene was conformable to Nature and Humanity. Can any thing be so beneficial to man, as breathing into his soul a sensible idea of joy?

I felt this, and was transported by it, when I was interrupted by an accident that happened to Celina.

As we came out, we stepped a little aside from the crowd, and leaned on each other for fear of falling. Deterville was a little before us, leading his sister-in-law; when a young handsome savage came up to Celina, and whispering a few words to her, in a very low tone of voice, gave her a bit of paper, which she had scarcely strength to receive, and retired.

Celina was so frightened at his approach, that it made me share the fright with her, but she turned her head towards him, in a languishing manner, when he left us: She seemed so weak, that fearing she was attacked by some sudden illness, I was going to call Deterville to her assistance; but she stopped me, and putting her finger on my mouth, gave me to understand that I should be silent: And I chose rather to feel uneasiness, than disoblige her.

The same evening, when the brother and sister came, as usual, into my chamber, Celina shewed the Cacique the paper she had received. By the little I could understand of their conversation, I should have imagined that the young man who gave it her had been her lover, if it had been natural to be frightened at the presence of what one loves.

Many other remarks have I made, my dear Aza, which you should have known; but alas! my Quipos are at an end, the last threads are in my hands, and I am now tying the last knots. The knots which seemed to me a chain of communication betwixt your heart and mine, are now the only sorrowful objects of my regret. Dear delusive thoughts now quit me, frightful truths take their place; my wandering mind, bewildered in the immense void of absence, will henceforth be annihilated with the same rapidity as time. I seem to be separated anew, my dear Aza, and snatched from your love. I lose you! I quit you! we shall meet no more! Aza, dear hope of my heart, how distant indeed shall we now be removed from each other!

## LETTER XVIII.

How much time has passed, my dear Aza! since I last enjoyed the artificial happiness of believing my soul held converse with yours; since that time the sun has run half his course.[131] How much courage was necessary to support it! I looked forward only to futurity, and the present time did not seem worthy to be computed. My thoughts were nothing but desires, my reflections only so many projects, and my sentiments a series of hopes. I have scarce learned to form these figures, and yet will I now endeavour to make them the interpreters of my passion.

I feel new life from this tender employ: Restored to myself, I exist anew.[132] Aza, how dear are you to my soul, and what delight do I take in telling you so, in painting these sentiments, and giving them every means of existence! I would trace them upon the hardest metal, upon the walls of my chamber, on my clothes, upon every thing that surrounds me, and express them in all languages.

Alas! how fatal has the knowlege of the language which I now use been to me! How deceitful were the hopes that prevailed on me to learn it! Scarcely was I acquainted with it, but a new world opened before me; each object took a different form, and every light I gained, shewed me a fresh misfortune.

My eyes, my heart, my soul, even the Sun himself, has deceived me. For I have been fatally convinced that he enlightens the whole world, of which your empire, and the various kingdoms that acknowledge your supremacy, are only a small portion. Do not think, my dear Aza, that I am imposed upon in these things; incredible as they may appear, they are indeed but too well proved.

Far from being amongst people subject to your dominion, I am not only under a foreign power, but so prodigiously remote from your empire, that our nation had still been unknown here, if the avarice of the Spaniards had not made them surmount the greatest dangers to come at us.

Will not love do as much as the desire of riches has done? If you love me, if you desire to see me, if your thoughts are still bestowed on the unhappy Zilia, I have every thing to expect from your tenderness and generosity. Could I but learn the roads that would conduct me to you, the dangers that may be to be surmounted, or the fatigues which are to be born, would be so many pleasures to my heart.

## LETTER XIX.

I am as yet so poor a proficient in the art of writing, that it takes me up a deal of time only to put together a few lines; and often does it happen, my dear Aza, that after having written much, I cannot myself divine what I have endeavoured to express. I am perplexed, my ideas are confounded, and I forget what I had with difficulty revolved in my memory. I begin again, do no better, and yet I proceed.

The task would be easier to me, if I had nothing to say but express my own tenderness; the quickness of my feelings would then overcome all difficulties.

But that is not sufficient, I wish to give you an account of all that has passed during the long interval of my silence. I would make you acquainted with every thing I do; and yet, of so little importance are my actions, so uniform has my life for some time been, that one day seems to me just the same as another.

The principal event that has happened has been Deterville's departure. As long a time as they call here Six Months, he has been gone to fight for the interest of his sovereign. When he took his leave, I was unacquainted with his language; but by the grief he shewed at parting from his sister and me, I understood that we were going to lose him for a long time.

I shed many tears, a thousand fears filled my soul, lest the kindness of Celina should decrease.[133] In him I lost the strongest hope I had of seeing you again. To whom could I have had recourse, if any new misfortunes had befallen me? nobody understood my language.

My fears were not ill-grounded;[134] in a short time I felt the effects of his absence: Madame, his mother, whose contempt I had before but too much felt, and who had kept me so much with her only to indulge her vanity on account of my birth, and to shew her authority over me, ordered me to be shut up with Celina in a house of virgins, where we now are; and there is such a sameness in our manner of life, that it can produce nothing that can give any entertainment.

This retirement would not be displeasing to me, if it had not cut me off, just as I began to understand, from the instructions I wanted in order to carry on my design of coming to you. The virgins who live here are so exceeding ignorant, that they cannot answer the most trifling questions.

The worship which they give to the Divinity of this country, requires that they should renounce all his blessings, all the feelings of the soul, all intelligence of the mind, and, I think, even reason itself, if I may judge from their conversation.

Though shut up like ours, these virgins have an advantage which is not to be met with in the Temple of the Sun. The walls are open in several places, secured only by cross bars of iron, so close, that there is no getting betwixt them. From places inclosed by these grates, which they call Parlours, they have the liberty of conversing with persons who are without.

And through one of these convenient places it is that I continue to have my instructions in writing. I speak to nobody but the master who gives them to me, and his ignorance in every thing but his art, is not likely to enlighten my mind. Celina seems to know no more than the rest; in the answers she gives to my questions, I observe a perplexity, which can proceed from nothing but aukward dissimulation or dark ignorance. Whatever it is, her conversation is confined only to the affairs of her own heart, and those of her family.

The young Frenchman who spoke to her as we came from the singing entertainment, is her lover, as I indeed imagined.

But Madam Deterville, who will not let them marry, forbids her his sight; and the more effectually to prevent her seeing him, will not permit her to speak at the gate to any person whatever.

Not that her choice is at all an unworthy one; but this haughty and unnatural mother, taking advantage of a barbarous custom established among the great in this country, obliges Celina to put on the virgin's habit, in order to enrich her eldest son.

From the same cruel motive, she has forced Deterville to enter into a particular order, from which he can not be disengaged, after he has pronounced certain words called vows.

Celina, with great resolution, opposes the sacrifice they would make of her; and her courage is supported by letters from her lover, which I receive from my writing-master, and deliver to her. Yet this contradiction so alters her character, that, instead of shewing me the same kindness she did before I spoke her language, she spreads such a sowerness over all our conversations, as renders my anguish the more acute.

Her sorrows, of which I am the constant confident, I hear without disgust. I lament them without deceit, and endeavour to sooth her with my friendship; but if my tenderness, awakened by the picture of hers, makes me seek ease to my oppressed heart, by only mentioning your name, impatient anger is immediately painted in her countenance; she disputes your understanding, your virtue, and even your love.

My very China, (I give her no other name, this having pleased so well that it has been continued) my China, who seemed to have an affection for me, and never disputed to obey me in any thing, now takes the liberty to tell me I must think no more of you; and if I bid her be silent, she quits me. Celina then comes in, and I hide my resentment.

This tyrannical government increases my evils. I have nothing left but the painful pleasure of covering this paper with expressions of tenderness, it being the only kind witness of the sentiments of my heart.

Alas! perhaps the trouble I take is useless; perhaps you will never know that I live for you alone. This dreadful thought enfeebles my mind, yet does not prevent my design of continuing to write to you. I please myself with the delusion, that my life may be preserved for you. I banish reason, when it cruelly tells me the contrary. If I had not the hope of seeing you again, I am very certain, my dear Aza, I must die; for life without you is insupportable to me.

## LETTER XX.

Hitherto, my dear Aza, engaged only in the affairs of my heart, I have said nothing to you concerning those of my mind; yet these are not less perplexing because I have omitted to write them.[135] I experience one entirely unknown among us, and which nothing but the equivocal genius of this nation could invent.

The government of this empire, quite opposite to that of yours, must certainly be defective. Among us, the Capa Inca is obliged to provide for the subsistence of his people in Europe; the sovereigns subsist only on the labours of their subjects,[136] by which means their crimes and misfortunes proceed chiefly from unsatisfied necessities.

The unhappiness of the nobles arises in general from the difficulties they are under to reconcile their apparent magnificence with their real misery.

The common people support life by what is called commerce or industry, the smallest evil arising from which is insincerity.

Some of the people, in order to live, are obliged to depend on the humanity of others, which is so bounded, that those wretches can scarcely be said to exist.

Without gold, it is impossible to be possessed of any part of that land which Nature has given in common to all men. Without having what they call wealth, it is impossible to have gold; and by a false conclusion, contrary to reason and the light of Nature, think it a shame[137] to receive from any other than their sovereign, the means of life, and the support of dignity. By this method, they give that sovereign so small an opportunity of bestowing his liberality,[138] that the number of his subjects who are provided for by his favours are so few, in comparison of those who are miserable, that there would be as much folly in pretending to any share in them, as there would be infamy, in obtaining deliverance by death from the impossibility of living without shame.

The knowlege of these sad truths raised in my heart at first, only pity for the unhappy people, and indignation against their laws. But, alas! how many cruel reflections does the contemptuous manner in which I hear them speak of those who are not rich, cause me to make on myself! I have neither gold, land, or title, and yet I am forced to make one of the citizens of this place. Oh! Heaven! in what class must I rank myself?

Though I am a stranger to every sense of shame, which does not arise from the knowlege of a fault; though I am convinced it is foolish to blush for things which depend neither on my power nor will, I cannot help feeling[139] from the idea which others conceive of me; and my sufferings would be insupportable, if I did not hope that your generosity would one day put me in a condition to return those favours, by which I once thought myself honoured, but which now humble me to the lowest degree.

Not that Celina omits any thing in her power to quiet my uneasiness in this particular; but what I daily see and hear in this country, gives me a general doubt of their sincerity. Their virtues, my dear Aza, are as superficial as their riches. The moveables, which I once thought were of gold, have only a thin covering of that metal, their true substance being wood. In the same manner, what they call politeness, has all the outward appearance of virtue, and lightly veils their faults; but a little attention will discover the falseness of them, as well as of their artificial magnificence.

I am indebted for part of this knowlege to a kind of writing they call books; which, though I found it very difficult to understand them, have been very useful to me. I draw ideas from them; Celina explains to me as far as she understands, and I form such notions as I think are likely to be just.

Some of these books teach me what men have done, and others what they have thought. I cannot explain to you, my dear Aza, the exquisite pleasure I should take in reading them, if I did but better understand them; nor the earnest desire I have to be acquainted with some of those divine men who compose them.

As they are to the soul, what the sun is to the earth, I should, with them, find all the assistance, all the light I require; but I have no hope of meeting with that satisfaction. Though Celina reads often, her mind is not sufficiently improved to satisfy mine. As if she had never reflected that books were made by men, she is ignorant not only of their names, but even that such men ever lived.[140]

I will convey to you, my dear Aza, all that I can collect from these surprising geniuses: I will explain them in our language, and shall taste supreme happiness in giving a new pleasure to him I love. Alas! shall I ever be able to perform my promise?

## LETTER XXI.

I shall not be at any future loss for matter to entertain you with, my dear Aza; they have suffered me to talk with a Cusipata, whom they hear call a Religious; he understands every thing, and has promised to instruct me in all his knowlege. He is as polite as a great Lord, and as learned as an Amatas; he is as well versed in the customs and manners of the world, as in the tenets of his religion. His conversation has been more instructive than a book, and has given me that pleasure which I never before felt since my misfortunes separated me from you.

He came to instruct me in the religion of France, and exhort me to embrace it; which I should certainly have done, if I had been well assured he gave me a true picture of it.

By what he says of the virtues he teaches, they are quite agreeable to the law of Nature, and of equal purity with our own; but either I want discernment, or the customs and manners of this nation seem not to agree with their religion. On the contrary, I find such a want of connection between them, that my reason cannot submit to the belief of what my tutor tells me.

The origin and principles of this religion did not appear to me more wonderful or incredible than the history of Mancocapac, and the lake Tisicaca:* I should therefore readily have embraced it, if the Cusipata had not treated the worship of the Sun with great contempt; and wherever we perceive an instructor partial, we lose our confidence.

I might have used the same arguments against him which he did against me; but as we are forbidden by the laws of humanity to give a blow to a fellow-creature, because it is doing him an injury, is there not more reason that we should not hurt his mind by despising his opinions. I satisfied myself, therefore, with explaining to him my own thoughts, but did not attempt to contradict his.

Besides, a tenderer concern made me change the subject of our conversation. As soon as I could interrupt him, I asked him how far the city of Paris was

---

*        See the History of the Incas.

from that of Cuzco,[141] and if there was any possibility of getting from one to the other? The Cusipata kindly satisfied me on this head, and though the distance he told me there was betwixt the two cities was sufficient to make me ever despair of reaching Cuzco; though the difficulty of performing this voyage seemed almost insurmountable; yet it was enough for me to know that it was possible, in order to confirm my courage, and communicate[142] my design to the good Father.

He seemed astonished, and endeavoured to divert me from my project by such tender words, that I was myself moved at the dangers I was likely to be exposed to; but my resolution remained unshaken, and I pressed the Cusipata, in the warmest manner, to tell me by what methods I could return into my country. He declined entering into particulars, and only said, that Deterville being in great credit, through his high birth and personal merit, could do much for me;[143] and that having an uncle who had great interest in the court of Spain, he might, with more ease than any other man, procure me news from our unhappy country.

The better to persuade me to wait for his return, which he assured me was not now far off, he added, that after the obligations I owed this generous friend, I could not, with honour, dispose of myself without consulting him.[144] I acknowledged the truth of what he said, and with pleasure heard the encomiums he made on Deterville, and those rare qualities which raise him even above his rank. The weight of favours is light, my dear Aza, when one receives them only from the hands of Virtue.

This learned man informed me also, by what chance the Spaniards were conducted to your unfortunate empire; and that the thirst of gold was the only cause of their cruelty. He then explained to me, in what manner the right of war had made me fall into the hands of Deterville, in a fight by which he was conqueror, after having taken several ships from the Spaniards, among which was that in which I had embarked.

It was some advantage, my dear Aza, that though he has confirmed my misfortunes, he has, however, drawn me out of that dark obscurity in which I lived, with regard to all those extraordinary events. This is no small comfort to me, and for what remains, I must wait the return of Deterville. He is humane, noble, virtuous; I have every thing to hope from his generosity; and if he restores me to you, what a blessing! what joy! what happiness!


## LETTER XXII.

I was in hopes, my dear Aza, to have made a friend of the learned Cusipata; but a second visit from him has destroyed that good opinion which the first had given me: In short, we have quarrelled.

At first he appeared to me gentle and sincere, but in the last visit he appeared all rudeness and falsehood.[145]

My mind being easy with regard to the object of my tenderness, I desired him to satisfy my curiosity concerning the wonderful men who write books: I began by enquiring what rank they held in the world; what acts of veneration were paid to them; and in fine, what were the honours and triumphs conferred on them, for so many blessings as they bestowed on society.

I know not how my questions were productive of mirth; but he smiled at every one of them, and answered me in so uncertain a manner, that it was easy to perceive he deceived me.

Ought I to believe that persons who understand and delineate so well the nicest delicacies of virtue, should not be possessed of more; nay, that they should sometimes be possessed of less than other men?[146] Can I believe that interest can be the guide of a labour more than human, and that so many pains are rewarded only by a few compliments, or at most a little[147] money?

Can I persuade myself, that in this haughty nation,[148] men of an acknowledged superior understanding, are reduced to the sad necessity of selling their thoughts, as people sell the poorest productions of the earth for bread?[149]

Falsehood, my dear Aza, is no less displeasing to me when it appears through the thin veil of pleasantry, than when concealed under a thick mask of gravity:[150] This behaviour of the Father provoked me, and I did not descend even to give him an answer.

But, finding I should not be able to satisfy myself with regard to this enquiry, I changed the conversation to that of my intended voyage; instead of dissuading me from it with the same gentleness as before, he opposed such striking and potent reasons against it, that I had nothing to argue in favour of it but my passion, and this I frankly confessed.

At first he put on an air of gaiety,[151] and answered only by jokes, which, insipid as they were, gave me offence. I earnestly endeavoured to convince him of my truth; but, in proportion as my expressions grew stronger, and proved the sincerity of my heart,[152] his countenance and words grew severe. He dared even to tell me, that my love for you was incompatible with virtue, and that I must renounce either the one or the other; for it was impossible to continue my passion, without being criminal.

My indignation rose at these words,[153] and I forgot the moderation I had prescribed myself, so far as to load him with reproaches. I told him the opinion I had of his veracity,[154] and protested to him a thousand times that I would love you for ever; then, without waiting for an answer I left him, and shut myself up in my chamber, where I was sure he would not follow me.

Oh! my dear Aza! how incongruous is the reason of this country! always at war with itself; I cannot understand how I am to obey some of its precepts without contradicting many others.

It agrees in general, that to do good is the first duty; it approves of thankfulness, and forbids ingratitude.

It allows that it would be laudable in me to re-establish you on the throne of your fathers, were it in my power;[155] but it is a crime to preserve for you a greater good, in the truth and sincerity of my own heart,[156] than the empire of the world could bestow.

They would commend me, if I could reward your virtues with the treasures of Peru. But, stripped of all, and dependent for every thing upon others, I possess only my love: That they would tear from you, and call it virtue to become ungrateful. Ah! my dear Aza! how much should I deceive them, if I allowed that I could for one moment cease to love you. Faithful to their laws, I shall be so to those of my own heart, and live for you only.

## LETTER XXIII.

Nothing, my dear Aza, can surpass the joy which I felt at the return of Deterville, except the seeing you; but surely I am never more to taste unmixed pleasure, or it would not so soon have been followed by a sorrow, which still sensibly affects me.

I was yesterday morning sitting with Celina in my chamber, when somebody coming to whisper her, she went out; she had not been long gone, before I was sent for to the parlour. I ran thither, and how much was I surprised to behold her brother at the gate.

I did not disguise the pleasure I received at seeing him to whom I owe so much.[157] As feelings of this kind are quite agreeable to virtue, I expressed them with all the ardour that I felt.

I saw my deliverer, the only support of my being; I spoke without any restraint of you, of my love, of my designs, and my joy increased even to transports.

Not speaking French when Deterville left us; how many things had I to tell him? how many questions to ask? and how many thanks to return? desirous to say all at once, I spoke bad French, and yet continued to talk on.

During this time I perceived that Deterville changed countenance; the chagrin which I remarked in his face when I entered, disappeared; joy took its place; and I, pleased to give him pleasure, did every thing in my power to increase it. Alas! ought I to have feared giving too much delight to a friend to whom I owe every thing, and from whom I hope every thing? yet my sincerity threw me[158] into an error, which now costs me many tears.

Celina left us as soon as I came in; her presence perhaps might have prevented so cruel an explanation.

Deterville, attentive to my words, seemed unwilling to interrupt me;[159] I was desirous of gaining from him instructions relating to my journey; the motives for which I would have explained to him, but wanted words, which I in vain endeavoured to find: I was silent and embarrassed,[160] he availed himself of this moment, and falling on one knee before the grate, which he took hold of with both his hands, he said to me, in a passionate tone; To what sentiments, divine Zilia, must I ascribe the pleasure which I see so artlessly exposed in your fair eyes, as well as your conversation? Am I the happiest of men, at the very instant when my sister persuaded me I was the most worthy of compassion? I am not answerable, replied I, for any uneasiness which Celina may have given you; but I am very sure you will never receive any from me. She has told me, returned he, that I must not hope for your love.

Not hope for my love, cried I! is it possible she could say that you had not my love? Oh! Deterville, how could your sister blacken me with such a crime! I detest ingratitude, and should hate myself if I thought I could ever cease loving you.

While I spoke those few words, Deterville looked at me with an earnestness[161] which seemed to read my soul.

You love me then, Zilia, said he, and it is your own lips which tell me so! I would have given every thing that was dear to me in life to have heard this charming confession; but, alas! now I do hear it, I cannot believe it. Zilia, my dear Zilia, is it indeed true? Do you not deceive yourself? Your voice, your eyes, my own heart, every thing helps to seduce me. Perhaps it is only momentary,[162] and I am again to be plunged into the despair from which I have just escaped.

You astonish me, replied I, from what can arise your distrust? Since I have been acquainted with you, if I was incapable of making myself understood by words, surely all my actions must have convinced you that I loved you? No, returned he, I cannot now flatter myself with such a happiness; you do not as yet understand French sufficiently to dispel my just apprehensions. I know you have no design of deceiving me; but tell me in what sense you mean those adorable words, "I love you." Let my lot be decided; let either grief or pleasure kill me now at your feet.

These words, says I to him, (a little frightened at the manner in which he concluded his speech) these words, I think, ought to convince you that you are dear to me; that I interest myself in your fortune, and am attached to you by the most grateful friendship; these sentiments please my heart, and, I should imagine, ought to be satisfactory to yours.

Ah! Zilia! answered he, how your expressions grow more feeble, and the tone of your voice more cold! Celina then told me truth: Do you not feel for Aza all that you now say to me? No, said I, the sentiments I have for Aza are quite different from those I have for you; they are what you call love in another sense. What pain can this possibly give you? added I, (seeing him grow pale, leave the grate, and cast a melancholy look towards heaven.) I have this tender love for Aza, because he has the same for me, and we were to have been united. There is nothing in all this that at all concerns you. You should have felt this for me, says he, instead of feeling it for him, since I have a thousand times more love than he ever felt.

How can that be? said I, interrupting him, you are of a different nation; and so far from being chosen for your wife, it was chance only that brought us together; this is even the first day in which we have been able to communicate our thoughts to each other. What reason then could you possibly have to entertain such sentiments as these for me?

Was any other reason necessary, replied he, than your charms and character[163] to attach me for ever to you? I was tenderly educated, had a natural indolence in my temper, and was an enemy to deceit. The trouble it must have given me to engage the heart of a woman, and the fear of not finding there that sincerity I wished for, gave me only a vague and transient relish for the sex. I lived without passion till the moment I saw you, when your beauty struck me; but its impression perhaps had been as light as that of many others, if the sweetness and artlessness of your character had not made you appear to me all that my imagination had so often formed. You are sensible, Zilia, whether I have not shewn you proper respect. What has it cost me to resist the seducing opportunities which the familiarity of a long voyage gave me? How often must your innocence have yielded to my transports, if I had listened to them? But, far from doing any thing to offend you, I forced myself to be silent: I even desired my sister not to mention a word to you of my love; determined to owe nothing but to yourself alone. Ah! Zilia, if this tender respect does not move you, I will give you up; but I perceive that death will be the price of the sacrifice.

Your death! cried I, (affected at the grief which I saw painted in his countenance) fatal sacrifice indeed! I know not if my own would be more dreadful to me.

Well then, Zilia, said he, if my life is really dear to you, command me to live. In what way must I do it? said I. Love me, said he, in the manner that you have loved Aza. I loved him always the same, replied I, and shall love him till death. Whether your laws permit you to love two objects in the same manner I know not; but our customs, and my heart forbid it. Be satisfied with the friendship[164] I promise you; I can feel no more. Truth is dear to me, and I tell it to you without disguise.

How you assassinate in cold blood, cried he; ah! Zilia, how great must that love be which venerates even this cruel frankness. Well, continued he, (after some moments silence) my love shall be greater even than your cruelty. Your happiness is dearer to me than my own. Be not afraid to treat me with this torturing sincerity, but tell me what hopes you have with regard to the love you still feel for Aza?

Alas! said I, my hopes are only in you. I then told him that I had found there was a communication between the Indies and his country; that I flattered myself he would procure me the means of returning thither, or at least be kind enough to get me an opportunity of conveying my knots to you, which would inform you of my condition, and procure me an answer to them; that by being informed of your destiny, I might know how to proceed.

I am going, said he, (with a coldness which he endeavoured to assume) to take all possible measures of discovering the fate of your lover; you shall be satisfied in that particular, but vainly do you flatter yourself with seeing the happy Aza again, he is separated from you by insuperable obstacles.

These words, my dear Aza, gave a mortal blow to my heart; my tears flowed in torrents, and it was a long while before I could answer Deterville, who on his side kept a melancholy silence. At last, recovering speech; If it is true, says I, that I shall not see him any more, yet will I live for ever for him. And if you have generosity enough to procure us some correspondence, that will make life less insupportable; but should that not be the case, and I should sink under it,[165] I shall die content, if you will promise me to inform him that I loved him with my latest breath.

Oh! this is too much, cried he, rising with precipitation. Yet, if it is possible, I will be the only unhappy person; you shall know this heart which you disdain; you shall see what a love like mine is capable of doing; and I will at least force you to lament that I was not more fortunate. Speaking these words he hastily left me, in a condition which I am unable to describe. I continued immoveable in the same place, with my eyes fixed on the door thro' which Deterville went out, lost in such a confusion of sad ideas, that I was entirely unable to regulate them. How long I should have continued there I know not, if Celina had not come into the parlour.

She asked me, in a sharp manner, why her brother was gone so soon; and I did not conceal from her all that had past betwixt us.

At first she seemed concerned for what she called her brother's misfortune; then, suddenly changing her sorrow into anger, she loaded me with the most cruel reproaches, to all which I dared not answer a single word. What could I say to her? my sorrow did not give me the liberty of thinking. I therefore went out, and she did not attempt to follow me. Retiring into my chamber, I spent the whole day alone,[166] without speaking to any person, and in such a disorder of mind, as did not permit me to write to you.

Celina's anger, her brother's despair, and last words, to which I could not give any favourable sense, continually tortured my imagination, and filled it with uneasiness.

At length, in order to soften my anxiety, I determined to impart it to you, and to endeavour to gain from your love, that advice of which I have so much need. This error supported me whilst I was writing; but how short a time did it last? My letter is written, and the characters are drawn for myself only.

You are utterly ignorant of my sufferings; you do not even know if I exist, if I continue to love you. Aza! my dear Aza! these things will never be known to you.

## LETTER XXIV.

I may justly call that time an absence, my dear Aza, which is elapsed since the last letter I ever wrote to you.

Some days after the conversation which I had with Deterville, I fell into a disorder which is here called a fever. If, as I believe, it was caused by the dolorous passions which then agitated me; I have no doubt but the continuance has been the longer, for the sad reflections that have since occupied my mind, and the regret which I have felt at having lost the friendship of Celina.

Though she seemed concerned at my disorder, and took of me all imaginable care, yet it was with such an air of indifference, and so little sympathy for my afflictions, that I have no doubt but her sentiments, with regard to me, are entirely changed. The extreme friendship she has for her brother, sets her against me; and she continually reproaches me for having rendered him unhappy. The fear of appearing ungrateful intimidates me. The affected kindness of Celina only tortures me: Every thing that is soft and agreeable is banished from our conversation, and restraint has taken their places.

But, notwithstanding all[167] that I feel through the brother and sister's means, I am not unaffected with the fortunate events by which their destiny is changed.

Madame Deterville is dead. This unnatural mother has kept up her character to the last, by leaving her whole fortune to her eldest son. But there are great hopes that the law will set aside this unjust bequest.

Deterville, though quite disinterested with regard to himself, neglects nothing that may save Celina from oppression. Her misfortunes seem to increase his friendship for her; he not only visits her every day, but writes to her morning and night; his letters are filled with tender complaints against me, and such anxious solicitude for my health, that though Celina in reading them to me, only makes a pretence of informing me of their own affairs, I can easily see the real motive.

I have no doubt but Deterville writes them with a design they may be read to me, and yet I am convinced he would not do it, if he knew the heavy reproaches that always follow the reading. They make such an impression upon my heart, that sorrow consumes me.

Hitherto, though in the midst of storms, I have enjoyed the small satisfaction of living at peace with myself. Not a spot sullied the purity of my soul, nor any remorse troubled me; but now I cannot think, without feeling a contempt for myself, for being the cause of two people's unhappiness, to whom I owe my life, who, but for me, had enjoyed that serenity of which they are so worthy! Yet, though I am the cause of their misfortunes, I must still continue to be so. My tenderness for you triumphs over my remorse. Aza, how do I love you!

# LETTER XXV.

How much do we sometimes deceive ourselves, my dear Aza! when we think that prudence guides our actions. I have a long time refused the urgent request which Deterville sent me, that I would grant him a moment's conversation. Alas! I shunned my own happiness. At length, not through complaisance, but because I was weary of continual importunity,[168] I went to the parlour. At sight of the great alteration in Deterville, which makes him scarcely to be known, I was in the utmost confusion, and immediately repenting the step I had taken, I stood trembling, expecting the reproaches which I thought he had a right to make me; far from divining what was really true, that he was going to fill my soul with the utmost pleasure.

Pardon, Zilia, said he, the violence I do you; I should not have forced you to see me, if I had not brought you as much joy as you inflict torments on me. Is the sight of me for a moment too much for you to bear, in return for the sacrifice I am going to make you? Then, not waiting for an answer; Here, says he, is a letter from that relation you was talking of. This will inform you of Aza's situation, and in so doing, prove in a greater degree than all the oaths I can make, the excess of my passion. He then read the letter aloud to me. Oh! my dear Aza, how could I hear it and not die with joy? It informed me that your life is preserved; and not only your life, but your liberty; and that you now live unmolested in the Spanish court! What an unhoped-for joy!

This pleasing letter was written by a man who knows you, who sees you, who converses with you. Perhaps your eyes were for a moment fixed upon this happy paper. How could I think that, and remove mine from it? It was with the utmost difficulty I suppressed the exclamations of joy that were ready to escape me, and tears of love overflowed my countenance.

Had I followed the emotions of my heart, I should have interrupted Deterville a hundred times, to tell him all that my gratitude inspired; but I considered that the expression of my happiness, would only increase his pain; I therefore concealed my transports, and my tears only were visible.

You see, Zilia, said he, as soon as he had finished the letter, that I have kept my word: You are informed of Aza's situation; is there any thing more to be done? you may freely command me; for there is nothing which you have not a right to exact from me, that can at all contribute to your happiness.

Though this excess of goodness was the less surprising, from what I had experienced before of Deterville's generosity,[169] yet it nevertheless affected me exceedingly.

I was some moments in distress for an answer, fearing to increase the pain which I had already given to this generous man. I searched for terms that might express the sincerity of my own heart, without offending the sensibility of his;

but could find none, and yet was under the necessity of speaking; at length I stammered out something. My happiness, said I, will never be unmixed, since it is out of my power to reconcile the duties of love with those of friendship. I would regain the friendship both of you and Celina; would wish never to part from you; would for ever admire your virtues, and through my whole life, pay the tribute of gratitude which I owe to your unexampled goodness. I am sensible, that in removing to a distance from two people so dear, I shall bear with me everlasting regret. But –

How, Zilia, cried he, will you leave us then? Alas! I was not prepared for this fatal stroke, and want courage to support it. I had formed resolution sufficient to see you live here in the arms of my rival; the strong efforts of my reason, and the delicacy of my love, had taught me to submit to that mortal blow which I had contributed to give myself; but I cannot bear the thoughts of a separation; I cannot give up the sight of you for ever: no, you shall not go, cried he, with warmth, do not think of it; you play with my tenderness, and without pity, tear a heart which is distracted with love. Zilia! cruel Zilia! see my despair; it is your work. Alas! in what manner do you repay the purest love that was ever felt!

It is you, answered I, (terrified at his resolution) it is you that are to blame. You wound my soul, by forcing me to be ungrateful; you give to my heart, the most poignant anguish! by the fruitless sensibility of your own. Let me conjure you, by our friendship, not to tarnish a generosity like yours, by a despair which will for ever embitter my life, without being of any use to yourself. Do not condemn in me those very feelings which you cannot overcome, and force me unwillingly to see a blemish in you. Let me for ever reverence your name, bear it to the farthest end of the world, and make it adored by a people who are the true admirers of virtue.

I know not in what manner I pronounced these last words; but Deterville fixed his eyes upon me, without seeming to look, but appeared shut up as it were within himself. He continued a long time in this deep meditation, during which I did not dare to interrupt him; but we both kept silence till he resumed speech, and, with a forced appearance[170] of tranquillity, said to me: Yes, Zilia, I know I feel my own injustice; but is it possible coolly to renounce the sight of your charms? Yes, you will have it so, and you shall be obeyed. Oh! heavens, what a sacrifice! my unhappy days will roll on without the least hope of ever more seeing you. At least if death — Let us talk no more of it, added he, interrupting himself, my weakness betrays me; give me two days to confirm my resolution, and I will wait on you again, that we may, together, concert the necessary measures for your journey. Adieu, Zilia; may the happy Aza enjoy the pleasures that fate has designed him. At saying these words, he went out.

I must confess to you, my dear Aza, though Deterville is truly dear to me, and though his grief made a deep impression on my soul, yet was I too impatient to enjoy my happiness in quiet, not to be very well pleased with his departure.

How delicious is it, after pains like mine, to yield one's self up to joy! I passed the remainder of the day in the most rapturous imaginations. I did not write to you, because a letter would not have been able to express the feelings of my heart, and would only have put me in mind that you was absent. As it was, I fancied I saw you, and spoke to you, dear Aza; what had been wanting to my happiness, if you had sent some tokens of your tenderness, in company with that precious letter? Why did you not do it? They mentioned my situation to you; you knew where I was, and yet you send me not a word of your love. But can I entertain a doubt concerning it? No, surely my own is a proof of it. You must love me, your joy must be equal to mine; the same fire consumes you, and the same impatience devours you. Let doubt[171] be for ever banished from my soul, and love and confidence[172] reign there unmixed: Yet, what can I think! you have embraced the religion of that savage people who overrun our country.[173] What is that religion? Does it require the same sacrifices as that of France? No, surely, or you would never have submitted to it.

However it may be, my heart bends to your laws, my understanding submits itself to yours; and will, without enquiry, adopt whatever may render us inseparable. From whence can my fears proceed? In a short time re-united to my prince, to my being, to my all, I shall think for you alone,[174] and live for nothing but to love you.

## LETTER XXVI.

Here it is, my dear Aza! that I may again hope to see you; my happiness every day grows greater by this particular circumstance. The interview assigned me by Deterville is just passed, and whatever pleasures I promised to myself in overcoming the dangers and difficulties of a long journey, of preventing you, of meeting your foot-steps, I sacrifice it all, without regret, to the welcome prospect of seeing you sooner.

Deterville has proved to me in so indisputable a manner, that you may be here in less time than I can travel to Spain, that though he generously gave me my choice, I did not hesitate a moment in my determination,[175] time being too precious to be unnecessarily wasted.

I should perhaps have examined this advantage more carefully, if, before I made my choice, I had not gained such intelligence with regard to my journey, as made me secretly resolve what part to take, and that secret I can trust to you only.

I remember, that in the long route which brought me to Paris, Deterville gave pieces of silver, and sometimes of gold, at all the places where we stopt. I enquired if this was expected from him, or if it was merely the effects of his generosity; and was informed, that in France, travellers pay not only for their food, but even for their lodging.*

Alas! I have not the smallest portion of what would be necessary to satisfy the cravings of this greedy people; all must come from Deterville: And you are already sensible how much I owe him, and how shameful it would be to renew my obligations! which if I did, it would be with the utmost reluctance, such as nothing but absolute necessity could oblige me to submit to. Can I willingly make myself a still greater debtor to the man who has done and suffered so much for me?[176] I cannot, my dear Aza; and this is sufficient to make me resolve to remain on this spot. The pleasure of seeing you sooner, is a stronger motive to confirm my resolution.

Deterville has, in my presence, written to the Spanish minister; he strongly presses him to let you come, and points out the means to him of your being conducted hither, with a generosity which at once excites both my admiration and gratitude.

How very delightfully were my thoughts employed during the time that Deterville was writing! I planned out the manner of your journey, I settled the preparations for my own happiness, of which I have now no longer any doubt.

If I at first felt some pangs in renouncing the design of preventing you, I confess, my dear Aza, that in so doing I found the source of a thousand pleasures which I did not before perceive.

Many circumstances, which did not at first strike me as considerable enough either to hasten or retard my journey, become to me now pleasing and interesting. I followed blindly the strong desires of my own heart, forgetting that I was going to search for you among those cruel Spaniards; the very idea of whom strikes my soul with horror. The certainty of seeing them no more, gives me infinite satisfaction. Tho' the voice of love at first stifled that of friendship, I now taste without remorse the sweetness of uniting them. Deterville has assured me that it is impossible for us ever to return to the city of the Sun; and after our own native country, can there be a more agreeable place of residence than this of France? You will be pleased with it, my dear Aza, though sincerity is banished from it. Here are so many pleasing things, that we shall forget the dangers of the society.

After the mention that I have made to you of gold, it is unnecessary to tell you to bring some quantity with you: you will here have no merit without it. A small part of your treasures would be sufficient[177] to confound the pride of the indigent magnificence of this kingdom: it will be necessary to display those before them,[178] to me your tenderness and your virtues will only be valuable.

---

*    The Incas established large houses upon the roads, where all travellers were entertained at the public expence.

Deterville has promised to find a conveyance for my knots and my letters, and assures me, that you will find interpreters who will explain to you the French language. He has now just sent for my packet, I must therefore conclude. Farewell, dear hope of my life; I will still continue to write to you, and if I have no means of sending my letters, will keep them till I see you.

How should I be able to support the length of your journey, if I was deprived of the only means I have of conversing with my joy, my transport, my happiness.

## LETTER XXVII.

Now that I know my letters to be upon the road, my dear Aza, I enjoy that tranquillity to which I was before a stranger. I am for ever pleasing myself with the imagination of what you will feel in receiving them; I share your transports with you; and my soul admits no ideas but agreeable ones; nothing is now wanting to complete my joy, for peace is restored to this our little society.

The judges have given to Celina that part of her fortune of which her mother had deprived her. She sees her lover every day, and all necessary preparations are making for her marriage.[179] Thus, happy to her utmost wish, her thoughts are employed in a more pleasing manner than quarrelling with me; and I am so happy in the appearance of her friendship, that I do not examine too deeply into the reality of it; for whatever the motives are that cause it, I look upon myself as always indebted to those who assist me in the enjoyment of agreeable sensations.

I felt it this morning in its utmost force, when, by an act of complaisance, she transported me in an instant from a tiresome anxiety to the calmest tranquillity of mind.

A prodigious quantity of stuffs, garments, and trinkets of all kinds had been brought her; and she sent for me into her chamber,[180] to consult me on the different beauties of so many ornaments. She then put together a quantity of those which had most attracted my notice, and[181] bid our Chinas carry them into my apartment, though I strongly opposed it. She at first laughed at my refusal; and the more strongly I declined the present, the more she persisted in forcing me to accept of it, I could then no longer dissemble my uneasiness.

Why, said I to her, (with tears in my eyes) why will you humble me in this manner? I owe to you not only my life, but all that I possess; but this extreme bounty is not at all necessary to keep my misfortunes continually in remembrance. According to your laws, presents should only be received by those who do not want them, those who do, are degraded by them.[182] It is with the utmost reluctance, added I, in a calmer tone of voice, that I conform to sentiments so contrary to the law of Nature. Our customs have more kindness in them, he that receives is honoured as much as he that gives; but you have taught me to think it is not so here, and after my knowledge of that, is not this offering me an insult?

This amiable girl, more affected at my tears than angry at my reproaches, answered in the gentlest tone of voice; My brother and I, my dear Zilia, would both of us be far from offending your delicacy; and indeed I could soon convince you that such airs, in your company, would fit very ill upon us: I only meant to beg of you to share with me the presents of a generous brother, as I knew it was the most agreeable manner by which I could express my gratitude to him. In my present situation, it is generally the custom to do these kinds of things; but since I see it makes you uneasy, I will drop the affair. You promise me you will then, said I: Yes, said she, smiling; but only give me leave to write a line or two to Deterville.

I was easy; and good-humour was once more restored betwixt us. We began again to criticize upon every particular of her dress, till she was sent for into the parlour; she would fain have persuaded me to go with her; but, my dear Aza, can any amusement be equal to that of conversing with you? Far from wishing any other, I am quite apprehensive of being engaged in the company and diversions of the wedding celebration.

Celina will shortly be married, and is desirous of my being with her: She wants me to leave this religious house and live in hers; but if you can believe my truth

***

Aza, my dear Aza, how agreeably was my letter interrupted![183] I thought every monument of our ancient magnificence was for ever lost;[184] I had even ceased to think of them; but I am now surrounded by the riches of Peru. I see it, I touch it, and yet can scarce believe my eyes or my hands.

While I was writing to you, Celina came into my chamber, followed by four men, bending under the weight of large chests which they carried on their backs. They laid down their burdens and retired; and I, imagining these were some new presents from Deterville, began to murmur to myself, when Celina giving me some keys, said, Open the chests, Zilia, and do not be angry, for they come from Aza.

Truth, which is inseparably fixed to every idea of you, left me not the least doubt. I opened them immediately, and my error was confirmed,[185] when I beheld there all the ornaments belonging to the Temple of the Sun.

The most confused thoughts filled my mind; sorrow, joy, pleasure, and regret were mingled there. I threw myself before the sacred remains of our altars;[186] covered them with respectful kisses, and watered them with my tears; I could not leave them: I even forgot that Celina was present, till she roused me from my reverie, by giving me a letter, which she desired me to read.

Still deceived, I thought it came from you, and my joy redoubled; but, though with difficulty I made it out, I soon perceived that it was Deterville's hand. It would be easier for me to copy than to explain it, my dear Aza!

## DETERVILLE'S LETTER

"These treasures belong to you, fair Zilia, as they were found in the ship in which you was captive. Some disputes which arose among the crew, prevented me from sending them till now. I would have presented them to you myself, but my sister acquainting me how much you was offended this morning, I did not dare to follow my inclinations: could I too soon dispel the uneasiness which the sense of dependence made you feel? I will, thro' my whole life, prefer your happiness to my own."

I blush, my dear Aza, to confess that I was for a moment less sensible of the generosity of Deterville, than I was of pleasure that I was able to give him proofs of mine.

I immediately looked out a Vase, which chance, rather than avarice, had made fall into the hands of the Spaniards. It was the same, and my heart told me so, which your lips touched on that day when you desired to taste some Aca* prepared by my hand. Richer in this cup than in all the rest that was restored to me, I called the men who brought the chests, and bid them take the whole back again as a present to Deterville; but Celina would not suffer them to do it.

Is this acting right, Zilia? said she; you, who were offended at the offer of trifles, desire my brother to accept of immense riches? Observe justice in your own actions, if you would chuse that others should do so to you.

I was struck with these words, and could not help secretly confessing that there was more pride and disdain of obligation[187] than generosity, in what I was about to do. How very near does vice approach to virtue! I acknowledged my fault, and begged Celina's pardon: But what gave me most concern was, that I was afraid to offer her any thing.[188] Do not punish me as much as I deserve, said I, with great timidity, nor disdain to accept of a few specimens of the ingenuity of our unhappy country: You are in no want of any thing, and therefore my request cannot shock you.

While I was speaking, I observed Celina look attentively on some golden shrubs, with birds and insects on them of exquisite workmanship: I desired she would accept of them, together with a small silver basket, which I filled with flowers made of shells,[189] excellently imitated. She took them with a goodness which delighted me.

I afterwards selected several idols of the nations† [190] conquered by your ancestors, and a small statue,‡ representing a Virgin of the Sun; to these I added a

---

* A drink of the Indians.
† The Incas caused idols of the people they subdued to be deposited in the Temple of the Sun, after the conquered had conformed to the worship of that luminary. They had also idols themselves, the Inca Huyna having consulted that of Rimaca. See the History of the Incas.
‡ The Incas adorned their houses with golden statues of all sizes, even to the largest degree.

tiger, a lion, and other beasts of prey,[191] intreating her to send them to Deterville. Write to him then, said she, smiling; for a letter from you is, I am sure, necessary to make the presents well received.

I was too much pleased not to consent to every thing, and wrote to him in such terms as gratitude dictated. When Celina was gone out, I distributed some little things to her China and mine; and set some others aside for my writing-master. Now it was that I enjoyed the extreme delight of being able to give.

But I was careful, my dear Aza, in what I gave away, not to put any thing that came from you; whatever you will particularly remember, I have kept to myself.

The golden chair,* which was kept in the Temple, for the days of visiting from the Capa Inca, your august father, I have placed in a corner of my apartment, as a throne, by which is represented to my imagination your grandeur and high rank. The large figure of the Sun, which I myself saw torn from the Temple by the barbarous Spaniards, hung over it, excites my veneration. I fall down before it, and adore it, while my heart is offered to you.

The two palm trees, which you offered to the Sun as a pledge of your faith to me, I have placed on each side of the throne; and they continually call to my mind your tender vows of eternal love.[192]

Flowers, birds,† [193] elegantly disposed in different corners of my apartment, form in miniature a scene of those magnificent gardens where I have so often dwelt on your idea.

My delighted eyes can look no where without recalling to my mind your love, my joy, my happiness; in a word, every thing that can contribute to make the life of my life.

## LETTER XXVIII.

In vain, my dear Aza, has been my prayers, complaints, and remonstrances: I was obliged to quit my desired retreat; I yielded to Celina's importunity, and we have been three days in the country since the celebration of her marriage.[194]

What pain, what regret, what anguish did I feel at leaving the dear precious objects of my solitude! Alas! I had scarcely had them long enough to enjoy them; and I am sure I can find nothing here to make me amends for this loss!

The pleasures which enchant every one else, are so far from pleasing me, that they only make me look back to those peaceful days I spent in writing to, or at least in thinking of you, with the more anxiety.[195]

---

\*    The Incas always sit upon chairs of massy gold.

†    The gardens of the Temple, and those belonging to the Royal Palaces, were filled with various imitations of Nature in gold and silver. The Peruvians even made images of the plant Mais, with which they would fill whole fields.

The diversions of this country appear to me as affected and unnatural as their manners; they consist in extreme gaiety, expressed by loud laughing, in which the soul seems to take no part; of insipid games, in which money makes all the pleasure; or else in conversations so trifling, in which the same words are continually repeated, that it rather resembles the chattering of birds than the discourse of thinking beings.

The young men, great numbers of whom appear at Celina's, were at first much taken up in following and endeavouring to oblige me; but whether the coldness of my conversation has disgusted them, or that the little relish I shewed for theirs has tired them of taking any pains to serve me, I know not; but two days were sufficient to make them give me up, and deliver me from their troublesome notice.

The natural propensity which the French have to extremes is so great, that Deterville, who is in general exempt from the faults of his nation, does yet partake of this.

Not satisfied with keeping the promise he has made, of no more entertaining me with his passion, he avoids being at all alone with me; so that though we are obliged continually to see one another, yet have I not been able to find one opportunity of talking privately with him.

By the melancholy which appears on his countenance, in the midst of this general joy, I can easily see, that in thus shunning me he does violence to himself. Perhaps I am obliged to him for so doing; but I have so many questions to ask about the time of your leaving Spain, and when you may be expected here, and other such interesting subjects, that I am really angry at being forced to approve of his conduct. I have a strong desire to ask to speak to him alone,[196] but the fear of reviving his tender complaints prevents my doing it.

Celina, entirely taken up with pleasing[197] her husband, affords me no relief; and all the other company are really disagreeable to me. Thus alone, in the midst of a large assembly, I have no entertainment but my own thoughts, which are all addressed to you, my dear Aza, who shall ever be the sole confident of my heart, my only pleasure, my happiness.

## LETTER XXIX.

I was very blameable, my dear Aza, in so earnestly wishing to speak to Deterville. He has spoke to me but too much, though I believe no cause of those terrors which he has endeavoured to excite in my soul, yet are they not yet effaced.

I know not what it was[198] that yesterday made an addition to that usual melancholy that hangs about me; but the world, and its vanities, was more disagreeable than common. Every thing, except the tender pleasure which I saw expressed betwixt Celina and her Husband, gave me an indignation which bordered on contempt. Ashamed of the unjust pride of my own heart, I endeavoured to conceal what I felt, and retired alone to the most private part of the garden.

I sat me down at the foot of a tree, and the tears began involuntarily to wet my cheeks, leaning my forehead upon my hand; I was so buried in my own thoughts, that Deterville was on his knees before me ere I perceived he was near.

Be not offended, Zilia, said he, it was not design but chance which brought me hither. Tired of the continual tumult, I was coming to indulge my sorrow in peace. When, seeing you, I struggled with myself to keep at a distance from you; but the desire of soothing my unhappiness urged me on. In pity to myself I walked forward; but when I saw your tears, I was no longer master of myself; yet, if you command me to fly from you, I will immediately obey. Can you do it, Zilia? Am I really hateful to your sight? No, said I, far from it, pray sit down, I was wishing for an opportunity of speaking to you ever since the last favours you conferred on me.

Let us not talk of those things, interrupted he, briskly; but pray hear me, replied I; you cannot be completely generous, if you will not listen to acknowledgments. This is the first time I have ever spoken to you since I have received those valuable ornaments belonging to the Temple in which I was educated.[199] I am afraid, in my letter I but poorly expressed the sentiments that such an excess of kindness inspired me with; but I meant — Alas! interrupted he again, what pleasure does acknowledgment give to a heart torn like mine? Thanks are the companions of indifference, and are sometimes even joined with hatred.

Ah! how can you think this? cried I; how much would you deserve, Deterville, to be reproached, if pity did not prevent it! Far from hating you, from the first moment I ever saw you, I had a confidence in you which I never had in the Spaniards. Your gentle treatment made me, in proportion as I saw more of your character, wish to gain your friendship. I have long been convinced that you deserved all mine, and without mentioning the uncommon obligations I owe you, (since I find my acknowledgments offend) could I, when I thoroughly knew you,[200] help feeling for you all those sentiments which are so justly your desert.

You were the only one whose virtues I found allied to the simplicity of ours; a native of the Sun would be honoured by such a soul as yours; your reason seems to be guided by nature: could I have stronger motives for esteeming you? Nay, I may say, the majesty of your person, and your figure, pleases me; for friendship has eyes as well as love. There was a time when, after a short absence, I never saw you again without feeling my heart beat with pleasure.[201] Why have you yourself been the cause of changing that innocent delight, for such anxious pains as your presence now gives me.

Your reason is now continually disturbed, and I am always afraid of some violent sallies of passion. The sentiments you entertain me with, lay a restraint on the expression of mine, which deprives me of the pleasure of describing to you, without disguise, the charms I could find in your friendship, if you did not yourself forbid me to indulge myself in it. You even deny me the delicate pleasure of pleasing my eyes with beholding my benefactor; your looks confuse me, since I no longer observe in them that agreeable tranquillity which has given such exquisite pleasure to my soul. Your constant settled melancholy is an everlasting reproach to me for being the cause of it. Ah! Deterville, how unjust are you, if you look on yourself as the only sufferer!

My dear Zilia, cried he, (ardently kissing my hand) how does your kindness and innocent frankness add to my regret! What a treasure would the possession of such a heart as yours be! And with what aggravated despair do you now make me feel the want of it.

Mighty Zilia, continued he, how great is your power! Was it not sufficient to inspire me with love, who had never before been sensible of any thing but the most careless indifference, but you must likewise overpower me thus? How is it to be borne? Such an effort, says I, is worthy of your noble heart; so generous an action raises you above other men. But can I survive it? resumed he, in a sorrowful tone. Do not imagine, however, continued he, that I shall continue here the victim of your love. I must for ever adore your idea,[202] which will be the bitter nourishment of my life. I know I must love you, but I will see you no more. Yet, at least do not forget –

He here lost his speech, and hastily endeavoured to hide the tears which flowed down his cheeks. Equally affected by his generosity and his sorrow, I could not contain my own, but shedding tears, pressed one of his hands in mine. No, said I, you shall not leave us. Let me still keep my friend, and be satisfied with those sentiments which I shall feel for you to the end of my days. I feel for you almost as much affection as I feel for Aza, but it is an affection of a different kind.

Cruel Zilia, cried he, must every mark of your goodness be accompanied with such piercing strokes? Must a mortal poison continually destroy the charms which your words convey? Why do I suffer myself to be bewitched by their sweetness! How do I humble, how do I debase myself! But it is over, I am again master of myself, added he, in a firm tone. Farewell, you will soon see Aza, and I heartily wish that he may not make you feel some of those torments which now prey upon me; may you find him such as you desire him, and worthy of a heart like yours.

I can give you no conception, my dear Aza, how alarmed I was at the manner in which he pronounced these words. Suspicion filled my soul. I had no doubt but Deterville had stronger cause for his words than he chose to appear to have, and had received some letters from Spain which he concealed from me. In fine, (shall I dare to speak it?) I suspected that you were faithless.

I called him back, and in the strongest manner, conjured him to tell me the truth; but all that I could get from him, amounted only to vague conjectures, which sometimes confirm and sometimes lessen my fears.

However, I could not help reflecting on the natural inconstancy of your sex, the dangers of absence, and the ease with which you had changed your religion, and those reflections remained deeply engraven on my soul.

Now, for the first time of my life, did my passion appear painful to me; now did I first begin to fear the loss of your heart. Aza, if it is true, if indeed you cease to love me, oh! that my death had for ever separated us, before you had become inconstant.

But it cannot be, it was despair that suggested to Deterville these dreadful imaginations. Surely the trouble and distraction of his mind ought to be a convincing proof to me of it. Nay, might not even his self-interest be called in question by me, that might make him endeavour to fill my thoughts with doubts? These thoughts rushed into my mind, my dear Aza, and all my resentment was turned against him: I expressed it in strong terms, and he quitted me in a violent passion.

Alas! was I less violent than he? How many tortures did I suffer, before I found again any repose in my mind? nor can I say it is yet perfectly composed. Aza, is it possible you can forget me? I, whose tenderness for you is to such an excess!

## LETTER XXX.

I begin to think, my dear Aza, that the time is very long before I see you. With how much ardour do I wish your journey at an end! Time has dissipated my fears, and I now look on them only as a dream, of which the morning dawn has effaced even the impression. I cannot help thinking myself criminal for having suspected you, and my repentance increases my tenderness to such a degree, that it has almost erased my compassion for Deterville. I cannot forgive his having conceived so ill an opinion of you, and I now feel my regret much less for being, in a manner, separated from him.

We have now been at Paris a fortnight; and I live with Celina in her husband's house, which is so distant from that of her brother, that I am no longer obliged to see him every hour. He often indeed comes hither to eat; but Celina and I live in such a continual round of pleasures, that he cannot find leisure to speak to me in private.

Since our return, great part of the day is employed in the tedious work of dressing, and the remainder, in what is here called paying visits.

These two employments seem to me as useless as they are fatiguing. All that can be said for it is, that going into company procures me the means of informing myself more particularly of the customs of the country.

At my first arrival in France, being ignorant of their language, I could judge of things only by their appearances. Afterwards, I could learn but very little in the religious house, nor did I find the country turn to better account, where I saw only a certain society, with whose company I was too much tired to pay any attention to them. But it is here, that by conversing with what they call the great world, I see the whole nation.

The visits, or duties that we pay, consist of going to as great a number of houses as possible, there to give and receive a mutual tribute of commendations upon our beauty,[203] the fineness of our taste, and the elegant choice of our dress.

It was but a short time before I discovered the reason that made them take so much pains to acquire this homage: I found it was, because it was necessary to receive in person this momentary incense; for no sooner does any one take her leave, but they immediately give her another form. The charms which were before allowed to her when present, only serve for contemptuous comparisons betwixt her perfections and those of the next newcomer.

Censure is as much the reigning taste of the French, as incoherence is the character of the nation. In their books you find a general criticism on the manners of mankind, and in their conversation, a particular one on any person who happens to be absent.

What they call the mode, has not altered the ancient custom of freely saying all the ill that can be said of another, and sometimes even more than they think. People of the first fashion addict themselves to this custom, and only distinguish themselves by making a formal apology for their frankness and love of truth; that being once done, they reveal the faults, follies, and even vices of others, without scruple, not sparing even their best friends.

As this sincerity which the French use to each other is without exception, so is their confidence without bounds; there is no occasion for eloquence in order to gain attention, nor probity to obtain belief. Every thing is spoke, and every thing believed, with the same degree of levity.

Yet, would not I have you imagine, my dear Aza, that the French are in general born with bad inclinations; I should be more unjust than they are, if I gave them such a character.

By nature susceptible of tender feelings, I never knew one of them who was not affected by the history which they often oblige me to give of our sufferings,[204] and the account of the rectitude of our hearts, the candour of our sentiments, and the simplicity of our manners. Did they live among us, they would be truly virtuous; but example and custom are the tyrants to which they submit.

A man of good sense will speak ill of the absent only to gain the good opinion of the present; another would be honest, humane, and beneficent, if he did not fear being laughed at; and a third makes himself ridiculous, by endeavouring to conceal such qualities as would make him a model for others, if he dared to exert them, and assume his own just merit.

In a word, my dear Aza, their vices are as much affected as their virtues; and their very trivial character, will never suffer them to be perfectly either one thing or another. Like the playthings which they give to their children, these frivolous people are only a faint resemblance of those thinking beings which they ought to be in reality. There is show, softness, colour, and altogether a fair outside, but no intrinsic value. By this means, I find that other nations look on them only as the toys and trifles of society. Good-sense smiles at their airs, and gives them a low rank among the human race.

Happy that country which has Nature only for its guide, Truth for its mover, and Virtue for its principle.

## LETTER XXXI.

It is not all surprising, my dear Aza, that inconsistency is a consequence of the airy character of the French; but yet I cannot help being astonished, that as they certainly do not want for penetration, they should not themselves perceive the ridiculous contradictions which foreigners remark in them at the first sight.

Among a great number which strike me every day, I cannot help mentioning one, which I think much dishonours their understanding, I mean their manner of thinking with regard to our sex.[205] They respect, and yet despise them, my dear Aza, at the same time.

The first law of their politeness or virtue, (for I think the whole of their virtue consists in politeness) is the deference they pay to women. A man of the first rank shows the utmost complaisance to a woman in the lowest state of life, and would blush, and think it an everlasting reproach to him, if he offered her any personal insult. And yet a man of the lowest credit, may deceive and betray a woman of credit, and blast her reputation, without fear of punishment.

If I was not well assured that you would yourself soon see these things, I should hardly dare to tell them you, as the contrast is so great, to the simplicity of our souls, that you cannot easily conceive them. Led by the hand of Nature, our genius goes no farther: By her we are taught, that the strength and courage of one sex, is designed for the support and defence of the other, and our laws are conformable to this discovery.* Here, instead of looking with compassion on the weakness of women, those of the common sort, tied down to labour, have no relief, either from the laws or their husbands: While those of a more elevated rank, often become the prey either of the seduction or malice of the other sex; and have no resource from such perfidy, but a mere outside respect, which is continually followed by the most cutting satire.

---

*     The Peruvian laws exempt the women from all hard bodily labour.

I soon perceived, when I began to converse with the world, that the habitual censure of the nation falls chiefly upon women, and that men do not treat each other with contempt, without some reserve. I endeavoured to find out the cause of it, but could not, till an accident shewed it me.[206]

In all the houses which we have gone into for these two days past, the conversation has turned on the death of a young man who was killed by a friend; and this barbarous action is approved of for no other reason, but because the dead had said something to the disadvantage of the living.

This new extravagance seemed of so serious a kind, as to deserve my nicest enquiry. And I find, my dear Aza, that a man here is obliged to expose his own life, in order to take away that of another, if he hears that the other has been talking against him, or if he refuses to take so dreadful a vengeance, he is banished from society. I needed be told no more, in order to form a very clear idea of what I sought. I am convinced that the men are by nature cowards, without shame and without remorse, afraid only of corporal punishment. And that if women were allowed to punish the outrages offered them, in the same manner as the men are obliged to revenge the slightest insult offered to each other, such men as I see now well received in the world, would be shunned and detested. The slanderer must then retire into the desert, and there, by himself, conceal his malice with his shame.[207] But cowards here have nothing to fear, for their abuse has taken too deep root ever to be abolished.

Impudence and effrontery are the first sentiments that the men imbibe: Timidity, gentleness, and patience are the only virtues that are sought for in women: How then can they avoid being the victims of deceit?

Oh! my dear Aza, let not those brilliant vices of a nation, who have the art of disguising them so as to make them almost appear like virtues,[208] give us a contempt for the plain simplicity of our own manners! May you never forget that it is incumbent upon you to be my example, my guide, and support through the paths of life; and may I never forget that it is my duty to preserve your esteem, as well as your love, by not only imitating, but, if there is a possibility, surpassing my model, and meriting a respect founded on virtue, and not on a trifling custom.

## LETTER XXXII.

Our fatiguing visits, my dear Aza, have had a most agreeable conclusion. I yesterday had a most delightful day, owing to fresh obligations which Deterville and his sister have conferred on me. Oh! with what pleasure shall I share them with you?

After two days respite from noise and tumult, we yesterday morning set out from Paris, Celina, her brother, her husband, and myself, in order to pay a visit, as she said, to a very dear friend of hers in the country. The journey was short, and we arrived pretty soon in the day at a house which was delightfully situated. But I could not help being surprised to find the doors open, and meet nobody.

This house, too pretty to be uninhabited, and too small to conceal the people who lived in it, seemed to me like a little enchanted palace. I could not help diverting myself with the thought, and asking Celina, if we were in the dwelling of one of these Fairies, the history of which I had sometimes read to her, where the lady of the house and her domestics were all invisible?

You shall see the lady, answered she, by and bye; but some affairs of consequence have obliged her to be absent today, and she has desired me to prevail on you to do the honours of her house till her return. Come, says she, laughing, let us see how you will perform? I joined in the joke, and put on a serious air, to pay the compliments which I had heard on such occasions; and they told me I acquitted myself tolerably.

After diverting ourselves some time in this manner, Celina said, This politeness would be enough of itself, at Paris; but, I assure you, Madam, we expect something more in the country, that you should have the hospitality to ask us to dinner.

Indeed, said I, in this particular I shall not be able to please you; and I begin to think that your friend has relied too much upon my management. Well, I know how to rectify that, answers Celina; if you will only be kind enough to write your name, you shall see that it is no very hard matter to entertain your friends in a proper manner. You give me some comfort, said I, let me write immediately.

No sooner had I spoke those words, but a man came in, dressed in black, with a standish[209] in his hand, and paper already written upon. He laid it before me, and I wrote my name where I was directed to do it.

At the same moment another well-looking man appeared, who desired us to walk into the dining-room.[210]

We there found a table covered with equal propriety and elegance: As soon as we were seated, music, which was very fine, began to play in the next room. In short, there was nothing wanting that could make our meal pleasant. Deterville himself seemed to set aside his melancholy, and entertained us with great chearfulness, and in a very agreeable manner; and tho' he could not help expressing his passion to me, yet it was in a pleasant tone of voice, unmixed with complaint or reproaches.

The weather was very fine, and we all agreed to walk as soon as we arose from table. The gardens were more extensive than the house seemed to promise; and art and nature joined to render the charms of the country infinitely delightful.

The end of the garden was terminated by a wood: There we all sat down together on a beautiful green turf, and began to indulge ourselves in those contemplations which the beauties of the universe naturally inspire; when we saw, through the trees on one side of us, a company of peasants very neatly dressed, preceded by some instruments of music; and on the other, a number of young women, all in white, their heads adorned with the flowers of the field, who sung, in an untaught melodious manner, songs, in which, to my great surprise, I often heard my own name repeated.

But how great was my astonishment, when both companies being come up to us, he who seemed to be the chief man among them, kneeled on one knee before me, and presented me with a large bason,[211] in which were several keys; at the same time making me a compliment, which the perplexity of my mind would not suffer me perfectly to comprehend: All I could understand was, that he being the principal of the villagers of that country, came to pay his respects to me as lady of this manor, and present me with the keys of the house, of which I was also mistress.

As soon as he had finished his harangue, he arose and made room for a very pretty young damsel, who presented me with a bundle of flowers, adorned with ribbands, which she also accompanied with a short complimentary discourse, delivered with a good grace.

I was in too much confusion, my dear Aza, to answer compliments which I was sensible I so little deserved; though every thing had an air so much like truth, that I could hardly help believing what I at the same time thought impossible, my mind was so much engaged with those ideas, that I was incapable of speaking a word: And however diverting this might be to the rest of the company, it was far from being so to myself.

Deterville was the first who, taking pity of me, made a sign to his sister, who immediately dispersed some pieces of gold to the lads and lasses, telling them at the same time, that was only the earnest of my future kindness towards them; she then arose, and proposed taking a turn in the wood. I followed her with alacrity, resolving to reproach her for having diverted herself at my expence; but she did not allow me time; for, stopping before we had taken half a dozen steps, she looked on me with a smiling countenance, Now, says she, Zilia, confess that you are very angry with us, and that you will be still more so, when I tell you that this land and house do in reality belong to you.

To me! cried I; ah! Celina, whether it be an affront or a joke, you carry it too far! Hear what I have to say, said she, in a more serious tone; suppose my brother has disposed of some part of your treasure to purchase it, and, instead of the disagreeable formality that must otherwise have been, has only agreeably surprised you into it, when the thing was over, are we so very much to blame for doing it? and can you never forgive us for having procured you a dwelling, such as you seem to like? and secured to you an independency, which you wished for? You, this morning, signed the deed that put you in possession of both. Grumble at us now as much as you please, added she, smiling again, if we cannot contrive to do any thing that is agreeable to you.

Oh! my amiable friend! cried I, throwing myself at her feet;[212] I have so lively a sense of your generous actions, that I am unable to express my thanks. These few words were all I could utter, for my secret wish had indeed been such an independency. I dissolved in rapture, when I reflected at the pleasure I should find in bestowing on you this charming abode; my gratitude was so strong, that it stifled the expression of it. I tenderly embraced Celina; she returned my caresses in the same manner; and having given me sufficient time to recover myself, we returned to her brother and husband.

Fresh trouble seized me, when I beheld Deterville, and I found a new perplexity how to express myself. I therefore gave him my hand, which he kissed, without speaking, turning aside to hide the tears which he shed in spite of himself. This I took for marks of pleasure on seeing me so happy. It moved me so, that I could not help shedding some myself. Celina's husband, who had not the same concern in it as we, turned the conversation into a more pleasant vein, and complimented me on my new dignity; at the same time desiring, that we might return to the house, in order, as he said, to examine its defects, and convince Deterville that his taste was not so good as he had the vanity to imagine.

I must confess to you, my dear Aza, that every thing now seemed to put on a different form; the flowers looked more beautiful, the trees had a fresher verdure, and the gardens appeared better laid out.

I even thought the house more convenient, the furniture more rich, and the smallest trifle appeared now a matter of consequence to me.

I walked through the apartments with so much pleasure, that I did not give myself time to examine every thing minutely; the only room in which I stopped, was one of a moderate size, surrounded with cases curiously wrought, and adorned with gold, in which were a great number of books, of all colours and all sizes, elegantly bound. I was enchanted by them to such a degree, that I did not know how to leave them till I had read them all through; but Celina took off my attention, by putting me in mind of a golden key which Deterville had given me, and which belonged to a door in that room;[213] we endeavoured to find it out, but our search was in vain, till he himself shewed it us; it was so artificially concealed in the wainscot, that it was impossible to discover it, without being told where it was.

I opened it with eagerness, and stood amazed at the splendor which it disclosed to my view.

It was a closet hung with glass, and paintings; the ground of the hangings was green, upon which were figures extremely well executed, employed in the sports and ceremonies of the city of the Sun, done from the description which I had given of them to Deterville.

In many places virgins were represented, dressed in habits of the same kind which I wore when I first came into France; and the company told me they thought they resembled me.

The ornaments of the Temple, which I had left behind me in the Religious house, placed upon gilded pyramids, adorned the four corners of this magnificent cabinet. The figure of the Sun, in the midst of the cieling, painted with the most beautiful colour of the heavens, completed the embellishment of this charming place:[214] Every piece of furniture it contained was equally elegant,[215] and the whole was brilliant to the highest degree.

In reviewing it, I recollected that the golden chair was not there; this I took no notice of,[216] but Deterville seeing, I suppose, that I was looking for something, and guessing what, took the opportunity of letting me know what was become of it: It is in vain for you to look, fair Zilia, for the chair of the Incas, said he, which, by the power of magic, is changed into a house, a garden, and a piece of land: If I rather employed that science than my own in making this transformation, it was only in regard to your delicacy; for I must own it was with regret. Here, says he, (opening a little beaufet[217] which was ingeniously sunk in the wall) here are the remains of this magical operation. He then shewed me a strong box, filled with pieces of the French gold currency. You know, continued he, that this is not one of the least necessary things among us, I therefore thought it quite proper you should be provided with some.

I was beginning to express my gratitude in such thanks as it dictated, when Celina interrupted me, and led me into a room by the side of this wonderful closet. I would willingly, says she, convince you that I have some skill in magic too. She then opened some large drawers, which were filled with rich silks, fine linen, and all the ornaments that are worn in women's dress, in such quantities, that I could not help laughing, and asking Celina, how many years she wished me to live to make use of all these fine things? I should wish you to live as long as I and my brother do, answered she. And, for my part, replied I, I only desire you to live as long as I love you, and then I am sure you will not die before me.

When I had finished speaking, we returned into the Temple of the Sun, (which is the name we gave to that wonderful closet) and now having recovered freedom of speech, I expressed all the feelings of my heart, which must be great for such extreme goodness. What virtues are not this brother and sister possessed of!

We spent the remainder of the day in the utmost confidence and friendship; and I entertained them at supper with more gaiety than I had at dinner.[218] I gave orders, without restraint, to the servants, whom I now knew to be my own; I valued myself upon my own opulence and power, and was as chearful as possible, in order to shew my sense of the favours received from my benefactors.

I could not help thinking, however, that as it grew late, Deterville fell into his usual melancholy, and a tear now and then stole from Celina; but they soon resumed an air of content, and I thought myself mistaken.

I endeavoured to prevail on them to stay some days in the country, and let us enjoy together the pleasure they had procured for me: But in this I could not succeed; and we returned the same night, promising ourselves, however, to make soon another visit to my enchanted castle.

Ah! my dear Aza, how happy shall I be when I can enjoy it with you?

## LETTER XXXIII.

Deterville's melancholy, as well as that of his sister, my dear Aza, has increased, since the day we visited my enchanted palace. They are both so very dear to me, that I could not help being earnest with them to intrust me with the cause; but as they evaded the subject, I was fearful that some new misfortune had retarded your journey. The uneasiness of my mind, which I did not at all dissemble, was too strong for the resolution of my amiable friends.

Deterville owned that he did not design to let me know the day when he expected you, in order to give me an agreeable surprise; but my uneasiness made him determine to tell me: He therefore shewed me a letter from the guide who was ordered to conduct you; and, calculating the time when, and the place from whence it was written, he assured me that you might be here to-morrow, to-day; in short, that I might expect you every moment, and had no more hours to reckon to that which is to crown my wishes.

After having told me this, Deterville let me know how he had ordered every thing else. He shewed me the apartment which he designed for your use; for you are to lodge here till the time of our being united, as decency will not suffer us to live together in my delightful castle till that ceremony is past. I will never lose sight of you any more; nothing on earth shall separate us: Deterville has ordered every thing, and by every action daily shews me more and more the boundless excess of his generosity.

After his having told me all these things, I was no longer at a loss for the cause of that sorrow which consumes him. It is the thoughts of your approaching arrival: I pity him, I sincerely commiserate his passion, and wish him an happiness independent of me, such as may be a reward worthy of his merit.

I look on it as a duty to conceal the joy which overwhelms me, that I may not add to his affliction. This is all I am able to do; but it engages my mind too much, for me entirely to conceal it: Therefore, though I believe you are very near at hand, and my heart bounds at the least noise; though I cannot help leaving my letter at the end of every sentence, to run to the window, yet I still continue to write, finding it necessary to moderate the transports of my soul. You are near me, it is true; but is your absence less than if the seas still divided us? I see you not; nor can you hear me: Why then should I cease to converse with you by the only means left in my power? A few moments more, and I shall see you; but this moment is not yet come. Is there any way in which I can better employ that time of your absence which I have yet to wait, than by painting to you the greatness of my tenderness? Alas! you have hitherto known it only breathed in sighs! Let the remembrance of it be banished from my mind! Joy shall for ever erase it from my memory! Aza, dear Aza! how delicious is the sound of that name to me! the time is very near, when I shall cease to call you in vain; you will hear me, and fly to my voice. The tenderest expressions of my soul shall reward your eagerness – But I am interrupted: It is not by you; and yet I must quit you to attend to it.

## LETTER XXXIV.

To the Chevalier Deterville at Malta.[219]

Could you, Sir, foresee, without relinquishing your design, the extreme chagrin you were joining to the happiness you had prepared for me; how could you have the cruelty to let such agreeable circumstances be concluded by your departure,[220] unless it were to make me more sensible of despair for your absence?[221] But two days ago I tasted all the sweets of friendship, I now drink largely the bitterest pangs of it.

Celina, all affected as she is, has too well obeyed your commands. She presented me Aza, at the same time that she gave me your cruel letter; though the sight of him was the completion of all my wishes, yet at that moment grief darted through my soul; when I beheld the object of my most tender love, I did not forget that I had lost that of the sincerest friendship. Ah, Deterville! how severe is now your love! but do not think that you shall put in practice the hard resolution you have designed. The sea shall never make a total separation betwixt people so dear to each other. My name shall reach you; you shall receive my letters; you shall hear my prayers: Blood and friendship shall resume their right over your heart, and you shall again return to a family to whom I am answerable for your loss.

What! in return for so many benefactions, shall I embitter the future days of your sister?[222] Shall I break so tender an union, and fix despair in such hearts as yours, at the time I am enjoying the fruits of your benevolence? No, it shall not be. I cannot help looking at myself with horror, as the cause of filling this happy house with mourning. I acknowledge your kindness for that which I still receive from Celina, at the time when I think she would be quite excusable for hating me; but however pleasing this kindness may be, I will renounce it, and remove for ever from a place which is odious to me, unless you return.

Deterville, how very short-sighted you are, in suffering yourself to be carried away by a design so contrary to what you wish! You would render me happy, but you only make me guilty; you would wish to dry up my tears, instead of which you make them flow; and by your absence, destroy all the merit of your sacrifice.

Alas! you would have had some revenge in being a spectator of that meeting, which you so much dreaded! Yes, Aza, the object of so much love, is no longer the Aza which I have painted to you in such tender colours. The cold manner with which he approached me, the praises which he bestowed on the Span-iards, by which he many times interrupted the fond overflowings of my soul, the teazing curiosity, by which he was continually carried from me to visit the rarities of Paris; all these things contribute to fill my mind with a dread of such evils, the thoughts of which make me shudder. Oh, Deterville! you may not long perhaps be the most unhappy.

If regard for yourself will have no effect on you, let what you owe to friend-ship work on your mind. Friendship is the only asylum for unfortunate love. If what I dread should come to pass, surely you must reproach yourself for loving: If you give me up, where shall I find a friend to whom I may unburthen my sorrows? Shall generosity, till now so potent in your mind, at last give way to revenge for slighted love? No, I can never believe it: A weakness like this would be unworthy of you, nor are you capable of it; but come and convince me, for the sake of your own honour as well as my peace of mind.

## LETTER XXXV.

### To the Chevalier Deterville at Malta.

If your mind, Sir, was not the most noble of the human race, how low should I fall! If you had not the most generous soul, and the most feeling heart, surely I should not have made choice of you as the person to have entrusted with my dis-grace and my despair. But alas! what now remains for me to dread? what should I fear? every thing to me is lost.

It is no longer the loss of liberty, of rank, or banishment from my country that I lament; it is no longer an uneasiness at an innocent tenderness that draws tears from my eyes, but it is the violation of vows, it is love despised that tears my soul. Aza is unfaithful! Aza unfaithful! what force have those sad words over my soul! my blood freezes – a torrent of tears –

From the Spaniards I first learned to know misfortune; but none was equal to the last stroke. It is they that have torn from me Aza's heart; it is their cruel reli-gion that renders me odious in his eyes; that religion approves, nay commands infidelity, perfidy, and ingratitude; but it forbids the love of our near relations. If I was a stranger, and my family unknown, Aza might love me; but being united by the ties of blood, he must abandon me, he must take away my life, without feeling, without regret, without remorse.

Alas! strange as this religion is, if I could, by embracing it, have recovered what it hath taken from me, I would have submitted to all its laws, without suffering my mind to be corrupted by its principles. In the bitterness of my soul, I desired to be instructed in it, but my tears were not regarded; for I cannot be admitted into so pure a society, without giving up the very motives which make me desire to be received into it, without renouncing my love, that is to say, without altering my nature.

This extreme austerity, I must confess, struck me with awe, at the same time that my heart rebelled against it: I cannot help feeling a kind of veneration for laws which take away my life; but is it in my power ever to adopt them myself? and indeed if I did, what advantage could I gain from them? Aza no longer loves me! oh! wretch that I am –

The cruel Aza has lost all the candour of our manners, except that regard for truth of which he makes so savage a use. Seduced by the charms of a young Spaniard, and ready to be united to her, his only reason for coming into France, was to break his engagement with me, and frankly to confess to me his real sentiments; only to restore to me a liberty which I detest, or, rather let me say, to stab me with his sincerity.[223]

Ah! to what purpose is it that he tells me I am free; my heart is his, and will be so while life remains.[224] Let him take that life from me, but let him still love me. –

My misfortune was not concealed from you, why then did you only give me distant hints? Why did you fill my mind with suspicions, which made me unjustly upbraid you, without acquainting me with the plain truth? Alas! can I impute this to you, at a time when I knew I should have given no credit to your report? Blinded, infatuated as I was, I should have fled to meet my fatal destiny; I should have appeared before him a victim to my rival, to have fed her vanity,[225] and have now been – O ye Gods! save me from this horrible idea!

Deterville, too generous friend! am I worthy to be heard? Can you pity me? Can you forget my injustice? and weep for the misfortunes of a wretch, whose esteem for you rises superior to her weakness for an ungrateful man?

## LETTER XXXVI.

### To the Chevalier Deterville at Malta.

You would not surely, Sir, complain of me, if you were not entirely ignorant of the condition from which I have been revived by the cruel attention of Celina. It was not possible for me to write to you; I was not even capable of thinking. If any sense had remained in me, undoubtedly it would have been that of a thorough confidence in you. But surrounded by death, the blood frozen in my veins, I was long ignorant of my own existence: I was no longer sensible I was unhappy. Why, O ye Gods! in calling me back to life, have ye also recalled to me that dreadful remembrance.

He is gone! my eyes shall no more behold him! he flies from me; he no longer loves me; he tells me so: Every thing, with regard to my passion, is an end. He takes another for his wife, and religion forbids him to think any more of me.[226] Why! O cruel Aza! since the ridiculous fashions of Europe have such charms for you, why do you not also partake a little of that deceit which accompanies them?

 Happy Frenchwomen, it is true you are betrayed! but you are complaisantly indulged in that error which would now be a comfort to my mind. I receive at once the mortal blow, which has long been preparing for you. Fatal sincerity of my nation, which was once my pride, thou art no longer a virtue. Courage and firmness, which freely declare the sentiments of the heart, appear to me now to be crimes.[227]

Barbarous Aza, thou hast seen me at thy feet; those feet have been bathed with my tears, and yet thou hast left me – horrid moment! why does not the remembrance of it deprive me of life?

If I had not swooned beneath the weight of my grief, Aza should not have triumphed over my weakness – he should not have gone alone. I would have followed the ungrateful man, my eyes should have been fixed on him to the latest moment of my life, and I would have had the pleasure of dying in his sight.

Deterville, what fatal weakness has removed you to such a distance from me? you would have comforted me, in the midst of my despair; your reason, all-powerful as it is, would have taught me to have gained a victory over myself. Aza, perhaps, might have been still here, but, O Gods! already in Spain, and perhaps at the height of his bliss! – Useless regret, fruitless despair, extreme grief, overwhelms me!

Endeavour not, Sir, to remove the obstacles which keep you at Malta, out of a desire of seeing me; what pleasure would you receive here? Fly from a wretch who is no longer sensible of your kindness, who is a torment to herself, and only wishes to die.

## LETTER XXXVII.

### To the Chevalier Deterville at Malta.

Be not discouraged, too generous friend: I was determined to write to you no more till my life was out of danger, and my mind a little more at ease, that I might be able to calm the uneasiness of yours. I live: Fate will have it so, and I submit to my destiny.

The extreme care of your amiable sister has restored my health, and some returns of reason have supported it. The certainty that my misfortune is past remedy has, in some measure, reconciled me to it. I know that Aza is arrived in Spain, and that he has completed his crime; my grief is not gone, but the cause of it is no longer worthy. If any regret now remains upon my mind, it is for the vexation I have given you, for my sad mistake, and the dreadful wanderings of my reason.

In proportion as this reason enlightens me, I cannot help taking notice of its impotence. How small its power in an afflicted soul! Excess of grief throws us back to childhood. As in that first stage, so in this, objects alone have power over us: the sight seems to be the only sense that has any intimate communication with the soul. This I may say from woeful experience.

When I recovered from the long and senseless lethargy into which the departure of Aza had thrown me, the first desire which I felt was that of retiring into the solitude which I owe to your providential goodness. It was with great difficulty that Celina suffered me to return thither; but there I found such relief from despair, as neither the world, nor even friendship itself, could afford me. In your sister's house, even her conversation was incapable of banishing from my mind those objects which continually renewed the remembrance of Aza's perfidy.

The door through which Celina introduced him to me on the day of his arrival and your departure; the chair on which he sat; the place in which he made me sensible of my misery, by returning me my letters; even the remembrance of his shadow on the wainscot, where I recollected to have seen it; all these things kept the wounds in my heart still bleeding.

But here is nothing to be seen but what recals the pleasing ideas I felt at the first sight of the place. Nothing presents itself to my view but the image of you and your amiable sister, and the everlasting remembrance of your constant friendship.

If the remembrance of Aza forces itself upon me, it is in the manner in which I then thought of him. I fancy myself waiting for his arrival. I give way to this delusion as long as I am able; and when it fails, have recourse to books. I read with greediness. New ideas insensibly cover the horrid truth that surrounds me, and at length gives some relaxation to my sorrow.

Shall I acknowledge that the pleasure of liberty sometimes pleases my imagination, and I cannot help yielding to it? Amused with agreeable objects which surround me, I find charms which I cannot help enjoying. I suffer myself to be guided by taste, without much consulting my reason. I indulge the weaknesses of my mind; and by doing that, I make head against those of my heart. I find this the only method; for disorders of the soul will not submit to violent remedies.

Perhaps the rigid decency of your nation does not permit one of my age to live alone in this independent state; at least Celina, whenever she sees me, uses every argument to persuade me so; but her reasons have not yet been sufficient to convince me that there is any thing blameable in my doing it. Real modesty possesses my heart. It is not the image of virtue that I pay homage to, but virtue itself. I will for ever make her the judge and guide of my actions. To her will I consecrate my life, and to friendship my heart. Alas! when shall I be able to give the undivided possession to that sweet power?[228]

## LETTER XXXVIII, and last.

### To the Chevalier Deterville, at Paris.

It was almost at the same time, Sir, that I read the news of your departure from Malta, and that of your arrival at Paris. Whatever pleasure I shall find at seeing you again, it cannot overcome my concern, which the letter you wrote me at your arrival occasioned.

Can you, Deterville, after having so nicely dissembled your sentiments in every letter which you have before sent me; after having given me reason to hope that I should no longer have your passion to contend with; can you, I say, give yourself up to it in a greater degree than ever?

What end does it answer to affect a deference towards me, which you contradict at the same time that you profess it? You beg leave to see me; you assure me that you will submit to my decrees, and yet you avow sentiments which are the most opposite to my desires. This behaviour offends me, and I must assure you, that I can never approve of it.

But since I perceive you delude yourself with false expectations, and give a wrong turn to the confidence I place in you,[229] it is high time I should make you acquainted with my fixed resolves, which are different from yours, for they are never to be shaken.

In vain do you flatter yourself that my heart will ever wear new chains. The perfidy of another does not set me free from my engagement. Would to Heaven it could make me forget the ungrateful cause of it: but were it possible I could forget him, yet just to myself, I never would be perjured. The cruel Aza abandons one to whom he was dear;[230] but his right over her is not the less sacred. I may be cured of my passion for him, but never can feel any for another. All the sentiments that friendship inspires are yours, and I shall be ever faithful to them.[231] You have a right to all the confidence and sincerity of my heart, and shall enjoy them with the most unlimited freedom. Every tender and delicate feeling which love possessed in my mind, shall now turn to the advantage of friendship. With the same openness of soul, I will confess to you my regret that I was not born in France, and my invincible inclination for Aza. How happy would it have been for me, had I owed to you the advantage of thinking, and been destined to pay my eternal acknowledgment to him who procured me that blessing! We will read each other's soul; friendship as well as love can make time pass pleasantly away;

and there are a thousand means by which it may be made useful and instructive, and to prevent its ever losing its relish.

You shall teach me to know some of your arts and sciences, and, in so doing, find all the pleasure of superiority. I will reward you for your pains, by daily discovering virtues in your mind to which you are yourself a stranger. You shall give me that knowledge which will make solitude pleasing, and enjoy the fruit of your own work; while I will endeavour to make the native charms of simple friendship agreeable to you, and shall find happiness in succeeding.

Celina, dividing her love betwixt us, shall give that life to our conversations which they might otherwise want. What more can we desire?

Your apprehensions that solitude may be hurtful to my health, are without foundation. Believe me, Deterville, solitude is never hurtful but through idleness. Constantly employed, I shall be able to strike out to myself new pleasures, from things that otherwise would be insipid.

There is no necessity for searching deep into the secrets of Nature, since the examination of its daily wonders are sufficient continually to vary and renew employments that are always agreeable. Life itself is scarcely sufficient to acquire a small but interesting knowledge of the universe, of every thing which surrounds me, and of my own wonderful existence.

The pleasure of being; that forgotten, unthought-of pleasure, to so many people;[232] that sweet idea, that pure happiness of saying to one's self, *I am, I live, I exist*,[233] is alone enough to convey bliss, if we think of it as we ought, if we enjoy it, if we know the true value of it.

Come, Deterville, come, and learn of me to husband the resources of our minds, and the benefits which Nature allows us. Let us together renounce[234] those tumultuous feelings that imperceptibly destroy our being. Come and condescend to let me teach you the knowledge of lasting and innocent pleasures; come and let us enjoy them together. You shall find in my friendship, in my heart, in every sentiment of my soul, all that is wanting to make you amends for the loss of love.[235]

## END OF THE FIRST VOLUME.

# THE

# PERUVIAN LETTERS.

## VOL. II.

By R. Roberts,

Translator of Select Tales from

Marmontel,

Author of Sermons by a Lady,

And Translator of the History of

France, from the Abbé Millot.

London:
Printed for T. Cadell, in the Strand,
MDCCLXXIV.

# LETTERS
# TO AND FROM A
# PERUVIAN PRINCESS.[1]


## LETTER XXXIX.[2]

### Deterville's Answer to Zilia.[3]

Alas! Zilia, you permit me to see you, but on what hard conditions! Have you well considered on the request you have made? It is true, I did keep my complaints to myself when last in your presence; but it was a situation, that tho' I felt continual joy in seeing you, yet caused the chief misfortune of my life.

I took the utmost pains to procure you the sight of Aza. I did all in my power to gratify your passion for him,[4] though it was death to myself, even at a time that I suspected his inconstancy;[5] instead of giving myself up to the flattering hopes which I might then naturally have indulged, my mind was afflicted, because it was a circumstance which made you unhappy; but Aza came, he again beheld your charms, he found you the same faithful tender Zilia, whose mind was entirely filled with his idea, and the desire you had to make him happy.[6]

What a triumph ought it to have been for him to see those knots,[7] the precious monuments of your tenderness! What heart but his would not have rejoiced in[8] such chains? or indeed what heart but his could ever have broken them? As it was impossible for me to conceive him capable of such ingratitude, what was there remaining for me but to die. I determined to leave you for ever, and rather than not do that,[9] to fly my country and my family. I could not, however, help indulging the melancholy pleasure of making you acquainted with my resolution.

Celina, moved to the greatest degree by my unhappy destiny, took upon herself the delivery of the letter to you; and the time she chose for it, Zilia, was, as you have informed me, that moment that the faithless Aza appeared before you. Undoubtedly, the tender compassion of Celina for an unhappy brother, made her find a secret pleasure in embittering those moments, which were to have been given up to joy. She was not mistaken in thinking that would be the case. You felt for my despair, and were kind enough to let me know it by soothing expressions, which would have been sufficient to comfort a heart which could have been satisfied with your pity.

It was not long before I was informed of Aza's infidelity, and then I must confess my heart first felt a ray of hope; the delusion had such an effect on my mind, that I dared to flatter myself with being able to make you some amends for the loss of Aza: This was the first moment since I saw you, in which I could please myself with the prospect of a happy futurity; to these tender feelings, at once so soft and so new to me, the most afflicting ones succeeded. I found your life was in danger, and my mind sunk under the dread of losing you.

I endeavoured most ardently to overcome the difficulties which opposed my return. At last I obtained leave, and flew with the wings of love. My respect made me wait for your orders before I would appear before you; I begged this permission, in those expressions which are dictated by a heart like mine; but how can I express what I felt upon reading your answer! No, that is not possible! How many different feelings agitated my soul! How many senseless projects! At length, that of removing far from you, Zilia, was the only one which seemed feasable, and which I had the courage to form, but not to execute.

I yielded to my desire[10] of remaining still near you; my respect, my admiration, and my friendship shall be all that I will permit the ardour of my love to express; but will you forbid me, divine Zilia, to live in silent hope, that you may one day be touched with a passion, which will never be less than it is now?[11]

## LETTER XL.

### Zilia to Celina.[12]

My dear Celina, I am very unhappy; you leave me alone, and a more cruel enemy than myself could not be my companion. Incessantly haunted by the most bitter reflections upon misfortunes which it was impossible to foresee, and not philosopher enough to reconcile my mind to them,[13] I can by no means enjoy that peace of mind which this charming solitude seems to offer;[14] on the contrary, it seems only to bring back to remembrance the cruel Aza, with all his charms.

In vain do I call reason to my aid, in vain recollect my insulted love, returned by such ingratitude; I am convinced that time only can restore me to myself. Why was it not the fates' decree,[15] that such tender delicate sentiments should be reserved for Deterville? He would have been sensible of their value; but how could I see into events of which I never could conceive the least idea. The first time I ever beheld Aza, he appeared with every advantage that man could enjoy; birth, merit, and a noble figure, joined with the warmest love, authorised by duty.

Was there any thing else wanting to engage a virgin heart, by nature endued with tender sentiments? This heart was so given up without reserve, I breathed for him alone; if I was conscious of any beauty, or if I desired to make it more pleasing in the eyes of others, it was only that I might be more worthy of him, and, if possible, still more increase his passion. Our happiness was perfect, till that fatal revolution, which separated us; long absence, acquaintance with others,[16] and the loss of riches, have, doubtless, been the reasons that have made him give me up, that he may enjoy those advantages which are now offered him, and which he can never hope[17] to obtain by an union with me.

Besides, have I any reason to expect that his truth should continue to me, when it has not done so to his religion? One error is the natural consequence of another; but I see with regret, that I am incapable of entertaining you on any other subject than this ungrateful man. How weak am I, my dear Celina; and how much reason have I to wish for your advice, to strengthen my mind against an involuntary love! It shall be so, I am using my utmost efforts to overcome it.

Is Deterville at Paris? Is he willing to accept the tender friendship which I offered him? You and he are the only two in the world that are now dear to me; come then, and console me in my solitude; walking, reading, and conversation shall divide our time, and I cannot help feeling a desire to know something of your religion.[18] Aza, whose understanding is far superior to mine, who, as a son of the divine luminary, must have more penetration than I can have, has found defects in ours, which I am not as yet sensible of.

I may be deceived in looking on it as perfect. When I left Peru, I thought that the only country in the world which was favoured with the light of the sun, and that all other nations were involved in darkness, but I was soon convinced of my error; most likely then, the lessons which I may receive from Deterville, whose character is composed of rectitude, candour, moderation, and generosity, may yet make some farther impression upon me; let him add this one obligation more to those innumerable ones which he has already conferred on me. I will make only one condition with him, which is, that he shall employ alone reason and solid proofs to influence my mind; I am willing to be convinced, but not forced to believe; but lest this serious study should be too much for us, we will mix with it some innocent amusements, in which you, Celina, I hope will take a share.

One thing more I have to beg, which is, that you will tell Deterville, that he will bind me by everlasting gratitude, if he banishes love from our conversation. Such a society will be delightful, if I can enjoy it without this enemy to my repose breaking in upon it. Esteem and confidence shall reign among us, and what would he more desire? Come both of you, my friends, and breathe the free air which is enjoyed in the country, with people who are dear to each other; you will kindly bear with my weakness, you will strengthen my reason, and for the rest we must leave it to time.

## LETTER XLI.

### Celina's answer to Zilia.[19]

I should not have left you, my dear Zilia, if I had not supposed you more resigned to a misfortune, which is now past remedy. I should, indeed, have looked upon it as an affront to you, to have imagined that the inconstant Aza would still fill a place in your heart;[20] he is really unworthy of it, he who was so well acquainted with your merit, and could yet break his chains. It is too plain, that love is still a warm advocate for him in your heart; but it is impossible to justify him, even with all the pains you take to make him appear less guilty, which is only owing to the goodness of your soul, and the tenderness it still feels for this ungrateful man.

But do not, my dear Zilia, still deceive yourself; his passion was never like yours; he never felt any of those little uneasinesses which warm and increase love: jealousy, caprice, and coldness you was incapable of;[21] he was therefore secure of your heart, in which he found nothing but tenderness and softness of disposition: a passion, perhaps rather too ardent on your side, without any trial of his,[22] was the first source of your misfortunes; he was tired of love, because it had made him too happy.

It is no hard matter I think, my dear Zilia, to determine which it was; religion, or the beauty of the fair Spaniard, which made him give you up. If we charitably believe it to be the first, he is certainly justifiable; but as these two objects are joined, I cannot help very much suspecting him. However it be, you are very blamable, my dear friend, not to banish from your thoughts this perfidious man; you are nourishing an idea for ever fatal to your peace: let us talk no more about him, I beseech you, but if possible, let us forget there is such a being. You may certainly expect to see me, and I will do all in my power to amuse you; how much do I wish, that I may be able to contribute to the return of your peace of mind, and your future happiness.

I cannot help reproaching myself, for leaving you abandoned to your own sad reflections; but I flattered myself you was cured of your passion, and doubted not but agreeable company would sweeten your solitude; and in order to do this, I will bring with me two of my friends, who, I am sure, will give you pleasure. My brother is returned, and has seen your letter, which gave him great concern at perceiving from it, that your mind is still filled with the image of the perjured Aza. You owe to his delicacy, and that behaviour which none but himself is capable of, the violence which he does his passion by not seeing you; but he does not feel it the less,[23] and cannot always suppress the testimonies of it.

He fears your sight, because he apprehends, that in spite of himself some expressions may escape him contrary to your rigid injunctions; he incessantly laments, that sentiments so constant, so tender, and so delicate, and which he cannot but be sensible would have been justly bestowed on him, should be thrown away on one so undeserving.

You offer him your friendship, and press him to visit you; is not this a real cruelty? Can you desire, that he should every day behold an object for whom he continually sighs, who by her beauty, softness, and a thousand nameless charms, must still more and more enslave him; and yet severely forbid him to speak of that passion which is ever nearest to his heart, and uppermost in his thoughts?

However, he generously accepts the tender friendship which you offer him, since more you will not give; he is very sensible, this friendship would have a thousand charms for a heart less enamoured than his, but he feels that his passion is too strong to be satisfied with so weak a sentiment; unable to recal his own reason, think how difficult it will be to satisfy yours, if indeed, my dear Zilia, reason may be allowed to one, who still obstinately loves a person who neither can, nor indeed now ought to make any return for it.

If you have a desire to be instructed in the Christian Religion, be not afraid that Deterville will ever give you any lessons with tyranny; he will only assist you by such arguments,[24] as will be left to be choice of your reason, either to yield to or reject. You know his integrity and moderation; I am very sensible, those qualities will ever be his guide; though I am convinced it will give him the purest joy, should he be the instrument of your conviction; but, my dear Zilia, you cannot enter on this great work, without first freeing your mind from prejudice.[25]

We promise ourselves much pleasure in your conversation, and will use every means to make ourselves agreeable to you; this will not be hard to do, if both your hearts can be freed from love, and friendship in each take the place of it. Deterville, who we have at last engaged to be of the party, has firmly promised me, that he will give no marks of his passion, but observe all the rules of discretion which you prescribe to him; but you must promise him one thing in return, which is never to mention the faithless, but too happy Aza. I cannot help thinking this is a complaisance which he has a right to exact; perhaps, you may find a difficulty in it, but it is absolutely necessary it should be done,[26] in order to form that perfect harmony which ought to reign among us.

## LETTER XLII.

### Deterville to Celina.

At my return from Malta to Paris, my dear sister, I received the fair Zilia's letter, which was delivered to me by your order, with a mixture of joy and dread. This letter, in the beginning, expresses her design to forget Aza, in the strongest terms; but, oh painful and cruel thought! it likewise expresses her resolution afresh never to put another in his place. She even forbids me having the least hope of that kind; what a mortal blow, my dear Celina, was this! Do you thoroughly enter into it?

While Zilia imagined she could depend on the fidelity of her lover, I had no room either for hope or complaint; I was sensible, from the melancholy feelings of my own heart, that such a passion was not easily conquered.[27] While Aza was faithful, he had a right to Zilia; but when this Aza became faithless and perjured, had I not then a right to hope? Yet at the very moment that I conceived it, how cruelly was it crushed! Dear sister, how hard is my fate! Of what materials are those Peruvian souls composed? Is Zilia incapable of feeling that pleasure, which all women, I might say all mankind, enjoy in revenge? If she is, why does it not erase from her heart every idea of this ungrateful man. Surely it should, if it were only to shew her detestation of that crime.

How happy should I be, if amidst the variety of sentiments which fill her soul, one spark of love for me could find an entrance! I am sensible that my delicacy would be a little hurt by it, but no matter, if I have but her love. I shall owe a part of my happiness to revenge, but perhaps I shall likewise owe some to gratitude; shall I not then be infinitely blessed? Let me then for a moment enjoy the idea.

It is true, that this beauty whom I adore, offers me the warmest friendship, and expresses the charms of it with so much grace and delicacy, that had any but Zilia made me such an offer, it would have enchanted me; but can the most tender friendship on her side be sufficient to repay the most passionate love on mine? Weak shadow of a passion! how can it at all be answerable to that which I feel, if at the time that Zilia returns the most tender love with calm tranquil friendship only, her heart, at last forgetting the faithless Aza, should favour the passion of any other man? I shudder with dread and horror at the thought; alas! such an engagement would render me for ever miserable. To be always within sight of the object who alone could make me happy, and yet always far from happiness, is a situation, that instead of curing the evils I suffer, would serve to increase them to eternity. Pity me, my dear Celina, lament your unfortunate brother, if you have any idea of hopeless love.

## LETTER XLIII.

### Celina to Deterville.

I do indeed pity a distracted heart, which finds no relief either from itself or from any thing about it. Such is your situation, my dear Deterville; you love, with a passion which knows no bounds, the most amiable and most lovely girl that ever was; the purity of her soul, the natural delicacy of her conversation, her beauty, for ever new to your eyes, her candour, even her very tenderness for Aza, repugnant as it is to all your hopes, join to contribute to nourish in you a passion, which is continually increased by esteem. A passion the more tender, as it is the first you ever felt.

I would endeavour to cure you of it, if it were of such a nature as made it at all likely I should succeed; but I am not ignorant, that at the time you was master of this fair Indian, that she was yours by the laws of conquest, you respected her beauty, her sentiments, and her misfortunes. It was not for want of your strong endeavours, that what she prized as her only good, was not hers; and that even at the expence of the wealth which might have been your own.

I looked up to you as a prodigy, when I saw you send for the happy Aza from the Spanish court, in order to return to him, in company with his other treasures, the only jewel which you wished to keep. Surely this was the heroism of generosity. Afterwards, by an unexpected turn of fortune, when the infidelity of Aza rendered your favours useless, and you had more reason than ever to hope, the unexampled constancy of Zilia for an ungrateful man added the last severe stroke to your misfortunes.

But, my dear brother, while I indulge your grief, and lament your ill-starr'd passion, give me leave to say, that you suppose your case worse than it really is. Your anxious heart permits not the least glimpse of hope; but perhaps the indifference in which you formerly lived, makes you ignorant of the hopes which I think are still left you. As a woman, I ought to be true to my sex; but as a sister, I must a little betray it.

Hear me then, my dear Deterville: Aza was the only object in the world that Zilia could, in the early time of her life, be attached to; a prince tender, young, and handsome; and Zilia in all the force and sweetness of her first fires, authorised by duty, and agreeable to that virtue which ennobled both their souls; was it not likely a tender passion should be formed between them?[28] A dreadful misfortune, a cruel revolution separated them, and increases the idea of their happiness, of which they saw themselves fatally deprived.

Only recollect, what strength despair must add to a lawful passion before so warm: hers was the first impression of a heart formed for love, which could not know a more sensible pleasure than that of constancy to the first object it had chosen: In short, it was a heart enamoured to excess, whose passion was still more increased by difficulty, and which, just arrived at the height of its felicity, saw itself, in that instant, snatched from its expected enjoyment.

My dear brother, for a moment put yourself in Zilia's place; is it possible that a new lover could make her so soon forget a bridegroom who was so infinitely dear to her? Is it possible, that her tranquility could be already restored? Only recollect the innate nobleness of her soul, and you will own that a heart like hers must carry her attachment beyond the bounds of common sensibility, and may be capable of continuing to love an object which it is sure never to possess. This is a tuneful string, and it sounds a long time after it has been once thoroughly touched; but surely reason must convince you, my dear Deterville, that this is too contrary to nature, to last for ever.[29]

Can you doubt but that Zilia, when she can reflect more calmly on it, will see the injustice of Aza, will feel his indifference, and grow tired of a love which meets with no return; a sweet enchantment has hitherto supported her tenderness, but that will at last vanish; the image of Aza will become burthensome, and her heart, then disinterested and without an object to fill it, will not be able to continue in such an inactive state; a disagreeable languor will be tiresome to her active soul; she will find some pretence to get rid of it, and what pretence can better offer than that of gratitude? Zilia acknowledges her obligations, and is fully sensible how much she owes to your generous disinterested behaviour.

I come, in the next place, to that friendship she has offered you. By your refusing to accept of it, it seems to be displeasing to you; it is a sentiment not answerable to that of love; it seems like a payment in false coin, and you reject it because it is not comformable to your desires; but pray, dear brother, is it the name that gives you disgust? to me it appears so; or you would receive the friendship of Zilia with less reluctance; give me leave to tell you, that you ought to receive it with rapture; why do you oblige me to betray the secrets of my own sex?

This sentiment of friendship, so pleasing among men, and so rarely to be found between women, is always the strongest between people of different sexes. Men embrace it between each other with ardour, women with caution, but two people of different sexes, add to friendship a lively spark of that fire, which nature, true to itself, will always give; passion imperceptibly will attend this friendship, so pure in appearance, even in its birth, as friends of this kind generally find; let them be as much upon their guard as they will, it is of no consequence; all the precautions they can take, will not stop the progress of nature, and they will soon be surprised with finding themselves fall into that passion, of which they had no mistrust.

The friendship which is offered you, my dear Deterville, I look on to be the first act of that interesting play, the plot of which you so much desire to see unravelled; it is the first inlet to the heart, and if that is favourable to you, what cause have you for complaint? I must confess that the name of friendship spreads a veil over other sentiments, which conceals a part of them from your sight; but it is a veil wrought by the hands of love,[30] which conceals nothing from a penetrating eye, nor can long conceal the truth from him who is the object of it.

Confess now, my dear brother, that I had reason for surprise, when I heard you so bitterly complain of the only part which Zilia could take, reflect well upon it, and you will be of my opinion. Could a better method be thought of; one better suited to the delicacy of you both? Will not the lady always rise in your opinion, who was reserved, only to make your happiness the more complete? Who, by making your passion coincide with reason, intends to refine and increase your pleasure?

Indeed, my brother, you are much obliged to Zilia, who, under the veil of friendship, is preparing for you pleasures of a more exalted kind, than you could ever figure to yourself. She neither could, nor indeed ought to make at once such a return to your passion, as you requested. You must advise with our sex in affairs of this kind, and do not blush to confess that women understand them better than yourself; since without such assistance, men would be very ignorant in the art of love. Women are allowed, from the softness of their tempers, to have nicer geniuses than men; take notice, I distinguish this art of love from artifice; these two characters, though they resemble each other, are yet different.

Every sensible woman loves with art, but not with artifice; but as to your dear Zilia, her heart is honest, noble, and elevated. But she is ingenious beyond what I ever found in woman; that ingenious heart of hers, at present, wholly engrossed with the most tender passion,[31] but a passion cruelly slighted, you will at last find to be reserved for you; allow her only a decent time for grief, and without complaint, leave it to that time, to destroy in her the idea of constancy, which now flatters her vanity. That singular honour of remaining faithful to her first vows,[32] even when they are broken on the other side, without a possibility of re-union, is a sentiment which certainly she could not learn among us; she will therefore at last yield to our example; being then free, but afraid of enjoying that freedom, and at the same time fully sensible of your generous treatment, the friendship, which she now looks on as a pleasing harmony between souls, need go but one degree farther to become love, and that miracle will be accomplished without her perception.

My dear Deterville, what a charming prospect is before you? I think you must see enough of it to make you easy, and engage you with alacrity to accept the part which Zilia offers with so good a grace. From these intentions, which are disinterested in appearance, but more so from the gentleness of a female mind, expect the happiness of which you seem so much to despair.

## LETTER XLIV.

### Zilia to Deterville.

Ever since the misfortune which happened to me, in the loss of Aza, I could not have imagined, Sir, that any poignant affliction could have reached my heart; but fatal experience has convinced me of the contrary, from a discovery I accidentally made, and which has given me the most cruel uneasiness. Your sister came yesterday to see me, and after she had left me, I found a paper in my chamber. I opened it, but how great was my surprise to find it her hand, in a letter addressed to you;[33] in which, after condemning you for refusing my proffered friendship, she endeavours to persuade you to it, from motives very contrary to my thoughts.

Who could have imagined, that the ever tender, the ever generous Celina, the only comfort of my afflicted soul, would have proved unfriendly, after I had given myself entirely up to her, and had not the least reserve in the sincere love I felt? But I find her love to me is not without suspicion. Though your sister, at the beginning of this shocking letter, loads me with praises, yet surely they cannot flow so much from her own sentiments, as from her fear of displeasing you. For, on what pretences does she ground your hope, but the want of stability in those virtues which she allows appear in me. In betraying to you the secrets of her sex: Her art, or I will say artifice, does not turn to the advantage of her own mind: Mistaken girl! does she think the Virgins devoted to the Sun, and educated in his Temple, are to be looked on in that general light in which she makes women appear? Is there but one model for them, and but one rule to form a judgment by? The Creator, who gives endless variety to his works; who distinguishes every country by some particular property; who gives to us all faces so alike,[34] and yet so different; has he decreed that the characters of the mind should be in every nation similar, and that all reasonable beings should think in the same manner; I own this is what I cannot believe.

Besides, what right has she to allow to your sex such superior prerogatives? Can she think they are endued with a stronger portion of the breath of the Divinity? We have indeed in Peru, such an opinion of the divine Amutas, whose sublime knowledge, consecrated by a continual habit of virtue, raises them above the generality of men: But for others, if they have passions which are common to the species, we allow them only, common virtues to conduct and rectify those passions; and we judge of them from their actions, and not from any presupposed weaknesses.

How could she endeavour to persuade you, that there was so little firmness in my soul? Certainly, she cannot conceive it from any thing that is past. My heart, formed to frankness from my infancy, never used any other methods to persuade the faithless Aza of the sincerity of my passion, than by the natural manner in which it was expressed. I am entirely unacquainted, and wish ever to be so, with that art which degrades women in a much greater degree than it makes them appear charming, since it proves their weakness, their vanity, and their distrust of the object whom they would wish to enslave.

Nature knows no art, nor ever strives to adorn the graces, by adding superficial charms to virtue. In vain, doth Celina poorly distinguish art from artifice; I know no difference: Is there any need for disguise, where it is our interest to hide nothing? But she blushed to confess the arts she had made use of, to lead you into an error; however, I still hope every thing from the known generosity of your soul, worthy, as you are, to have been born among us.

I am sure no injurious suspicion ever yet found an entrance into your mind; and I shall be very sorry for your seeing this wicked letter, lest it should lead you to suspicion: But should I, Deterville, be at all worthy of your friendship, if the too credulous Celina had justly represented me? As you have too much candour to think I aim at any glory in barely performing my duty, you cannot expect that either time, or the supposed weakness of my sex, will make any change in me.

United with Aza, in ties[35] which death only could have dissolved, no other object can disengage me from him. Yet let me beg to see you, Sir, and let us together enjoy the tranquil fruits of friendship, which gratitude presents you with. Come, and at once enlighten and adorn my understanding, disengaged from all tumultuous passions. You will find that friendship alone, is worthy to fill our hearts, and make our destiny perfectly happy.[36]

## LETTER XLV.

### Deterville to Zilia.

I had set out, adorable Zilia, with a firm resolution to forget you, as the only relief to pains which were insupportable. I hoped a long absence might work this miracle; but, alas! the resentment which tenderness inspires, is soon stifled by its own principle. I am returned more enamoured, though with as little hope as ever.

In spite of the faint glimmerings which Aza's infidelity had kindled in my mind, my situation gives me more reason than ever to complain. But, notwithstanding your cruel manner of thinking, I still have no power to fly from you: The engaging manner in which you bind me, by the tender friendship you offer me, has such influence over my soul, that though the bounds you prescribe appear a species of ingratitude, yet I must own, that to make any complaint would be unjust; at the same time that I submit to the severity of your laws, my heart dares still to hope they may, in time, be softened. Pardon my distraction and my sincerity.

I express what my heart feels, and cannot help pleasing myself with these illusive prospects, or being sorry when my reason convinces me of the folly of them. It is true, it sometimes makes me blush for a moment, but soon the ideas of a happy futurity take place, and I triumph over my misfortunes. This is my weakness; I confess it; and though it so much mortifies and degrades me, yet does it raise the glory of the daughter of the Sun.

When I am with you, fair Zilia, a look from you will recal the respect that is your due. My desire to please you will be stronger than any other, and will be the rule of my actions; united to you, only by the pure feelings of the soul and similitude of mind, we shall have nothing to fear from those disgusts which the passions too often bring along with them; our calm and quiet days shall flow on in perfect tranquillity, like a perpetual spring, when all things seem to start afresh out of the hands of Nature. We shall together enjoy her benefits, and crown them by our gratitude:[37] If we at any time mention Aza, it shall be only to pity and detest his perfidy; perhaps Fate was more guilty than he: but however that may be, he was certainly not worthy of the Virgin of the Sun, after having breathed the native air of the barbarous enemies of Peru.

Let me beseech you to forget your anger to my sister; her tenderness for me, and her sense of my distress, has made her hope for what she has written; and her design was only to comfort me, and preserve me from despair. This is surely sufficient to excuse her; I must insist upon your promise of pardon, divine Zilia; let there be nothing to embitter the sweets of that society which we propose to enjoy in the country. Assured of this, I shall soon throw myself at your feet; I will look upon your new habitation as the Temple of the Sun, and there respectfully adore the luminary that enlightens it. My constant, my incessant care shall be, to pay to you the purest and most submissive homage.[38]

## LETTER XLVI.[39]

To the Chevalier Dubois,[40] at Malta.

My abrupt departure from Malta, without taking leave of you, my dear Sir, might justly give you disgust; but you know me too well, to suspect that friendship which, contracted in our earliest years, has ever since been increasing by that unreserved confidence which has always subsisted between us.

This early intimacy, this unrestrained freedom, must plead an excuse for my having so often lately interrupted the natural gaiety of your mind, to entertain you with my complaints. You know the affair which drove me to Malta; the same cause has hurried me back to France: Do not reproach me for not seeing you, my mind was then too much oppressed to bear the disagreeable ceremony of taking leave of my friends.

I left Paris with a full design never more to see this Peruvian Beauty; I hoped time, absence, and your company, would banish from my breast a fruitless passion: but oh! my dear Dubois; Zilia herself has begged, has entreated my return: alas! how cruel a task does she require of me? While she calls me her friend, and urges me to see her in the kindest manner, she forbids my ever thinking of her by another name; she imposes a cruel silence on my lips, and insists that love shall never be the subject of our conversation.

I know you smile at what you will call my little knowledge of the fair-sex; but indeed, my friend, you must not judge of Zilia by our countrywomen; such an invitation from a Frenchwoman would be an assurance of success, but Zilia, to all the sweetness, softness, and delicacy which can adorn her own sex, adds a steady constancy, which is rarely to be found in either; and a candour of soul, which makes her incapable of the least disguise.

Accuse her not of cruelty, for she is all gentleness; and, in spite of myself, I must admire those sentiments which destroy my hopes. Alas! why was the amiable Zilia born to waste such a profusion of love on the faithless, ungrateful Aza? Why was not I the happy object of her tender attachment? And why may I not yet be so? Pity my distraction, my dear friend! I know not what I say. I set out to-morrow for the country, with my brother and sister (to visit this lovely girl); they sometimes console and sometimes rally my distress: You shall soon hear of me again. Adieu.

## LETTER XLVII.

### To the Chevalier Dubois, at Malta.

I have now, my dear Dubois, been two days in this agreeable retreat: It is impossible to describe to you the agitation of my mind at setting out; I wished with ardency to see the charming Zilia, yet feared that sight might awaken such sensations in my soul, as I wished, if possible, might sleep.

I knew I should meet with her with all the warmth of the most lively friendship, but my heart whispered me, it was not likely to stop there: Thus wavering, thus perplexed, I was not much inclined to talk; my fellow-travellers observed my reverie, and endeavoured to draw me from it, by enquiring what passed in my journies to and from Malta, and how I passed my time when there; their questions teazed me, and I could scarcely answer with good humour.

At length we arrived, and I summoned all my resolution, to keep within the bounds I had prescribed myself. Zilia, after having saluted my sister, ran to me, with her usual frankness, calling me her dear brother; I caught her in my arms, and while I embraced her, felt a rapture, which told me, that was not the name I wished her to know me by: A sigh escaped me, as she disengaged herself; whether it was observed I know not, but she diverted our attention, by making us take notice of the little alterations she had made in the house and gardens, since my departure.

We dined together with great chearfulness; plenty, neatness, and elegance reigned at table, and Zilia did the honours with a grace that enchanted us. How comes it that this dear girl, without seeming to take pains, has, in so short a time, acquired that easy address, which is the study of great part of the lives of our French ladies?[41] Indeed she has learned all the politeness of an European court, without having lost that native simplicity which adorned the beauteous Indian.

After dinner my sister, who has much taste in music, entertained us on the harpsichord; and Zilia, who has great sweetness of voice, and who, while in the Convent, had improved her judgment, sung to the instrument: It was a new air, I think a pretty one; the words are tender, I applied them to my own passion: I send you the copy.

SONG.[42]

I.

When Delia leaves the blissful plain,
And in retirement veils her charms,
Tho' thousand beauties still remain,
No fair one now my bosom warms;
'Midst sportive nymphs and shepherds gay,
Musing, I sigh the hours away.

II.

But when she to the plain returns,
My joys revive, my sorrows die;
My breast with kindling transport burns,
My wish fulfil'd, to her I fly;
My speech attempts my love to paint,
Alas! in vain, all words are faint.

III.

Lend me thy power, oh! mighty love;
With eloquence, my lips inspire,
Such as my Delia's soul may move,
And touch her heart with fond desire:
So shall thy votary[43] e'er be bless'd,
Thy votary, still thro' life confest.

The tune was adapted to the words; soft and plaintive, it soothed and nourished my distemper. The effect it wrought on my mind was visible, after the little concert ceased; love took the entire possession of my soul; I continually repeated to myself the lines of the song; I applied them to my own passion; I grew insensibly pensive and melancholy; I was called upon, and endeavoured to resume my gaiety, but in vain; I sunk again into thought, and remained so the whole evening. Was I writing to any one but you, should I thus entertain them with the history of my heart? But you have ever been the confident of its foibles, as well as its virtues.

You, my dear friend, to whom love has been a sport, and women only the amusement of your lighter hours, will perhaps be inclinable to ridicule my folly; but, I beseech you, spare me, I am indeed too serious to bear raillery.

My God! what a trial! to love to excess, to have the beloved object for ever in my sight, yet condemned to eternal silence! I dread chance leaving us a moment alone together; how should I then command my tongue? Alas! these sad reflections dispirit me too much; I must conclude. Adieu, my dear Dubois,
Ever remember your
Deterville.

# LETTER XLVIII.

## To the Chevalier Dubois, at Malta.

I am now, my dear Dubois, at a little villa of my brother's, about three miles from the residence of my fair friend – What does that name express! Surely, with a female, every thing that is tender: Dull, insensible clods, who talk of Platonick love,[44] a dream, a chimera, which never did, nor ever will exist, but in the brains of monks and religious enthusiasts; who having deadened all tender feelings in themselves, endeavour to degrade the Deity, to whom all mankind have bowed, and set up this unnatural idol in his stead: Yet, my Zilia would persuade me, that it is possible for me to yield to their nonsensical jargon. Strange! that she, who judges so justly in all other things, should in this so much deceive herself; and that, while she cherishes a hopeless passion for a lover who is for ever lost, should imagine that I, the beloved object daily in my sight, can cease to wish her mine.

I am led into these reflections by an accidental interview we had this morning. My sister and Zilia being so near, and so fond of each other, are seldom asunder[45] a day together. I have carefully avoided being left alone with my lovely Indian, fearing I should give offence by expressing, what I vainly endeavour to seem not to feel.

My sister being fond of reading, has a small study, to which I have free access: There have we frequently formed little parties, and read favourite poets, and sometimes philosophers, to my dear pupil, and been often charmed by the observations she has made: And there, it was that this morning, I inadvertently surprised the lovely maid.

I passed the last evening with a friend; and returning home, when the family were retired to rest, I did not know that Zilia spent the night with my sister. That uneasiness which keeps me waking while others enjoy repose, made me rise earlier than usual, and walk to the study, with a design of diverting my anxiety by a book; when, on opening the door, I saw Zilia sitting with her back to me, leaning her head on her hand, which rested on a table, busy in perusing a paper which lay before her. I made but little noise in entering, and she seemed so absorbed in thought, that I advanced some steps without her perceiving me. As she lifted up her face, I perceived she had been shedding tears: taking the paper in her hand, she was going to throw it in the fire, but suddenly snatching it back, she clasped it to her breast, and wept over it. Having seen more than I wished, I would have retreated as quietly as I entered, but Zilia turning her head just as I was going out of the door, called me back. Oh! heavens, Sir, says she, is it possible you can thus steal on my retirement? Shocked at being looked on as a spy, I returned, threw myself at her feet, and told her by what chance I had been brought there, and how unexpectedly I had found her. I am satisfied, Sir, says she; but since it has so happened, sit down, and learn the occasion of the disorder in which you found me: This is an explanation which I owe to your friendship. You know to what excess I have loved; and that despair only could ever have forced me to drive the faithless Aza from my mind: you know how almost impossible a task I imposed on myself, when I resolved to think of him no more; however, to this sad necessity has he reduced me; and there was no means of accomplishing it, but by parting with every thing that was ever his. I thought I had done it; but, looking in a cabinet yesterday, I found this letter, which was the forerunner of our last fatal meeting: I bathed it with my tears; I was ashamed of my weakness, but was not able to assume sufficient courage instantly to destroy it; I carried it about me, with a design of doing it as soon as I could fortify my mind against the many tender ideas which were now renewed in it: I this morning thought it done, and was preparing to put my design in execution, when I could not help wishing to read it once more, to take an everlasting adieu; I dwelt on every sentence, not reflecting that my foolish heart was preparing tortures for itself: at length, on a sudden recollection, I determined to burn it; but just as I was committing it to the flames, my heart recoiled, and I pressed it to my bosom in a transport of affliction and grief: I find a tender reluctance in my mind, which will not suffer me to see it consumed; at the same time, I am convinced I ought not to keep it, as it is only feeding a hopeless, and unreasonable passion: let me beseech you to take it, and do with it what you will; but let me never see or hear of it more.

Alas! my dearest Zilia, says I, would I could, by taking this paper from your sight, banish the faithless Aza from your mind, who, I fear, has taken too deep root to admit of any other making an impression. Ah! Sir, says she, let me entreat you, proceed no farther; you know this is a subject with which you promised never to entertain me!

Oh! my Zilia, says I; how cruel is that injunction, yet, how religiously have I kept it, till inadvertently drawn into this conversation! why did you insist on my return? Can a man carry fire in his bosom and not be burnt? And can you, who have yourself felt a passion so tender, and, oh sad reflection! so unalterable; can you, unjust and partial girl, blame me, for feeling that love which the sight of you daily inflames? or, that now urged by what I have just heard and seen, I dare (though contrary to your hard commands) confess it?

Alas! says she, I feel the justice of your reproach, but surely I deserve some degree of pity: Did not your sister, my loved friend, unkindly condemn me, as the cause which deprived her of the society of a brother? Ah! still do I remember those upbraidings which pierced my soul; and though my tears, my innocence, my just excuses, and my real sorrow, made her cease to afflict me by words; yet her looks, though full of sweetness, seemed to me a silent reproach; and I never saw her without feeling the painful sensation of being the cause of uneasiness to the person I loved.

Whatever were the motives, returned I, since you have recalled me, and I am every day blessed with the sight of my lovely, my adorable Zilia, suffer me to breathe my passion, and to hope that the heart which has once been capable of feeling to such excess, will not be for ever insensible to me. Hold, Sir; for heaven's sake, spare me on this subject; I am quite unprepared for it, and must conjure you to leave me, that I may recover from the perplexity into which this meeting has thrown me.

I made no answer, but seizing one of her hands, pressed it to my lips, bowed, and left her. As soon as I got home, I endeavoured to ease my mind, by communicating its feelings to you, my dear friend: sometimes I flatter myself with hope, and sometimes her steady uniformity makes me despair. What are your sentiments of my situation? But why do I enquire of you, who form your judgment only from women in general, and know nothing of my Zilia! Adieu; you shall hear from me again soon: always love your

Deterville.

## LETTER XLIX.

### To the Chevalier Dubois, at Malta.

It is very well, my dear Dubois, you indulge your vein of raillery; it is your turn, and I must allow it you, especially as you always do it in a manner which pleases rather than hurts.

You seem to be highly entertained with what you call a very prosperous opening; we are all in the right train you cry, and do not doubt but by this time Zilia and I perfectly understand each other: how will you be surprised to find that I have drawn no advantage from that beginning; nor has love been the subject of our conversation since that day. No, believe me, our discourses and thoughts have been turned a sublimer way.

I do not pretend to say that love does not mix itself with all my thoughts, though I never talk of it but to you; a silence, which I should perhaps have found difficult to have kept, had I not been engrossed by another topic.

The day after I wrote you the last letter, my brother, sister, and self, dined with Zilia; the weather was sultry, and we sat in a delicious grove, where the trees formed an arched canopy over our heads; the shadow of the boughs, which were just moved by the wind, chequered the sunbeams on the ground, and made a constant tremulous motion; while the little choiristers,[46] that were perched here and there, seemed, by their various notes, to express their thanks for the crumbs they received from our table.

After our repast, we strolled through a winding path, which gradually opened to the banks of a river; here we seated ourselves in an arbour, composed of jessamine[47] and woodbines.[48] The prospect on the other side was delightfully romantic;[49] the green sloping hills, which descended to the water, were shaded round with woods and vineyards: and it being the time of the vintage, nothing could appear more luxuriant.

What added to the beauty of the scene, was a small rock which stood opposite to us, at the top of which rose a brook that ran down its craggy sides, till it was lost in the current of the river. The sweetness of the air, the soft melody of the birds, the continual murmur of the water, and the sublimity of the prospect, all concurred to give our minds a turn to something serious and solemn.

We began by admiring the fineness of the evening, and the charming diversity of scenes which surrounded us: we looked up to the cloudless sky, and were delighted with the blue ether which composed it. This naturally led us to contemplate the great first mover, and to express our grateful adoration in terms suited to hearts at that time warmed by his blessings.

We observed that devotion was implanted in the heart of man; since there was no nation under heaven, however rude and barbarous, that did not worship a Deity.

Zilia hearkened with silent attention to all that was said; then resuming the subject, As I can no longer, says she, look on the Sun as a God, but as a striking proof, among many others, of the wisdom and goodness of some all-powerful being, I wish to know as much of this revered Deity as possible; for this end, I have long secretly desired to be instructed in the tenets of your religion, but have yet never had it in my power. The priest, who formerly, in the Convent, pretended to enlighten my mind,[50] though there appeared the marks of divinity in what he attempted to teach, yet he so obscured and puzzled it by his manner, that I could by no means reconcile it to my understanding.

It may be, says I, that you was at that time less inclinable to attend to any arguments in its favour than you are now; however, as your mind is disposed, it is certainly worth a second enquiry. The great book of nature is before you, study it, an intelligent being must, in every page, behold the traces of its almighty Author. This will naturally lead you to wish a more perfect knowledge of him; which is only to be gained by reading, without prejudice, those books wherein he has revealed his will.

That is, returned she, what I wish to do, and in which you must assist me: let me not bewilder myself, in reasoning on what is difficult to be understood, but do you clear the way before me, remove error from my sight, and teach me to distinguish truth from falsehood.

Since that time our mornings have been devoted to this sacred employment: I look on myself as a missionary sent by heaven, to convert my Zilia. I have put into her hands those books which treat of the life and miracles of our Saviour; it opens to her a daily scene of wonders; she reads, she admires, she comments;

she makes her objections, I endeavour to obviate them; she seems pleased to be convinced.[51]

I will send you in my next, the substance of some of our conversations; in the mean time rest assured, that no one is nearer than yourself to the heart of

Deterville.

## LETTER L.

To the Chevalier Dubois, at Malta.

In my last, I sent you an account of the pleasing task I had undertaken; I now proceed to tell you how it has succeeded.

Sitting alone with Zilia, the other day; I have, says she, with equal pleasure, and surprise, read the life and discourses of your great Lawgiver: every example, every precept it contains, seems calculated to render mankind a set of happy social beings. The way which leads to heaven seems to be the only path they could tread, by which they could ensure to themselves a constant succession of calm and peaceful days on earth; yet, by some strange perversion of human nature, among you who glory in being called after the name of that divine person, how many miseries abound, owing to that wickedness and folly which prompts you to act contrary to reason, and the dictates of that religion which you profess; these things stagger my newly received faith.

Satisfy me, if you can; and tell me, why avarice, revenge, and all those unruly passions which trouble the repose of life, find a passage into the minds of men, who acknowledge the Gospel as a rule of action, and call themselves the followers of a disinterested, mild, and forgiving Saviour?

It is, says I, perhaps a question not easily answered; if men were not liable to be influenced by those passions, there would be no exertion of virtue, as there would be no vice to counteract: nor would it have been necessary for a God to have descended from heaven, where he reigned supreme, to pass a life of poverty and subordination on earth, when he might have been born a prince, and had nothing more to do, than declare his will, to creatures so prone to obedience. On the contrary, our Saviour, Christ Jesus, became man, in an humble station, and was invested with passions incident to human nature; that he might shew, by a practice of constant self-denial, that it was possible to controul desires, which, under proper regulation, are beneficial to the world, but if let loose, must prove destructive.

Undoubtedly, returned she, some passions are amiable, and tend to the good of society; but surely avarice must destroy every seed of humanity; and the breast that is open to such a guest, must be shut against every tender sentiment.

Avarice is, indeed, replied I, the mark of a mean and sordid soul; yet there is, perhaps, no vice which so imperceptibly creeps into the mind of man. The person of scanty fortune, whose income is spent in his daily bread, sees it at a distance, and looks with contempt on the wretch, who sits brooding over the hoard, which his contracted heart will not suffer him to use: but let an unexpected flow of riches pour in upon him, how often does he dwindle into the very wretch he so despises; or, what is full as bad, spends it prodigally on himself, insensible to the calls of pity, alike deaf to the cries of distress, and blind to the mute petitions of silent suffering merit.

Again, as you say, we are commanded, as well as excited by the great example before us, to forgive injuries received; and as perhaps no task is harder than to forgive, while the sense of ill-usage remains, we are told to endeavour to forget; lest, by cherishing the remembrance in our minds, we should be tempted to revenge.[52]

Man naturally finds a pleasure in revenging an insult, but the laws of Christianity forbid him to indulge it; nay, it goes yet further, it commands us to love our enemies. By loving, I do not apprehend we are to treat them as friends; that would be absurd and ridiculous: but we are to be willing to do them every good office, to oblige them, when it is in our power to do it, without hurt to ourselves or others; and, by a noble forbearance of evil, and perseverance in good, shew them the distinguishing character of the Christian Religion.

By this means, we may at last overcome them; and by subduing ourselves, become the happy instruments, of leading them to a proper sense of their unworthy conduct. If we fail in this, we shall at least have the satisfaction of quieting all turbulence in our own minds, and conquer ourselves by regulating, not destroying our passions.

Even the most amiable of all that bear that name, Love, that cordial drop, designed by heaven to soften all our cares; by which we most resemble angels, and without which we degenerate into brutes; requires some controul. For if we indulge the desires of that sweet power to the extent, what fatal consequences does it often produce? Do not you, my Zilia, daily teach me the art of self-denial? continued I, lowering my tone of voice.

She said nothing, but seemed uneasy, and we immediately joined the rest of the company, who were walking in the garden. Madamoiselle St. Clare,[53] a young lady, with whom Zilia has contracted an intimacy, was of the party. This lady is about five and twenty; she is too little to be called a fine woman, and besides, wants that regularity of features, which connoisseurs say constitute beauty; but in which I, who judge of beauty only by the pleasing effect it has upon my mind, and not by rules which the painter and statuary[54] has laid down, disagree with them.

To a person whose judgment is guided by his feelings, Madamoiselle St. Clare must be inexpressibly pleasing; as the whole turn of her countenance is such as denotes great goodness of heart, and sweetness of disposition: perhaps her sensibility is too great, since a fine understanding, which she certainly possesses, has not been able to preserve her from love. Her story I am not acquainted with;

only know in general, it is an unfortunate one; and indeed the air of melancholy, which she constantly bears about her, is an indication of it.

She has a turn[55] for poetry, but deals in the pathetic; and there is something in her verse, which constantly alludes to the misfortunes of her life, and are generally soft plaintive soliloquies. I send you one, which was given me by Zilia.[56]

> No more, my soul, with unremitting grief,
> Thy hapless fate, unceasingly bewail;
> Those floods of sorrow, cannot yield relief;
> No tears, for evils past, can ought avail.
>
> From those black clouds, those veils of darkest hue,
> Oh! let me turn aside, my aching sight;
> Where fairer prospects, open to my view,
> And beaming brightness, drives away the night.
>
> Religion, only balm the wretched find,
> Thy healing comforts to my soul apply;
> Let love of God alone possess my mind;
> Teach me to live, and teach me more, to die.
>
> That idol, which so long usurp'd thy place,
> And left no room for any other guest,
> Despoil'd of every soft and pleasing grace,
> Shall to its God, resign this anxious breast.
>
> Lord sought-for peace, shall to my mind return,
> Calm resignation, hush my cares to rest;
> No pulses beat, no ardent wishes burn,
> Nor sighs for luckless love, shall me molest.
>
> To Heaven, my sighs and wishes now ascend,
> Where love immortal, my desires shall fill:
> For ever blest, when time shall have an end,
> I still shall live, and do my Maker's will.

Thus does she endeavour to reconcile herself to a fate, which most of her friends think will sink her to the grave. I find myself a little infected by her melancholy, and will therefore conclude this long letter, with assuring you I am faithfully yours,
    Deterville.

## LETTER LI.

### To the Chevalier Dubois, at Malta.

And do you really, my dear Dubois, believe that I am likely to change the object of my passion? What can I have said, that can induce you to such a belief? And Madamoiselle St. Clare is the person you have pitched on? Do you suppose then that I am determined, to fall in love always, where a prior prepossession precludes all hope? Be assured that can never happen a second time.

Indeed I am so well acquainted with my own heart, that I may venture to affirm it would never have been the captive of Zilia, lovely as she is, had I suspected any pre-engagement; but it yielded to her charms, when I thought her as free as myself; and was flattered by the pleasing delusion, that the little services I had been able to render her, would incline her to favour my pretensions. The frankness of her manners, the softness of her deportment, and the winning sweetness of her looks, served to confirm me in what I so ardently wished: nor was she sufficiently conversant in our language to undeceive me, till it was too late to banish her beauteous image from my mind. However, I sacrificed my love to her happiness; and went so far as to use every means in my power, to secure to her, her favoured lover; till he, like the base Judean,[57] threw a pearl away richer than all his tribe. Hopes I conceived from that circumstance, which certainly had no foundation, as experience has proved; and could I cherish any, the conversation I lately heard would totally destroy them.

Indulging my contemplative disposition in a walk by moonlight a few evenings since, a train of serious reflections which that produced, occupied my mind to such a degree, that I prolonged it beyond the time I designed; and having a key, which gives me access by a private door into my sister's garden, I let myself in, at an hour when I imagined every one, but my servant who waited my coming, in my apartment, were at rest.

I seated myself on a bench at the back of some trees, which inclosed a walk, and was giving a loose to that pensive melancholy, which my own turn of mind, and the solemn stillness of the night, inclined me to; when voices that I was well acquainted with, drew me out of my reverie: it was Zilia and Miss St. Clare, who seemed to be arguing together.

My dear Maria, says Zilia, I can by no means admit of what you say, That I was born to love, and shall ever love; my own experience proves the contrary: taught to look on Aza, as a man whom the laws of my country designed for my husband, and won by the amiable dignity of his countenance, and the awful sweetness of his manners, he had full possession of my heart. My soul bent before him alone, as to a superior being, and looked up to him, as to the arbiter of its destiny. When he forsook me, I seemed to have lost a part of myself: the whole creation, without him, was a blank, and gave me no real delight. Time, though it lessened my regret, would never have enabled me to conquer my passion, had not a new, and indeed glorious pursuit, engaged my mind; the study of religion. As my faith has increased, my love has died away;[58] and I can now hear his name without emotion, and look on any thing which was once his, without feeling any thing more than a kind remembrance: instead of condemning, I venerate the principles which induced him to forsake me; nor do I wish that he should ever return: but be assured, that no other person, has usurped his place in my breast; on the contrary, I have the pleasure to feel that calm tranquillity, and general benevolence, that I think will never give way to a second passion.

My friendship for Deterville makes me hope otherwise, replied St. Clare; nay, forgive me, if I say a tender regard for your own happiness, inclines me to wish it. Your heart has now a vacancy, which that general benevolence you boast of, can never fill.

You are mistaken, Maria, returned she; my heart feels no such want as you intimate. Happy in your friendship, and that of some others, it is no longer susceptible of any other impressions: that I feel in the strongest degree for Deterville; more, I am fully convinced, it is not possible I ever should.

As they were now advancing towards the house, I heard no more; but sat some time reflecting on what had passed, then retired to my chamber, with a mind full of uneasiness, at a conversation, from which even your sanguine disposition (I think) can draw no favourable conclusions. However, as I suppose you are by this time heartily tired, and wish me to conclude, I subscribe myself,

Yours,

Deterville.

## LETTER LII.

To the Chevalier Dubois, at Malta.

Nothing has indeed happened, my dear friend, which can at all countenance your prognostics. Zilia's looks are more placid, but not less firm than before. She behaves with great sweetness, but joined with that kind of reserve which gives no hope; nor have I the least reason to imagine she will ever change her sentiments. However, as you wish me to change the subject, I will not dwell for ever on the same, but entertain you with what you so much wished to be acquainted with; the history of Miss St. Clare, as she gave it in writing to my sister: it is a melancholy one, and, I think, upon the whole, will give you more pain than pleasure. But I will no longer anticipate.

Here begins her story.[59]

"I comply with your request, my dear Madam; which I am the more willing to do, as I have reason to think my life will not be long: and I would wish my unhappy story to be told (after my decease) without any extenuations or aggravations; nor falsely represented, as it already has been, by those whose curiosity tempts them to supply, by their invention, a want of finding out whatever they desire to know.

You know that my father possessed a very genteel[60] appointment under the government; the salary of which, joined to his own paternal estate, which, though not large, was far from despicable, was sufficient to provide for his family, so as to set them above dependence. I had a brother older, and a sister younger than myself: I may say that adversity was my early portion; for the great partiality my mother shewed to them, and the unnecessary severity with which she treated me, embittered those days which are generally passed without anxiety.

The daily discouragement I met with, damped the natural vivacity of my temper, and gave me a turn for gravity, which is seldom found in young minds. I was fond of reading, to an excess; and my father, who was a man of literature, and whose indulgence to me had been the only support to my spirits, cultivated this taste in me, because it gave pleasure to himself. I spent whole days in his apartment, reading to him, and hearing his observations; which I was the more pleased with, as his mind was such, as I wished to form my own by.

As I grew up, my mother's severity decreased; and as my understanding improved, my father's pleasure in my company grew with it; that what I believe was at first the effect of compassion, became at last the result of judgment and approbation. This was the only period of my life, from about fifteen to eighteen, that I can be said to have passed with tranquillity, and, indeed, the only part of it that I can think of with pleasure.

It was at that time, that my brother, having finished his studies at the university, brought a fellow-collegian to spend the summer with him in the country. I had been prepared to admire the genius and understanding of this young gentleman before I saw him, by the encomiums my brother had, at different times, bestowed on him. He had certainly the most extensive knowledge, without the smallest degree of affectation: every thing he spoke, seemed the genuine sentiments of his heart, expressed with a graceful freedom, yet modest deference, to the opinion of others.

As to his person, he was of a middle size, well made, and his face such as appeared to me very handsome: he had a dignity in his countenance, which, while he was silent, inspired awe; but the moment he spoke, the courtesy of his manner dispersed it. But here I will make a little digression.

It is commonly said, that beauty is of no consequence in a man;[61] that any degree of plainness less than frightful, is not a thing to be at all considered in the choice of a husband; and that custom makes it as pleasing to look continually on a disagreeable object, as it is to behold the reverse. These assertions have always surprised me: whether they are meant as a compliment to our sex, or the contrary, I cannot certainly determine. If men searched only for the intellectual qualities of the soul, and looked on living beauties with the same degree of sensibility that they would feel on examining a fine picture, without even a wish that the woman they married should be possessed of any, I should think they designed to compliment us with having minds like their own, that looked down with contempt on outward graces, and only prized the inward gem.

But, as I believe few men would chuse to confess themselves so devoid of taste, I think it is setting us too much in the scale of creatures formed only for their pleasure, and whose senses were not refined enough to be pleased by beauty, or disgusted by ugliness. That the beauty of the sexes is totally different I allow; and that we can no more be pleased with the dimpled cheek, the delicate red and white, and the extreme smoothness of the countenance in the one, than with the rough masculine air, the coarse-grained skin, and the bearded chin in the other: but there is certainly a manly strength, which is quite consistent with grace of body, and symmetry of features, and is so far from being despicable, that it is truly desirable, I had almost said essential, in the person for whom you would wish to feel a tenderness, mixed with reverence, as for the image of his maker, and lord of this lower world.

These external graces Monsieur de St. Far possessed in the highest degree: too fatally powerful were they over my mind. I daily saw, I heard, I admired, I loved: sad consequence of a too tender heart! How was it possible for me to penetrate the deep recesses that hid from me my gloomy destiny? Though it was easy to perceive, by all the little nameless attentions which St. Far constantly paid me, that I was not indifferent to him; yet they were the only methods by which he declared his attachment, till very near the time of his leaving us, when mere accident disclosed his sentiments.

We were one very fine evening walking on the banks of the river near which my father's house was situated; the various beauties which the view of the land and water afforded us, gave us continual images for conversation. Our party consisted of St. Far, my brother, my sister, and myself. We were all pleased with each other, and the objects which surrounded us, increased our happiness, when, in the midst of this delightful converse, my sister pointed out to me a view, which we had not before observed: I turned short to look at it; but being nearer the edge of the river than I imagined, my foot slipt, and I fell into the water. My sister screamed, and my brother and St. Far immediately leaped into the river, and brought me senseless to shore. I was carried home and put to bed, where I soon recovered my senses; but the shock which my frame had undergone, produced a fever, which for some days filled my friends with the most anxious concern for my life, which appeared in danger. St. Far seemed distracted; he came ten times a day to my chamber-door, to inquire if there was any hope; he kept no guard on his words, but recommended me to the physician's care, in terms which shewed that his own life and health depended on mine. In a week I was pronounced out of danger."

And now, my dear Dubois, having put you out of the pain which I am sure the goodness of your nature inclined you to feel for the fair Maria, I will conclude this very long letter, and give your mind a respite, which I think it has occasion for during the detail of this mournful story, which indeed fatigues my own too much to proceed very far at once. Ever remember, with your usual kindness, your

Deterville

# LETTER LIII.

## To the Chevalier Dubois, at Malta.

Nothing material, my dear Dubois, has occurred since my last. Zilia is obliging in her deportment, and attentive to her studies. My brother, sister, the fair Indian, and myself, are seldom asunder: Miss St. Clare generally makes one in all our little parties; and though she is never chearful, yet is there a complacency in her manners, which makes even her melancholy pleasing. As you express a curiosity to know the remainder of her history, I will gratify it, by making it the subject of this letter.

"The day after I was pronounced to be out of danger, continued she, my maid brought me a letter, which, by the superscription, I knew to be from St. Far: I opened it with some emotion, and found it contained these lines:

"When a general joy, my dear madam, is spread over a family, instead of that universal horror which so lately reigned in it, shall not he, who so bitterly shared the grief, express the raptures which fill his heart at the happy vicissitude? I must, I do, amiable Maria: your parents, your brother, your sister, felt all that paternal, and fraternal love could excite; but there is an affection, which produces feelings too strong for words to express, and in which the mute language of the eye is more eloquent than any phrases which the tongue can furnish. Such feelings for you, lovely Maria, pardon the confession, has possessed my soul; surely, my eyes must have been faithful interpreters of it. That timidity which restrained me from breathing my passion, before your late dreadful accident, gave way to despair; and in the bosom of friendship, I poured out all my complaints. Your brother heard, and pitied me: he has encouraged me to hope, he has promised to be a warm advocate in my cause; but let me not be deemed presumptuous or ungrateful, if I reject all advocates but love; if I wish only him to plead for me in a heart, where I have no desire to succeed but by his influence. False delicacy may, perhaps, condemn this sentiment, as too presuming in a lover, but a mind like yours, which is inspired by nature, with every truly delicate sensation that the female breast can feel, rises above those arts, which the common mind thinks itself obliged to practise, but which can please only the lover, who is charmed with studied graces rather than real refinement. In a few days I shall hope for the honour of seeing you, and hearing my destiny from those lips where guile never yet dwelt.[62] I wait that hour with a restless anxiety, and a fear, which, being the effect of love, is inseparable from the heart of your devoted

St. Far."

I read this letter over several times, and the pleasure I took in perusing it, convinced me that St. Far was not indifferent to me. I indulged the prospect of an union so desirable, to which I foresaw no reasonable obstacle. St. Far was introduced to us as the son of an officer, who had been killed, soon after this son was born, in defence of the invaded rights of an unfortunate English Prince: his mother was a widow, who lived in a distant province of France, possessed of an easy fortune, which was to descend to this her sole heir. Sad remembrance of those delightful scenes which my fancy then painted, how do you torture my imagination! I saw St. Far, I heard him; eloquence dwelt on his tongue, persuasion in his looks; every thing seemed to concur to render me happy.

My friends were little less pleased with St. Far's avowal of his passion, than with my recovery. Two months passed without the smallest interruption of our happiness, except when sometimes St. Far talked of leaving us, to visit his mother, and paying her the compliment of asking her consent to a marriage, with which he did not at all doubt her being pleased. This short absence, made with a design of soon meeting to part no more, as it drew near, gave us a degree of uneasiness: every thing was fixed for his departure, and his return to be at the end of one month, and during that time he was to write every post; when one morning, a few days preceding that on which he was to set out, St. Far came hastily into my dressing-room: his melancholy air alarmed me; but before I could inquire the cause, he laid a letter on the toilette. Read that, my dear Maria, says he, and you will judge of the necessity I am under of leaving you this day. I read it instantly, and found it from his mother: the purport of it was, an earnest conjuration to come to her with all expedition, to see her for the last time, for Death had already begun his work, and, she feared, might not allow her sufficient respite to give him her last blessing: it concluded with some dark hints of a secret which was to be unfolded to him alone, and a dread lest her understanding might fail before that could be done.

You see, my dear girl, resumed he, there is no time to be lost; I have already ordered post-horses,[63] they are now at the door: you shall hear from me as soon as possible, and I hope on my return Heaven will bestow on me all that can console me for the loss of an indulgent mother, in giving me Maria. He then pressed me in his arms, and with a tender embrace bid me farewel.

I do not pretend to argue for secret presages; but I could by no means account for the horror which seized my soul, as soon as he had left me: it seemed as if something supernatural had whispered me it was for ever. I sunk down in my chair, and spent many hours in tears, for which I could assign no reasonable cause; for I own, the short absence of my lover did not appear to be one. When my tears ceased, the agitation of my mind still continued; and when I retired to rest, I found none, for many hours. At last, worn out with anxiety, I fell into a short slumber, which, instead of refreshing me, fatigued my mind, by presenting it with frightful images of my future destiny.

I dreamt that St. Far and myself were walking alone in a forest, where every tree was blasted, and the verdure under our feet withered. A cold northern wind blew over our heads, and the heavens were darkened with clouds: nor were we, methought, less melancholy than the scene which surrounded us, but were bitterly bewailing some dreadful reverse of fortune, which made it necessary we should meet no more; when on a sudden St. Far stopped short, and gazing on me with an eager wildness in his eyes, It shall not be! cried he; no power on earth shall separate us; why must we be punished for the faults of others? Saying these words, he attempted to snatch me to his arms, when he was pulled back by an invisible hand, and remained some paces distant from me, fixed to the earth, loaded with chains, which he in vain endeavoured to break. I was running towards him, when a gleam of fire flashed in my eyes, and the thunder rolled over my head in so dreadful a manner, that the horrid sound awaked me in terrors not to be described.

I rose, but in vain endeavoured to compose my mind: my frightful dream continually obtruded itself upon my thoughts, in spite of reason, which would have persuaded me it was the effect of a disordered imagination. I passed several days without hearing from St. Far, which surprised and alarmed me much."

And now, my dear Dubois, let us for a time leave the unfortunate Maria in that suspense, a release from which will be only a change to despair. Adieu: I will continue my mournful narration in a few days.

Deterville.

## LETTER LIV.

### To the Chevalier Dubois, at Malta.

I again resume the subject, my dear Dubois, and go on where I left off in my last.

"When St. Far had been absent about a fortnight, continued Maria, as I was sitting in the garden, ruminating on what could be the cause of this strange silence, a servant brought me a letter: the superscription told me it came from my lover. I opened it hastily; it was truly obscure. He lamented the loss of his mother in the most pathetic terms, but gave some dark hints of a misfortune which touched him still nearer than her death. The conclusion was such as I could by no means fathom. These were his words: "Oh! Maria, how hard to renounce sentiments so dear, and once so cherished! Alas! must that passion which I looked on as my glory, now become my shame! Horror shocks my soul. Oh, Maria! when you are acquainted with my misfortunes, your tender mind will feel all the distress with which mine is overwhelmed. I can no more pity, but do not condemn    St. Far."

What could I think? I formed a thousand conjectures, but none that could give the least light into this cruel secret. I leave you, my dear friend, to guess at my sensations in this fatal moment; for I am utterly unable to describe them: but surely nothing more dreadful can be conceived, than the seeing all my promised happiness thus overthrown, without being at all able to discover by what means.

I held the letter in my hand in a kind of stupid grief, while the tears trickled down my cheeks, almost insensibly. In this condition I was surprised by my father, who started at the sight of me; but recovering a little, I see, Maria, says he, you have received a letter; may I know the contents? I presented it to him without speaking a word, turning away my face, to wipe off the tears with which it was bedewed. Having read it, he returned it again. Be comforted, my dear, says he; I have received a letter too. Have patience a little; this mystery will soon be cleared. I made no answer, but walked with him into the house. In our way he desired me to conceal my uneasiness from the rest of the family. I promised to endeavour to obey him; but it was not possible for me to erase the traces of it from my face, which was rather increased than diminished every time I cast my eyes on my father. He seemed afraid to look on me, and the horrors which I from time to time observed on his countenance, convinced me that he knew more of this dark affair than I did.

I retired early to bed, but not to rest. In some broken slumbers, I saw St. Far fleeting before me; I endeavoured to catch him, but grasped a shadow.[64] At another time I thought myself with him, and reproached him in the most bitter terms with inconstancy: while he, in the most pathetic manner, lamented the cruel destiny which made him appear deserving of my reproach.

I arose, not at all refreshed, and soon after saw my father enter my dressing room. As soon as he looked on me, his countenance lost that firmness which it had assumed on his first appearance. He came forward, and took me by the hand. Your eyes, my dear Maria, says he, too much indicate the uneasiness of your mind. How gladly would I give my life to make you happy, instead of being as I am, the fatal cause of your unhappiness! I leave this paper with you to read. Can you, my good girl, forgive your father, who has rendered himself more wretched, even than he has you? Saying this, he hastily left me, so thunderstruck at his words, that I scarcely knew where I was.

It was some time before I could acquire courage to open the paper, the contents of which I so much dreaded to know. Dear indeed did that knowledge cost me; and the melancholy which constantly clouds my brow, the tears which I daily shed, are but faint images of the agonies which then tortured my soul. It was addressed to St. Far from his mother. I will give it you in her own words, as I know none more expressive.

## To the Chevalier St. Far.[65]

[Not to be opened till after my decease.]

"Could I, my dear son, bury the sad secret which I am now going to reveal, in that grave to which I am hastening, how truly thankful should I be to Providence, for having bestowed on me a greater blessing than I deserved! I once flattered myself that I might have spared so mortifying a recital, and have injured no one; but an unhappy attachment of yours, has made this humiliating confession necessary: I submit to it as a punishment due to my crimes, and bend to the will of Heaven.

You know you have always passed for the son of an officer. The son of an officer you indeed are, but not killed, as you have been taught to suppose. What will you say, my dear St. Far, when I tell you this officer is the father of your loved Maria?[66] As soon as you have a little recovered the horror and surprise which this news occasions in you, read the rest.

It was at a very early time of life that I became acquainted with that gentleman, who, in appearance at least, was passionately in love with me. You know enough of him now in his decline, to believe that in his youthful days he was very amiable. You cannot then wonder that a young heart, naturally inclined to tenderness, should be touched by him: mine felt all that passion which he wished to raise in me.

At that time I lived with my mother on a small jointure,[67] which was to descend to me at her decease, and was all the inheritance I was born to possess. The father of Maria was heir to a good estate, besides the expectations of a lucrative place at court, if he kept on good terms with the Prime Minister, who was his patron and relation. These circumstances made it absolutely necessary to keep our amour[68] a secret: but as these were obstacles which did not seem as if they would soon end, I was prevailed on, by the importunity of my lover, to yield to a marriage, so very private that there were no witnesses present at the ceremony.

My mother and I lived very retired, as well on account of the narrowness of our income, which would not admit of mixing with the great world, as our peculiar situation, which made it prudent for us to do so. My husband visited me as often as possible, and for some months we gave ourselves up to transports, which knew no abatement. I then perceived him sink by degrees into a melancholy, which much alarmed me; and though he still seemed fond, yet it was certainly with less ardour. I feared to inquire the cause; but when I sometimes ventured to take notice that he was more pensive than usual, he always evaded the conversation. This reserve made me very unhappy, and I had one day been weeping alone, when my mother returned from a visit, which she sometimes made to a few select friends; and coming into my apartment, I think, says she, I have heard something this evening, which accounts for the great change which we see in Mons. St. Clare. I am at a loss to determine whether it is right or wrong to acquaint you with it; but some secret impulse inclines me to tell you, in hopes that when you know there is a cause, you may find your mind a little relieved from doubt and perplexity, though you find a fresh reason for uneasiness.

This preamble made me eager in my inquiries after what she had heard. The substance of it was, That both his father and the Minister had been very pressing with him to enter into an alliance with the daughter of a general officer, whose great interest would be very serviceable to him; that the obstinacy with which he

refused this union, provoked and surprised them much, as the person and qualities of this lady were such as were generally admired. This news overwhelmed me:
I began to look on myself as the evil genius of a man, whom I loved to excess, and
to whose happiness I would willingly have sacrificed every worldly consideration.

I saw him next day; and as it was always impossible for me to conceal any
uneasiness which passed in my mind, it plainly appeared that I was much agitated: he took notice of it, and pressed me earnestly to tell him the cause. Was
I of a temper, says I, to conceal my thoughts from you, I might dissemble with
you; but the hiding what I feel, is the only thing in which I cannot follow your
example. I own I am wretched, from a knowledge of what you daily suffer on my
account. He turned pale while I spoke. As soon as I had done, with the utmost
melancholy painted in his countenance, he acknowledged the justice of my
reproach, but excused himself by saying, that he could not bear my heart should
be torn in the manner his had been for some time past. I could not help weeping
bitterly. My tears put him in despair; he exclaimed against the malignity of his
fate, and seemed quite frantic; so that I was obliged to endeavour to comfort him.

Some weeks passed, and the resentment of his friends increased to such a
degree, that he was obliged to give a seeming consent to their desires. It was now
the will of Heaven to deprive me of the only comfort I had left, my mother, who
was snatched from me by an apoplexy.[69] It is impossible to express what I felt on
this occasion. Your father did every thing in his power to alleviate my affliction;
but as his visits were obliged to be circumscribed, so that he could not be often
with me, I begged his leave to retire for a few months to a religious house, at least
till the first period of mourning was expired. He consented, and conducted me to
one, in the environs of Paris, where he settled me as a boarder, and taking a most
tender leave, promised to see me frequently. For the first month he kept his word;
after which I was a whole fortnight without either seeing or hearing from him.

My mind had been so harassed of late, that I lived in a continual expectation
of something dreadful. It was not therefore to be wondered at, that when I was
one morning told I was wanted in the parlour, my knees shook under me, and
I had scarce strength to support myself thither. It was a servant of Mons. St.
Clare, who gave me a letter, and disappeared. I retired to my chamber to read it:
the impression it made on my mind was such as never can be erased; nor have I
occasion to consult any thing but my memory, in order to write it in the words
it was couched.[70]

"I am become, my dear girl, the dupe of my own artifice. Deceived by appearances, which he wished real, my father has carried the treaty with the Count de
—,[71] for a marriage with his daughter, too far for him to recede with honour.
He was so sure of my consent, that he the other day mentioned to me a lawyer
that he had engaged for drawing the writings. I was thunderstruck at the news;

which my father observing, told me, he was not to be trifled with; that it was my happiness and advancement in life he was seeking, both which he looked on as promoted by this match; but that if I was obstinately bent against my own interest, he must suffer himself to be exposed by my folly: But think not, says he, that I will submit to it patiently; for, by the Author of my being, when that is once over, I will, if I can help it, never see you more, and will settle the whole of my fortune on a stranger. I have several times since endeavoured to mollify him, but my endeavours have a contrary effect, and he gives me hints, that he suspects some dishonourable amour is the cause of my reluctance. My situation is truly dreadful, for I feel for you, and for myself. Think for me, my dearest life; in your hands my destiny is placed. I never can love another; but if urged by necessity, I give my hand, where I cannot give my heart. Who knows but Providence may one day bless me, by putting it in my power to acknowledge the wife of my soul, my first, my only choice? In the mean while, to free you from all idea of dependence, I will give you a bond for twenty thousand crowns,[72] payable on demand. After all, you shall dispose of my fate; and if you think penury to ourselves, and posterity, can be supported by our mutual love, I will renounce all other enjoyments, for the sake of spending my life with you."

It is impossible to describe what emotions agitated my soul on this occasion. I plainly saw I was no longer loved, and felt an indignation rise in my mind, which determined me not to assert my lawful claim as a wife. I despised the idea of living with a man who seemed to wish to give me up. I should have rejected the offer of the bond, had there not been a private reason for accepting it. This reason, which was indeed an expectation of bringing another person into being,[73] determined me not to refuse, what would be of future service, to a creature who was to depend upon me.

My pride, however, made me resolve not to acquaint Mons. St. Clare with my situation, lest he should imagine I wanted to draw that from pity, which I could not gain from love. I therefore summoned all the resolution I was capable of, and wrote him an answer, in which I conjured him, in the most pressing terms, to comply with his father's desires, solemnly abjuring all future right to the title of his wife. The business was soon concluded, as it was certainly what he wished; and as soon as I had received the stipulated sum, I retired to a remote part of the country, where I boarded at a farm house till after your birth.

Upon my return to town, I found Mons. St. Clare married, and heard that he had taken every method to find out the place of my retirement; but I had taken such precautions as made all inquiries fruitless. However, the possibility of being found by him made me very uneasy; but Lady R.[74] my particular friend, and only confidant, proposed an effectual means of eluding all search, by accompanying her into England, to which place she was going for three years. I gladly embraced the opportunity, which carried me for a time from a country which was grown hateful to me. The only thing which gave me concern was the leaving you behind, who were too young to be taken with me. However, I was obliged to be satisfied with placing you with a very careful nurse. Absence, and the variety of objects, which engage the attention in travelling, if they did not lessen my passion, at least abated the poignancy of my regret.

I found you at my return, what mothers generally think their children, a most engaging prattler. I grew fonder every day; and determining to superintend your education, I constantly resided in a convent near your school, till you left it, for college, when I settled in this province; anticipating the time when I should be happy enough to see you enjoy that fortune, which, by living upon a part only of my income, I have been increasing for you from the hour of your birth. This is a happiness which has not been permitted me. I am truly sensible I have deserved the punishment inflicted on me, for having, through a false principle of pride, and offended love, consented to give sanction to an unlawful marriage,[75] and by that means deprived you of the claiming a father, and all the advantages arising from such a claim.

Into what a dreadful error has this wrong action of mine plunged you! Oh, my son, what an escape! Be thankful for it; make use of your wonted[76] fortitude, and love Maria as your sister; her virtues deserve it. My last request is, that you would forgive your mother, the only fault she ever committed against you, and which arose from a mistaken notion of honour; and, Oh! may I not hope, that my memory will be ever dear to you?"

The reading of this paper for some time bereaved me of the power of thinking; but as soon as I had returned to my unhappy self, the sluices of grief were opened, and I was drowned in tears. In this condition I was surprised by my mother, who, astonished at my despair, examined the contents of the paper, which lay on the couch by me; while I was so absorbed, as not to endeavour to prevent her. Real sorrow was painted on her visage: she shed tears at the certainty of never having possessed her husband's affections, but at the same time endeavoured to comfort me, with a tenderness which was rather unusual in her.

My father and sister, ever kind and affectionate, contributed every thing in their power, to alleviate the distress of my mind, but in vain. I became a prey to sorrows which found no relief. What did not a little contribute to my afflictions, was the seeing that all appearance of friendship and confidence, between my parents, was totally at an end, and mutual sullenness, and dislike succeeded. However, this did not last long. My mother, ever of a delicate constitution, perhaps hurt by the perturbation of spirit she had undergone, fell into a disorder, which terminated in a fever, that put an end to her life. My father was sensibly touched with her death, looking on himself as the cause of its being hastened:

he lamented her with more real affliction, than is often felt by those, who have through their lives had the appellation of tender husbands.

Quite overcome by this scene of melancholy, I begged leave of my father to retire from a world where I had no longer the smallest prospect of happiness. He willingly consented to my request, but made me promise not to take the veil for at least three years. By that time, my dear girl, said he, your good sense may overcome your misfortunes, and reconcile you to the world; but should you after that probation, prefer a cloistered life, I think you may trust to it, and not fear the mortification, which often comes too late, for having mistaken a sudden disgust, for real piety.

I acknowledged the justness of my father's caution, and taking a tender leave of him, my brother and sister, was conducted to the same convent where the mother of St. Far had formerly resided. I found a melancholy pleasure in preferring that to any other. I had been there about two months, when I was one day told that a young gentleman, desired to speak with me in the parlour. I asked if it was my brother, but was told it was a stranger, who had not been there before. This alarmed me, and I went trembling to the grate. It was St. Far. I turned pale at the sight of him, and sunk into a chair which stood behind me: he seized my hand through the grate, and pressed it to his lips. Alas! my dear Maria, says he, with what horror do you behold me! Am I then grown odious to your sight? I wept, but was incapable of returning any answer. He still continued to press my hand, which I had at last resolution enough to draw from him.

What end, says I, can our meeting answer, but the recalling to our minds scenes, which ought to be for ever banished from them? To avoid all intercourse with you and with the world, I have sought this retirement. Why will you disturb my repose in the only place where I can now expect to find it? For a few years at least, let us not see each other, till time, and perhaps a more happy engagement, may make you forget our ill-fated love, and look on me with indifference.

With regard to a new engagement, Maria, says he, I think I know my heart better than you do: nevertheless, I allow the justice of what you say: absence indeed is the only thing left for us; but do not reproach me with this last interview: I own I could not resist the strong desire I had of seeing you once more, and taking my eternal farewel. Perhaps, from your example, I may acquire resolution to put that design in execution which I have planned. I eagerly asked what his design was, but he evaded the question, and we took a mournful leave of each other.

After we had parted, the most gloomy melancholy took possession of my soul. I wept incessantly. My passion still continued, in spite of my remorse, in spite of my prayers. Fatal passion! which seemed as if it would only find a period with my life. At the altar, in the grove, his idea still met me; nor could the most solemn acts of devotion, chase it from my mind. What contributed more than any thing to the calming my grief, was a letter from St. Far, in which he told me,

That, from a certain conviction that while he was in the world, he should never be able to seclude himself from my sight, and yet dreading the consequence of seeing me, finding himself unable to look on me only with the eyes of a brother, he had, as a certain prevention of guilt, dedicated the remainder of his life to religion, by entering into the order of the monks of La Trappe.[77]

I found myself gather strength from this intelligence of St. Far. For the first time since our last meeting, peace dawned on my soul. Religion seemed to gain some influence in my breast, and I determined to follow his example, as soon as that time was expired, which I had promised my father to wait, before I finally took the vows. His death, which happened a few months afterwards, rather confirmed than weakened my resolution, and I should have immediately put it in execution, had I not looked on the promise I made him as sacred.

The earnest importunity of my sister, who is lately married, has prevailed on me to pass a little time with her. I know her kindness makes her hope, that the death, and the retirement, of those whose misfortunes were interwoven with my own, joined to the amusements of the world, may in time make me forget the cause of my uneasiness. Vain hope! every painful scene is daily present to my view. No amusement has charms for me; nor can the company of a sister whom I love, nor your friendship,[78] which has given me more pleasure than any thing that has happened to me for some years, at all reconcile me to life. My fixed and settled purpose is, to return to the convent, and there wait till Almighty Goodness, puts a final period to my life and my misfortunes."

Thus, my dear Dubois, I have concluded the story of this amiable and unfortunate lady. How undeserved her misfortunes! May we not with justice say, she ought to have been more happy? But how vain is man, when he presumes to account for the ways of Providence! Short-sighted as human reason is, how many things do we daily see which it cannot solve? Shall it then dare to solve the inscrutable decrees of Heaven? No, let it acknowledge its weakness, and cease to boast. Perhaps a time may come, when what now appears so hard to be understood, may be made clear to our enlightened minds: but I will leave you to make your own reflections on these subjects, and wish that your heart may remain as free from the disquiets of love, as it is now, nor ever be sensible of the pangs, which has torn that of your friend

Deterville.

## LETTER LV.

### To the Chevalier Dubois, at Malta.

You tell me, my dear friend, you now wish to hear something of my own affairs; but of them I have nothing new to say. Our little circle of friends divide their time between reading, walking, and conversation; I mean in general. Music comes in for its share; in which science, we have variety, sufficient to please every taste. My sister, whose present happy circumstances suit with the vivacity of her mind, deals in the sprightly.[79] Poor Maria, all tender and melancholy, like her own feelings. My lovely Indian (who is now become a true convert to Christianity) is all sublime, and in the most melodious tone of voice, chaunts[80] forth divine songs, in praise of the Deity, and his works; whilst I and my brother, are entertained by each alternately. But we are not such selfish, unsociable creatures, as to shut out the rest of the world entirely, but receive and return visits, at stated periods, so as not to be looked on in a disagreeable light by the neighbouring gentry, among whom some are pleasing enough.

The Abbé de V. is one of our greatest intimates, whose knowledge of the belles lettres, and fine taste in all works of genius, makes him very agreeable. He is the only one, whom we admit of our select party; when we meet, on an evening, in a delightful grove in the garden, where the height, and thickness of the trees exclude every other object, which is indeed what we wish; since, whenever the weather permits, we employ the hours from four to six, in all the luxury which books, and unreserved conversation can give. One of the company is deputed as reader, while the rest sit attentively to hear, till they find themselves all sufficiently interested, to deliver their opinions on what has been read: and here, though Zilia always gives hers with diffidence, yet is it such, as in general every one joins to approve and admire.

What then, my friend, are my emotions? Is this, do you think, the way to cure a despairing passion? Alas! no. I am sensible I am daily adding fresh fuel to the flame. To what purpose then, do I continue here? I am well assured I have nothing to hope; and were I again to urge my love, Zilia would take the alarm, and lose that sweet frankness, with which she now treats me. This is what I dread. But as such continual restraint grows more and more irksome, and will at last be insupportable, I think of returning to the duties of my profession, at Malta,[81] where I shall endeavour to console myself, for all that I quit, by that faithful friendship, which you have ever shewn me, and which has always been productive of the greatest, in the heart of your

Deterville.

## LETTER LVI.

### To the Chevalier Dubois, at Malta.

I sincerely rejoice, my dear Dubois, that I am recalled to Malta. However pleasing the society I am in, would be to a mind at ease, the particular feelings of mine make it, if I may so call it, a very painful enjoyment. You endeavour to persuade me to throw aside this boyish passion, as you term it. The advice, I own, is salutary; but the difficulty is in the execution; a difficulty of which you can be no judge, having never felt what you think so easily cured. Indeed, if you had, you would be convinced it does not at all depend on the will. The heart is no longer master of its desires, but is subject to an idol,[82] without being able to form a wish for liberty.

I could not help expressing my sentiments pretty warmly on this subject, in a little conversation which we were led into in the grove, sacred to friendship and the Muses.[83] Zilia seemed uneasy; for which reason I would have dropped it, but by accident it was continued much longer than I wished. My brother, designedly, as I have since thought, drew me on, without my being sensible whither I was going. I stopped, but he replied in a manner that shewed a desire of still prolonging the discourse. You are in the right, says he, and have given us a very just portrait of a lover. Certainly, added he, smiling, you must have been long learning, so well to delineate him; but surely his state is truly pitiable; and if Ovid,[84] that great adept in the science, had but taught us a cure for hapless[85] love, he would have been an able master indeed. I know not how you understand it, replied Zilia, with some confusion; but to me the thing appears not at all impracticable. It is certainly natural to desire the cure of an evil. Ask any one whose lot in life has condemned him to slavery,[86] if he would not gladly throw off his chains, and he will not hesitate a moment in saying Yes. Is not an unsuccessful lover in the same situation with such a slave? Nor can he want the wish to be free: but a certain indolence too often attends that passion, which prevents their using the necessary means for casting off the yoke.

Ah, Madam! replied the Abbé, you know but little of love, if you think there is any resemblance between that and other calamities, those which the iron hand of Necessity compels us to suffer, and to which we submit in the anguish of our souls, because we have no power to rise against them. But amidst the greatest torments which love can inflict, there is yet a cordial drop, which sweetens the bitter draught; and the heart accustomed to sigh, finds a pleasure in that expression of tenderness. The experiment, I own, is dangerous; and if we find this sentiment rising in our breast, we should use our utmost efforts to stifle it in its birth; but how much better, if we are happy enough never to feel it!

If that sentiment should grow unfashionable, says my brother, pleasantly, the empire of Love would be totally abolished, his darts[87] become useless, his fires extinguished, and mankind be delivered from the power of a despotic tyrant. But, alas! continued he, the susceptible heart is insensibly betrayed; pleasure leads the way, and we eagerly pursue: we give a loose to our desires, and experience alone convinces such a mind, that it is easier to live a stranger to the passion, than, having once felt it, to be able to submit to the rigid laws of prudence. How seldom do we hit the golden medium in any of our actions! That first of virtues, Generosity, often overleaps the bounds which œconomy[88] would prescribe. Œconomy dwindles into avarice, and courage degenerates into rashness. But love is of all feelings the most liable to extremes, and to prove its truth by its extravagances. The advice which you have just now given, of conquering it in its birth, I acknowledge to be good; but, I believe, never to be put in practice; for if the passion but weakly assails us, we don't find it of consequence sufficient to resist it; and if violent in its attacks, resistance will be found vain.

The weak attacks of love, rejoined I, are the only ones which admit a cure. Could any means be found to open the eyes of lovers, recal their wandering reason, and enable them to conquer that passion when in its utmost violence, it would be a great work indeed: but that is impossible; and the only remedies which can in any degree re-establish our peace of mind, and prevent dangerous, and perhaps fatal relapses, are absence and employment; for indolence gives that languor to the soul, which must, of consequence, nourish the disease.[89]

Pronouncing those last words, I involuntarily cast my eyes on Zilia, and perceived her covered with blushes. I feared it might proceed from what I had inadvertently said, and the apprehension of having offended her, made me, feel the same degree of confusion. My sister saw it, and endeavoured, in her sprightly way, to draw us out of it. After all then, says she, laughing, this powerful deity, of whom you talk, is but the child of Idleness, and surely he has infected us, or we should not throw away this fine evening in talking of him, and lolling in this close retreat, when we could so much better employ it in air, and exercise. For my part, continued she, I am determined to be lazy no longer, but to walk out in quest of adventures; and let those who have no mind to fall asleep, and dream of their mistresses, or lovers, follow me.

Every one laughed at this sprightly sally, which concluded a discourse that was growing irksome to many of the company. We cheerfully obeyed the summons, and finished the day by a very agreeable saunter.[90]

Adieu, my dear Dubois; I hope very soon to have the pleasure of embracing my friend, and holding a more pleasing intercourse than writing will afford

Deterville.


## LETTER LVII.


### To the Chevalier Dubois, at Malta.

I date this, my dear friend, from Paris; it is the only letter you will receive before I see you, which I hope will be in a fortnight: it is the sole comfort I promise myself, after having parted with those who share my heart with yourself, and whom I left with more regret that I ever felt on the same occasion before. There was something in Zilia's manner of taking leave, which, could I form any hopes of a change of her sentiments in my favour, would flatter such hopes.

Having previously informed my brother and sister of my design, I waited on Zilia, whom I found sitting in her dressing-room, resting her cheek on her hand, which leaned on a table; her eyes fixed on the ground, and in all appearance buried in thought. The noise I made in entering, awaked her from her reverie; she rose hastily, and seemed offended at being surprised in so abrupt a manner. Pardon me, my dear Zilia, says I, the having broken in upon your more pleasing contemplations, to mention any thing which relates only to myself; I wish I had been more fortunate in my choice of the time. I know already, says she, interrupting me with great quickness, what you would say: your sister has spared you the trouble of acquainting me with your departure: I sincerely wish you all the success your merit deserves, and hope to see you returned crowned with laurels, and free from fears.

While she spoke, her countenance betrayed evident signs of confusion and uneasiness. I own it struck me, and I was at a loss what to reply; when my brother unexpectedly entered the room, and clapping me on the shoulder, in his gay manner, You are in the right, my boy, says he, to try what absence will do with this insensible mistress. Take my word for it, it will forward your passion more in a few days, than whole months of assiduous attention can do, when present. I felt for my Zilia, whose confusion redoubled; but recovering herself a little, It is very cruel of you, Sir, says she, by this ill-timed raillery, to chill the effusions of friendship, and prevent those kind reciprocations of it, which a few hours will cut us off from. I joined in the accusation; he pleasantly asked pardon, and good-humour was restored among us.

We spent the evening together, and Zilia gave me every mark of the warmest friendship; she even seemed anxious for my return. I set out the succeeding morning; and surely I do not flatter myself too much, when I ascribe the melancholy which appeared on the countenance of my Indian maid, to my own account. When I took leave, a tear stole down her cheek, which I unperceived kissed off; and by so doing, hid it from the eyes of the rest of the company.

I know you will conceive great hopes; but, I beseech you, in pity to your friend, do not delude me into a belief of what will only render my disappointment the more intolerable. Alas! I have had great proof of the steadiness of Zilia's temper, though joined with the utmost softness; to which disposition alone I must place the tenderness shewn to your
Deterville.

## LETTER LVIII.

### Deterville to Zilia.[91]

You will be surprised, my lovely friend, to hear of the voyage I am going to take; but every thing at Malta seems to be safe: we have nothing to dread from the

Turks,[92] who are certainly too much intimidated to think of attacking us, and will be well satisfied if we will let them remain unmolested. This state of security has made me yield to pressing solicitations from my friend Dubois, to accompany him to England, at the invitation of a very agreeable nobleman of that country. We have obtained permission of the Grand Master,[93] and shall leave this rocky island, as soon as we shall have made the necessary preparations for our departure.

I think you would be pleased with the acquaintance of Lord Bruton; he has that native openness of character which is said to have distinguished the ancient inhabitants of Britain; he is brave and generous, and all his actions have that true dignity which ought to distinguish nobility, of every nation. My Lord has a sister, who is reckoned very handsome, as well as accomplished. The father of this amiable brother, and sister, was what is called a man of pleasure; that is to say, he preferred the gratification of his own appetites to the future welfare of his children; by which means he has left an estate to his son, too much loaded[94] to support his dignity in his own country, and his daughter too small a fortune to match her suitable to her rank.

Lord Bruton had too much spirit to sit down satisfied with a nominal[95] large estate; he has therefore spent some years in study and travel, and, by œconomy without parsimony, has gone great lengths in paying off the incumbrances of his estate: but while he has spared from himself, he has been liberal to his sister, and annually makes such an addition to her income, as enables her to live elegantly, under the protection of an aunt. My Lord only proposes a visit of a few months to this dear sister, whom he has not seen for five years; for he is determined not to reside in England, till his estate is perfectly clear,[96] and he can live suitable to the dignity of his character, and the generosity of his disposition.

I promise myself much pleasure in seeing a country which I have long desired to see, in company which will add charms even to novelty. Yet so greedy am I, that I cannot help wishing, to add to it the little circle of friends that I have left behind at your enchanting villa, which will ever contain what is dearest to the heart of

Deterville.

## LETTER LIX.

### Miss St. Clare to Deterville.

I am infinitely obliged to you, my dear friend, for the entertaining letter inclosed in Zilia's: it gave me as much pleasure, as a mind so dead to enjoyment as mine, is capable of receiving. However, there is a joy which the benevolent, though unhappy breast, will find some share in, that of communicating pleasure to others: it affords me a transient comfort, to be the channel of conveying pleasure to you.

Perhaps this is the only moment of your life in which you could find yourself pleased, to hear that the amiable girl for whom you have felt so much, felt any pain herself. Think me not cruel, my good friend; but I repeat it, Zilia is really unhappy: nor be not astonished, when I say her unhappiness is on your account. Yes, I repeat it, Zilia's happiness is certainly in your power. I am convinced she loves, and that she loves Deterville.[97] My heart, alas! has had too fatal an experience to be deceived. Was I not satisfied, that by revealing a secret which she would die rather than reveal, I was doing an essential service to two valuable friends, I should not look upon myself justified in acting the part I now do: but born, as Zilia is, with all that ardour of affection, which is consistent with unaffected modesty; formed with qualities capable of shining in the characters of wife, and mother, as well as that of friend; shall we suffer her, from a mistaken delicacy, to pine away in silent discontent, and never fulfil those social duties, for which Nature designed her? No, before I quit this world for ever, let me be instrumental in bringing about an event, which I am sure will be productive of the greatest future happiness to my friends.

But I will, without any further preface, give you an account on what I form my conjectures; I may, indeed, say my certainty. From the time of your departure, I have observed a pensiveness in Zilia, which of late has not been usual with her: she has affected solitude, and I have more than once surprised her in tears; but as, on these occasions, she has always forced a smile, and endeavoured to conceal her disorder, I have constantly seemed not to take notice of it: but going accidentally into her chamber, the other morning, I found her drowned in tears, with your letter in her hand: she hastily put it up, and endeavoured to conceal her confusion; but that was impossible. I hope, says I, you have no ill news. No, returned she, still more confused; but I find a melancholy, which oppresses me much this morning: but let me not, my dear Maria, infect you, but leave me till I have chid[98] myself into good humour. Indeed, my dear, replied I, you require more to be soothed than chid; but you shall never find my friendship impertinent; I will leave you till you wish to see me.

I then turned myself, and was walking along the gallery which led from her chamber, when she followed and stopt me. Excuse me, my dear Maria, for being so capricious; but I am sure I shall be happier with you, than alone. We sat down, and I endeavoured to enter into conversation; but she seemed confused and absent. At last, says she, you have had, Maria, an entertaining letter from our friend; I am glad, methinks, to hear that he is making this tour, and is likely to make so agreeable a friend as Lord Bruton; he certainly must be a worthy character. What do you think of his kindness to his sister? I wonder how Deterville will like her. I smiled at her curiosity, and was silent: she observed it. What makes you smile, says she? Is there any thing extraordinary in what I say? No, surely, not at all so, my dear, replied I; it is natural to be curious about those we are concerned for. And why, returned she, blushing, should I not be concerned for him? Does he not deserve from me all that affection which a grateful mind can feel? If I cannot be happy myself, I should at least rejoice to see him so. I have a notion Lord Bruton has a design with regard to his sister: I am certain, should that be agreeable to him, his whole family would concur in obtaining a dispensation,[99] from this order he has so lately embraced.

While she spoke, her eyes expressed the most eager anxiety. My dear Zilia, says I, you were not made for dissembling: why will you attempt any thing so foreign to the Peruvian character, and in which you can never possibly succeed? You are cruel, Maria, replied she, peevishly; I hardly know myself what I mean; how then can you? I begged her pardon; and some morning visitants[100] coming in, the conversation took another turn.

Tell me, my dear friend, is there no hope to be formed from this opening? I think there is. There is no event can now happen which will give me equal pleasure to that of seeing two such worthy characters joined. For myself, I must say, the world grows daily more and more irksome to me: I long to leave it, and indulge the melancholy of my soul, in that quiet retreat, where I propose to wait for the final period of my griefs: yet believe me, when I say, no convent, can shut out friendship from the heart of

Maria St. Clare.

## LETTER LX.

### Deterville to Miss St. Clare.

I have your letter now by me, my dear Maria: I know not how to give way to the delusive hopes you would have me entertain: is it possible my Zilia can love again? and can that passion be renewed in favour of Deterville? Transporting thought! Ah! let me not deceive myself; it is not the first time I have been betrayed by hope. Be watchful, my good friend; in your hands is my destiny: let me not proceed too far, till I have a certainty what that destiny is.

I have seen the lovely sister of Lord Bruton; nor have I seen a lady in whose favour, at first sight, I have been more prepossessed; but Zilia knows I have not a heart to give; and indeed if I had, I have reason to think hers is occupied by another. I do not wonder at her brother's attachment to her; the charms of her person alone, are such as must give pleasure to the partial eye of so near a relation: she is tall, and elegantly formed, with an air of true dignity, without that assured confidence, which is so often mistaken for it: her features are not perfectly regular, but there is that sweetness and sensibility, diffused over her countenance, that delights every one, and makes her have as many admirers as she has beholders; but the qualities of her mind are such as make her truly valuable to her friends: she has a superior understanding, joined with a diffidence, which, I believe, no French woman ever possessed, and indeed is rarely to be met with in any country. However, I must say, that English women have more of it in their general character, than I have found elsewhere. She has a frankness in her manners, which shews the unsuspecting simplicity of her heart: it would be the height of cruelty ever to impose on such a mind; so totally free from guile, that she seems not to suppose it exists in any breast. Her gratitude to her worthy brother, raises her affection almost to adoration.

The pleasing society of this amiable brother and sister makes my time pass agreeably. In their company I not only see every thing that is curious in the metropolis, but we sometimes form little parties, and make excursions to places adjacent. England is really a fine country;[101] and if it does not spontaneously produce the fruits, which warmer climates abound with, yet, with proper cultivation, there is scarcely any thing which, being transplanted, would not grow here. As to the natives in general, I own they are a people who please me, and yet I am at a loss to characterise them; for indeed there is more variety in their composition, than in any other people I ever saw, who received their birth in the same place. However, there is one thing in which I may speak of them in pretty general terms; they seem to have a natural openness in their manners, tinctured with a reserve, which prevents their falling into a disgusting familiarity. The women have much beauty among them, and I have scarcely seen a plain woman about the English court: their complexions are very fine, and they have not the character of using art: but what renders them truly lovely, is that modesty and gentleness which they almost all possess, and which are so rarely to be found in our countrywomen.[102]

My dear Maria, I must return to the old question: Does Zilia really love Deterville? Ah! if she does, can I purchase so great a blessing at too high a price? My whole fortune should be employed to release me from that cruel vow I have taken.[103] My good angel, let me hear from you soon; you have once more renewed the wishes of my soul: I am impatient to know how they must end. Ah! how dreadful, if I am again to be plunged into the horrors of despair! Remember poor Deterville.

## LETTER LXI.

### Miss St. Clare to Deterville.

I write with pleasure, my dear friend, because I am convinced you will receive infinite, by the contents of this letter. Zilia indeed loves; her own lips have confessed it. For some time after the conversation, of which I sent you an account, she avoided being alone with me. This behaviour grieved me, and I reproached myself, with having said any thing which gave occasion for it: the making an apology was aukward, and I knew not well how to begin it; but she spared me the trouble: for one evening, asking me to walk with her in the grove, where you, and all our little party of friends, have been so often pleased with each other, some reflections on those past times, opened the conversation, which she began.

Here, says she, my Maria, I think I have enjoyed the happiest hours since I left Peru; indeed, I may say happier than any I ever spent there; for I was then happy only in my ignorance; but here my enlightened mind, first learnt those truths, which restored peace to it, after its being so long a stranger to my soul. And here, replied I, my dear Zilia, may you long enjoy, that peace which your virtues have procured you.

Alas! said she, happiness flies me; I fear I shall never overtake it. Since you are disengaged from your tender cares, my dear, replied I, I was in hopes there was nothing could prevent your happiness: but I have already been impertinent, and will not repeat my fault.

Indeed, my good friend, returned she, I am capricious; I am conscious I have not behaved well to you; your friendship will make kind allowances for it. I would fain hide that from myself, which I cannot conceal from you. Good Heaven! continued she, is it possible I should again be sensible of that passion for which I have suffered so much? And why, my Zilia, rejoined I, do you oppose this second passion? What have you to fear from it? Ought you not rather to be pleased you have it in your power to return the faithful love of Deterville? Indeed, says she, Maria, I blush at the thoughts: after my steady opposition, how can I own my weakness? Besides, have I not suffered him to bind himself by insuperable vows, which I will never tempt him to break through? Perhaps they are not insuperable, replied I; at least, I am certain there is no means Deterville will leave untried to procure a dispensation; and money, joined with power, will do much.

Do not, Maria, says she, mention it; I cannot bear the idea. If you are determined then, says I, to be unhappy, I have nothing further to offer. Would you, says she, enter into a second engagement? The case is widely different, replied I: St. Far, by laws human and divine, forbidden the indulgence of a passion for the only woman he ever could love, far from forming a connection with another, as Aza has done, has only given up me for God; has sacrificed his earthly affection to a heavenly one, and endeavoured to find that peace from religion which the world has denied him. Incapable as I am of loving any other man, can I do otherwise than follow his example? Is there any part but that to be taken? On the contrary, Aza gave you up; influenced, perhaps, in a degree, by religious motives, but more by his own wayward inclinations. Resentment, joined to the religion you have embraced, has entirely driven him from your heart. That heart, after being long vacant, does by your own confession feel a tenderness for another; and who is that other? One who is an honour to his species; one whom Nature has enriched with every quality, both of body and mind, which can charm the eye, and delight the understanding. Such is Deterville. Add to this, he regards you with a passion little short of adoration. On what do you pique yourself?

What reasons can you find for resisting your tender emotions? It is neither deserved nor required by the unworthy object of your first vows; yet are you obstinately bent to render your own life unhappy, only to make another so, who so well deserves to be happy.

Do not chide me, my dear friend, returned Zilia, but act for me as you think proper: I submit to your direction. I embraced her with tears, and assured her, that if there was any thing yet remaining in this world, from which I could derive pleasure, it would be in seeing you both blessed to the height of your desert. From her last words, I think myself perfectly at liberty to send you this account. Write to me soon, and let me, if possible, see my friends united, in bonds which death only can dissolve, before I unite myself by those which will last to eternity.

Maria St. Clare.

## LETTER LXII.

### Deterville to Mademoiselle St. Clare.

How shall I express my thanks to my kind friend for the part she takes in my affairs! Had it not been for your friendly interposition, I had never known to what degree I was happy; Zilia had for ever buried the secret in her bosom, and sacrificed her peace to her refinement. Ah, amiable girl! what pity you, who delight in making others happy, should be fated to so hard a lot yourself! But we must submit to the inexorable hand of Destiny.

I propose leaving England immediately, and setting out for the court of Rome, to solicit, in person, a dispensation from vows[104] which I can now never perform. Perhaps there is no precedent of such a thing granted, because it may have never been asked; but I have no doubt of success: my ever faithful Dubois has promised to be my companion in this undertaking, and to assist me with all his powers.

I part with Lord Bruton with great regret; but he flatters me with a visit from himself and his amiable sister, and that he will make one of our little circle at Zilia's enchanted castle. Oh, Maria! why will not you continue among us? I am impatient to set out; Rome is a place I have never yet seen, and I promise myself much pleasure in visiting the ancient seat of the Muses, and being made acquainted with Italian music and Italian painting. These amusements will serve to make the necessary time of waiting less irksome to me. I shall inclose a letter to your fair friend, which you will take a favourable moment to deliver to her. I own I am at a loss in what manner to express myself, so as to paint my feelings, and yet not offend her delicacy; but I must write, and trust to her tenderness to excuse the faults of love.

I am, my dear Maria, with all the sentiments which gratitude and the tenderest friendship can inspire, yours,

Deterville.

## LETTER LXIII.

### Deterville to Zilia.

I am going to Rome, my lovely Zilia; from which place I hope to revisit your charming villa. May I venture to say, I shall see it with hopes which I never before durst[105] conceive? Shall I have the happiness to find those hopes confirmed by my adorable girl? Ah! in pity do not drive me to despair; that despair which will inevitably follow a second disappointment. Let the whole future life of Deterville be employed in contributing to the happiness of his Zilia. Maria, our mutual friend, has given me reason to think that delightful employment may yet be mine. How valuable a recompence shall I then receive for those past hours of uneasiness I have sustained! Can so great a pleasure be purchased at too high a price?

Pardon my transports, my Zilia; perhaps they are too lively. I would not shock the nice delicacy of your soul; but remember these are the overflowings of a heart in love; and let that plead my excuse. While my mind is ingrossed by one subject, and that so pleasing a one, how can it find room for any other? or where shall I find words to talk of any thing else? But I ought to say something of the society, and the country I am in; but for those accounts, I must refer you to the letter I have sent to Miss St. Clare. Yet I cannot help telling you, though a Frenchman, that the English manners are more suitable to my taste than those of my own nation. And can I, my dear Zilia, help admiring their ladies, when I tell you, that they have an ingeniousness in their carriage, which is nearly Peruvian? The country, in general, is well cultivated; and those parts which are not, have a romantic wildness, which is beautiful in the highest degree.[106]

The city of London is large, and well built; and the public edifices are not only magnificent, but elegant. Their theatres are well furnished with actors, and their theatrical pieces are, many of them, most justly admired.[107] Indeed, as I daily improve in the English language, I daily find new beauties in their works of genius.[108] Their poetry, in particular, has a sublimity which the French tongue will not admit of. However, that I may not seem to have learnt entirely to despise our own writers, I must allow there is a sprightliness in our gayer compositions, which they but poorly imitate, and for want of which theirs cannot give equal pleasure. But I hope, in our social circle, to entertain you with a more perfect account; which will be the more agreeable, as I shall have the pleasure of answering the questions my Zilia asks. To that happy time I look forward with an impatience which can only be conceived by those who love like

Deterville.

## LETTER LXIV.

### Deterville to Zilia.[109]

How cruel, my lovely friend, are those delays! I am grieved to the soul while I am detained from you. I have now been two months in this ancient seat of greatness, where I might perhaps find entertainment for a much longer time, if my mind was not too anxiously engaged in the pursuit of what I came here to solicit, to be capable of being amused by any thing without.

I have received great civilities from, I may say, all the nobility of Rome, and acquired the friendship of those whose good qualities make it most valuable: they have generously joined their interests in my behalf. I have no doubt of success; but the length of time makes me impatient. May I flatter myself, that Zilia feels any thing like a wish that my petition was granted, and that I had once more joined her in her charming retreat? Let me enjoy that dear thought; it will animate my endeavours, and I may breathe some of my ardour into the court of Rome, to make them speedy in determining my suit.

As I am now in the first city in the universe for the fine arts, you will naturally expect I should say something about them; but I beg you will excuse me: when I write to you, one favourite theme fills my thoughts, engrosses all my desires; nor can I find words to express myself on any other subject. Love, mighty Love, has taken possession of my soul, and leaves no room for any other guest. So entirely is he master, that he looks on every thing that would share with him as impertinent intruders. But lest I should tire you with a repetition of the same things, I must conclude with assuring you, I am your ever faithful and affectionate

Deterville.

## LETTER LXV.

### Zilia to Deterville.[110]

If it will be any pleasure to my dear friend to hear that my wishes coincide with his, I frankly confess they do. I please my imagination with anticipating the happiness I shall feel in meeting you again in my little villa. If that love which has once been bestowed on another, can be worthy the acceptance of a man of merit, it is yours without allay. This is an affection which is not liable to change; since it was not the mere effect of what pleased the eye, nor lighted up by a sudden gust of passion, but the consequence of long knowledge of such virtues as perhaps were never before possessed by any human mind.

Rely on those, for preserving a tender remembrance in my breast; and let that make you easy, while your affairs oblige you to remain at Rome.

I trust to that Being, who, by a particular interposition, has taught me the true knowledge of himself, for granting his choicest blessings to the man who was his chief instrument in doing it; and that I may one day be the means, in some degree, of conferring happiness on the favourite of Heaven.

Surely, my dear Sir, after so many evils as we have sustained, we shall enjoy those halcyon[111] days, which, I hope, are yet in store for us, with more serene delight, as well as gratitude to the great Author of all our good. Be assured that my desires for success in what you now solicit are equally strong as yours, since the happy conclusion of your suit will bring you nearer to your

Zilia.

# LETTER LXVI.

### To the Chevalier Dubois, at Malta.

My suit is granted, my dear Dubois; I am free from my vows, and again with my Zilia. Oh, my friend, how chang'd my situation! I fear giving way to the transports of my soul, lest some envious stroke of fortune should dash the cup of joy from my lips. At present, indeed, all is smiling: my lovely Indian received me with all the expressions of the most lively friendship, mixed with a soft confusion, which indicated something more.

As soon as we were alone together, I may now, my dearest girl, says I, without offence, venture to mention that passion which I once scarcely dared breathe even in secret. Zilia blushed. All the pleasure you can derive from that liberty, replied she, will be ever yours, if that will make you amends for the pains I have given you. I pressed her hand, with excess of joy; and whilst I still held it trembling within mine, Such a permission, my dearest Zilia, makes me ample amends for all the past evils of my life: I shall now daily have it in my power to remind you of a lover who is no longer disagreeable to you. She recovered herself, and with a sweet smile replied, You will certainly have opportunities enough; but at present it is proper you should pay what you owe to friendship, and not deprive those too long of your company who are so fond of it.

I was ravished with her words; and pressing her hand, which I still held in mine, to my lips, kissed it with rapture. Let them wait, says I, however, while I first pay what is due to love. Whilst I thus express my thanks for this extreme kindness, Oh! teach me, Zilia, how to return such mighty obligations. Mention not obligations, added she; I owe you already more than I can ever pay: but all I have to give is yours, my hand, and my heart. Your hand, your heart, my love, what can the world bestow of half their value? May I give credit to words so full of sweetness! Yet why should I doubt, when they fall from lips which never knew deceit! Will this fair form then give itself to me, and receive a heart overflowing with tenderness in exchange?

Henceforth, returned she, you may dispose of mine; it was yours long before I was myself sensible of it. My loved, my adorable girl, says I, what words shall I find to express the feelings of my soul on this occasion, but the constant uniform tenor of my life will be to make myself worthy of this excess of goodness. You daily, replied she, merit every return, both of affection and gratitude, which I can ever make: but our friends wait us, in that favourite room of yours, which fronts the garden, and commands a view of the fountain.

We immediately joined them, and passed the afternoon very agreeably together; in which time I endeavoured to give satisfactory answers to the many inquiries which were made of me concerning England, and other places I had seen during my absence. However, as the evening came on, I stole off unperceived, being impatient to indulge in solitude those thoughts which engrossed my whole soul. I strolled along the banks of that river which had so often been the scene of my most melancholy reflections: I wandered through the grove where I had formerly lamented my hard destiny, and enjoyed the happy change; while my delighted imagination dwelt on every tender expression my Zilia had uttered, and my fancy painted her in every point of view which the most ardent love could inspire.

My heart was unable to contain the mighty extasy, and I returned to my company, which I found increased by the addition of two agreeable neighbours, who were come to sup with us, and to welcome me back to the country. A society more willing to please and be pleased were never assembled. Our conversation turned on various subjects, and every one spoke their own opinions, while others acquiesced with complacency, or differed with candour; and the evening concluded with the utmost good-humour. Though you, my friend, laugh at the follies of love, yet I know you will sincerely share in what gives such exquisite pleasure to your

Deterville.

## LETTER LXVII.

### To the Chevalier Dubois, at Malta.

Rejoice with me, my dear Dubois, for all is accomplished, and Zilia is mine. A fortnight is past since I received every worldly bliss, in receiving her. The day was remarkably fine; the Sun seemed to display all his glory, as a compliment to her who was once stiled his daughter, the innocence of whose countenance made her still appear like a virgin of that luminary. The simplicity of her dress corresponded with her looks; it was of white Indian taffety;[112] and all together, she looked and moved an angel.

Oh! my dear friend, I have indeed reached the summit of earthly happiness: but as all sublunary happiness must have its allay, ours has received no inconsiderable one, by the loss of the tender and amiable Maria, that constant, faithful friend, to whom we are both so much indebted. She has left us about a week, and retired to that convent where her wishes had so long been: yet I believe we should not so soon have lost her, had it not been for a melancholy piece of news she received a day or two after our marriage:[113] it was the death of the unfortunate St. Far, who with his latest breath bequeathed a few jewels of his mother's to Miss St. Clare. These, with a letter written some hours before his death, were conveyed to her by a trusty friend of that gentleman. Poor Maria, after having in solitude given vent to the first effusions of her grief, came to my wife, and addressed her in these words:

"The pleasure, my dear Zilia, I had in seeing you happy, made me willing to spend a little more time with you, before I quitted the world for ever. I had designed to give you a month, but this last dreadful event has totally changed that design: I shall set out for the convent to-morrow, and immediately embrace the only state in which I can support life. Religious exercises, and frequent prayers, will by degrees calm my stubborn grief, and teach me to submit to the unalterable decrees of Providence with decent resignation. For me, to whom the light of the sun affords no pleasure, a gloomy cell can surely be no hardship: the finest scenes which Nature, dressed in her gayest livery, can exhibit, yield not one ray of cheerfulness to my mind. It is true, had St. Far lived, our peculiar unhappy circumstances made it necessary we should never meet; but I was conscious he breathed the same air, existed in the same manner, and our employments might casually be the same. Now, you will say, a pure, ethereal being, he no longer bears about him a load of matter, whose wants must be continually supplied; subject to fatigue, sickness, and many other inconveniences. To the truly pious this is satisfactory: it ought to be so to me: perhaps time, reflection, and prayer, may make it so; but it is religion only which can do it. Could any intellectual converse be held between us and our departed friends, death would be stripped of half its terrors. That, you will tell me, is not the lot of mortality. I know it is not, and I weep that it is not. Do not, I beseech you, condemn me; I know my wishes are wild and unjustifiable, but I cannot conquer them. Far from priding myself on these sentiments, I feel I am greatly humbled at being the prey of such new and fatal sensations; but if they are wrong, I suffer for them. Such uncommon feelings have, thro' my life, been their own punishment, by consuming me with sorrows, which not only philosophy, but reason, ought to have overcome: but let me retire from the gaieties which I am unfit for, and there shall be no means left untried to moderate my passions, and teach me to wait patiently for that time when the mysterious ways of Providence shall be made clear to our enlightened understanding."

Zilia embraced her with tears. I will not, says she, my dear Maria, attempt to dissuade you from your design; perhaps it may be the best thing you can do: your too tender sensibility deprives the world of the pleasure it would otherwise receive from your society: the keenness of your feelings is a sufficient punishment; think me not cruel enough to add to it, by condemning as a fault what I see as a misfortune. I must ever regret the loss of your company; but your friendship I shall not lose; a cloister will not shut me out from your heart; and I shall sometimes be able to indulge myself with a visit to you, in your retirement.

This estimable and unfortunate friend, my dear Dubois, is now settled in her convent. We much regret her loss; but being dead, as she was, to all earthly happiness, the world only added to her affliction, and a retired, religious life, was the only one from whence she could derive comfort. We long, my dear friend, for that visit which you have promised us. Come and share the happiness of a little circle of friends, who at present feel no wish ungratified, except that of seeing you once more joined with your faithful

Deterville.[114]

## FINIS.

# EDITORIAL NOTES

## *Letters from Juliet Lady Catesby*

1. *why this departure! this haste*: The French edition does not contain these words.
2. *Ossory*: 'd'Ossery' in the French edition.
3. *his air of sorrow strike me*: The French edition adds 'Qu'il étoit bien!' ('How good-looking he was!').
4. *But, are they not all so*: The French edition adds 'N'en parlons plus; ah n'en parlons jamais!' ('Let us talk about it no more, ah let us never talk about it!').
5. *Castle-Cary*: 'Carlile' in the French edition.
6. beech: Although the Académie française's 1762 dictionary, 4th edn, indicates that this word should be spelled 'hêtre', Riccoboni spells it 'être'. Brooke interprets it correctly, with 'être' meaning 'being'.
7. *Aston*: 'Warthy' in the French edition.
8. *still more disagreeable*: This detailed and insightful portrait as well as numerous others that follow recall the work of Jean de la Bruyère (1645–96) in his *Caractères* (1688). Riccoboni cites la Bruyère in her correspondence on two occasions: see *Mme Riccoboni's letters to David Hume, David Garrick and sir Robert Liston: 1764–1783*, ed. J. C. Nicholls (Oxford: Voltaire Foundation and Taylor Institution, 1976), pp. 338, 439.
9. *one of those men*: The French edition adds 'qui font tout mal-à-propos' ('who do everything at the wrong time').
10. *proud, with a termagant air*: These words are absent from the French edition; instead, it says 'avançant d'un air boudeur une petite tête' ('moving forward sullenly a small head').
11. *Harry*: 'Henry' in the French edition.
12. *Danby*: 'D'Erby' in the French edition.
13. *a court*: The article in the French edition here is definite ('la Cour') and so whereas Riccoboni refers to the royal court specifically, Brooke makes the 'toilsome inactivity' generic to any court.
14. *The man knows not what he would have*: The French edition states differently that 'Cet homme est inquiet, on ne sçait ce qu'il a ...' ('This man is anxious, one does not know what is the matter with him').
15. *friend*: While sibling and parent relationships are virtually non-existent in Riccoboni's work, friendship among women constitutes an important theme, for female friends can be relied upon and trusted even when men cannot. For an analysis of female friendship, see R. Thomas, '"Ma Soeur, mon amie"': Friends as Family in Madame Riccoboni's Fiction', *New Perspectives on the Eighteenth Century*, 5:1 (2008), pp. 13–19.
16. *Biddulph*: 'Bidulf' in the French edition.

17. *and not coquet*: The French edition adds that she is 'trop négligee même' ('too unrefined even').
18. *scolds his servants*: The French edition adds that she 'aime son mari' ('loves her husband').
19. *Mortimer-House*: 'Château d'Hastings' in the French edition.
20. *widow*: Numerous young widows appear in Riccoboni's oeuvre who have usually suffered during their marriage to an older husband. The most pertinent example is her 1767 *Lettres d'Adélaïde de Dammartin* in which three young widowed friends remarry; see M. Kaplan, 'Widows and Riccoboni's *Lettres d'Adélaïde de Dammartin*', in N. Bérenguier, C. R. Montfort and J. Rogers (eds), *Eclectic Expressions: Women's Triumphs, Past and Present. Selected Essays from Women in French International Conference 2006, Women in French Studies*, special issue 2008, pp. 58–65. See also the article by R. Thomas, 'Remarriage and its Discontents: Young Widows in Mme Riccoboni's Fiction', *Women in French Studies*, 17 (2009), pp. 54–65. Having lived separated from her abusive husband for many years while cohabiting with Marie Thérèse Biancolelli, a fellow actress, Riccoboni became a widow herself in May 1772, an event about which she expresses her relief in her correspondence (*Mme Riccoboni's Letters*, pp. 247–8).
21. *polite circles*: The French edition reads 'nos cercles' ('our social circles') so while Riccoboni has Juliet Catesby include herself in this milieu, Brooke separates her heroine from it by additionally stating that it is where '*they* have found the contemptible art of forgiving mutually every defect of the heart', emphasis added.
22. *displeases him*: The French edition adds 'le fâche, ou le chagrine' ('angers or distresses him').
23. *I am out of patience with him*: The French edition adds that 'quelque mal que je reçoive ses avis, il s'obstine à m'en donner' ('no matter how badly I receive his advice, he continues to give it to me').
24. *nosegay*: a small bouquet of flowers, often sweet-smelling. Since people did not bathe frequently in the eighteenth century, women often carried nosegays for their scent.
25. *Winchester*: 'Vinchester' in the French edition.
26. *Ought I to speak of him*: The French 'falloit-il me parler de lui?' would be better translated here as 'did you have to speak of him?' This would explain the following 'vous avez réveillé ...' ('you have awakened') in the French edition (but not in English), indicating that Henrietta's mention of Ossory has given rise to certain thoughts and memories in Juliet.
27. *Wednesday*: In the French edition it is 'lundi' ('Monday').
28. *I should despise myself indeed*: The French edition repeats neither this nor 'forgive him, Henrietta – If I could'. Through the repetition, Brooke emphasizes Juliet's horror at the thought and possibility of forgiving Ossory.
29. *with my friends*: The English leaves out the following sentence: 'La confiance ne reçoit pas deux atteintes; il le pense comme moi' ('Trust does not get attacked twice, he agrees with me on this').
30. *Wilton*: 'Vinchester' in the French edition. Brooke does not keep the same name for the person and the location.
31. *madrigals, in which Cupid, Venus, Hebe, all Olympus, find themselves*: A madrigal is a short poem that expresses a clever or gallant idea. The latter is obviously intended here since the Roman god of erotic love and beauty, the Roman goddess of love and beauty and the Greek goddess of youth, respectively, are all included; Mount Olympus is the home of the gods in Greek mythology.
32. *rhyme*: The French edition adds 'ou la mesure' ('or metre').
33. *he is always at my side*: The French 'il est près, tout près de moi ...' ('he is near, very near me') expresses how Sir Harry literally comes toward Juliet while she is writing, preceded

by 'il gagne du terrain' ('he is gaining ground') and followed by 'il lit presque ce que j'écris' ('he almost reads what I am writing'). Brooke generalizes the expression, thus reducing the reader's almost voyeuristic experience.

34. *Tuesday night*: The French edition specifies both the exact time and the fact that it is still the same day: 'Toujours mardi à minuit' ('Still Tuesday at midnight').

35. *Ranelagh*: 'Ranallagh' in the French edition.

36. *Southampton*: 'Bristol' in the French edition.

37. *any man*: The French edition does not indicate that this person is male ('on' meaning 'one'), but Brooke specifies his sex by repeating 'her attention to what *he* (my emphasis) is to say'.

38. *Sir William Manly*: 'Sir Manly' in the French edition.

39. *Sydney*: 'Sidney' in the French edition.

40. *the snare thou hast spread for us*: Riccoboni refers to Book IX of John Milton's *Paradise Lost*, first published in 1667. Able to read English, she possessed at least two books by Milton in the original English (see E. Crosby, *Une Romancière oubliée: Madame Riccoboni, sa vie, ses oeuvres, sa place dans la littérature anglaise et française du XVIIIe siècle* (Genève: Slatkine Reprints, 1970), p. 171). In this summary rather than literal translation, Riccoboni compares Man to the snake trying to ensnare (marry) Eve (Woman) in paradise. Brooke alters the French '... pour fixer notre attention & la détourner du piége qu'il nous tend' ('in order to engage our attention and divert it from the snare it has spread for us') so that the snake (Man) escapes from the snare (marriage) meaning Man abandons Woman, just like Sir Charles and Lady Selby (and of course, Ossery and Juliet), rather than simply diverting Woman's attention. See also R. Chai-Elsholz, 'Textual Allusions and Narrative Voice in the *Lettres de Milady Juliette Catesby* and Its English Translation', in A. Cointre, A. Rivara and F. Lautel-Ribstein (eds), *La Traduction du discours amoureux 1660–1830* (Metz, France: Centre d'Etudes de la Traduction, Université de Metz, 2006), pp. 122–3.

41. *I see only him*: The French edition adds 'il me cherche, me trouve' ('he seeks me, finds me').

42. *asks me for tea*: The French edition adds that he makes the tea himself: 'en prépare' ('makes it').

43. *I must think no more of him*: The French edition adds 'n'est-ce pas?' ('do you not agree?'). Brooke eliminates this direct reference to the internal reader of Juliet's letters, Henrietta.

44. *They would justify her choice in her own eyes*: While Riccoboni uses the future tense in this sentence ('justifieront' meaning 'they will justify'), Brooke uses the conditional, adding a more hypothetical dimension to the fact that there may be a woman who will love Sir Manly.

45. *if he had the generosity*: A more accurate translation of the French 's'il avoit eu la bonté' would have been 'if he had had the generosity' since it is apparent from the context that this is not the case.

46. *a philosophick attention*: The French edition uses the verb 'considérer' ('to consider') which Brooke gives a feminist twist by juxtaposing it with the word 'philosophick' usually reserved for male thinkers.

47. *the failings of my own sex*: Years later, in 1782, Laclos creates another infamous literary character who studies her sex carefully in order to survive in, and profit from, a male-dominated society, Madame de Merteuil in *Liaisons dangereuses*. After reading the novel, Riccoboni exchanges eight letters with Laclos because she wishes he had not 'adorned Vice with the attractiveness he bestowed on Mme de Merteuil' (C. de Laclos, 'Corre-

spondance de Laclos et de Madame Riccoboni au sujet des *Liaisons dangereuses*', *Laclos: Oeuvres complètes* (Paris: Gallimard, La Pléiade 1959), p. 687).

48. *difficult paths in which we tread*: The French specifies that these paths are distinguished by age: 'soit dans l'éclat de la jeunesse, soit sur le retour de nos ans' ('either in the bloom of youth or as we grow old').

49. *the sensibility of their hearts*: The French specifies that it is the pleasure which comes from the sensibility of their hearts: 'le plaisir que leur a donné la sensibilité de leur cœur' ('the pleasure which the sensibility of their heart gave them').

50. *will always be pleasing*: Brooke is more explicit than Riccoboni here, who describes it merely as 'un sentiment qu'on est sûr de conserver' ('a sentiment which one is certain to keep').

51. *Behold*: Before this word, 'Toujours jeudi' ('Still Thursday') has been omitted from the French.

52. *he lives for no other than myself*: Brooke's ambiguous translation implies that Ossory lives only for Juliet. The French, however, says that he is dead only to Juliet: '... il ne l'est [mort] que pour moi' ('he is dead to me alone').

53. *Marchioness of Dorchester*: 'Duchesse de Pembroke' in the French edition.

54. *white domino*: a loose cloak, worn at masked balls with a mask for the upper part of the face. The French edition does not specify its colour.

55. *masquerade*: a masked ball.

56. *even before I see them*: Brooke expands Juliet's dislike for Sir Harry by adding these words, absent from the French edition.

57. *my Lord Ossory*: The French edition specifies here that he is a 'Comte' ('Count').

58. *in the same manner*: Riccoboni uses one of her favourite themes here, the different standards men set for themselves and for women. Juliet's argument is premised on the fact that the same offence merits the same response, whether the victim be male or female.

59. *a widow at eighteen*: see n. 20.

60. *Anne*: 'Nancy' in the French edition.

61. *Osmond*: 'd'Ormond' in the French edition.

62. *Hertfordshire*: 'le Comté d'Erford' in the French edition.

63. *Mr. Ashby*: 'le Chevalier d'Orsey' in the French edition.

64. *Italy*: Although we learn later that Ossory went to France for a different reason, both countries were common destinations in the eighteenth century for the so-called Grand Tour, a trip undertaken by young British noblemen after they finished university, usually with an older and more experienced tutor. The main goals of this rite of passage were exposure to continental culture and art appreciation.

65. *Lady Dursley*: 'Lady Bedford' in the French edition.

66. *publick places*: Although Riccoboni mentions specific places where the British nobility gathered to see and be seen, 'la Cour, Bath & Tunnebrige' ('the Court, Bath and Tunbridge Wells'), Brooke prefers a generic term.

67. *every charm of art and nature*: The French is more specific here: 'les plantes rares, les bosquets & la quantité de fleurs' ('rare plants, copses and numerous flowers').

68. *these lovers*: The book is not identified. However, as R. Chai-Elsholz argues in 'Textual Allusions and Narrative Voice', the scene is reminiscent of the illicit lovers Francesca da Rimini and Paolo Malatesta reading a book together, an event that will also lead to their doom in Dante's *Inferno* (p. 120).

69. *Marquis of Dorchester*: 'Duc de Pembroke' in the French edition.

70. *which however he had the cruelty to conceal from me*: Brooke sometimes elaborates on the French. This is such a case as the French simply reads: 'qu'il me cachoit' ('which he concealed from me').
71. *Lord Newport*: 'Milord Portland' in the French edition.
72. *unusual melancholy*: Brooke expands on the French 'un peu de mélancolie' ('some melancholy').
73. *how my Lord did: they returned answer, that he was not in bed*: The French edition is more specific here ('... comment Milord avoit passé la nuit, on répondit qu'il s'étoit pas couché') ('... how Milord had done during the night, they returned answer that he had not gone to bed at all').
74. *My Lord Arthur, his lady, and son*: Brooke omits 'la comtesse de Lindsey' ('the countess of Lindsey') from the French edition.
75. *I lose you*: The French edition adds 'fatal voyage! ...' ('fatal journey').
76. *Who? – The author of my misery*: Brooke personifies the French here: 'quoi? ... mon malheur' ('what? ... my misery').
77. *duel*: Duels were illegal in France since 1602, but they still took place even in spite of anti-duelling campaigns by several kings.
78. *Fanny*: 'Jenny' in the French edition.
79. *hours*: The French states 'jours' ('days') instead.
80. *Penshurst*: 'Essex' in the French edition.
81. *Lady Bellvile*: 'Duchesse de Newcastel' in the French edition.
82. *to stay, least I should betray myself*: Brooke translates the French incorrectly here, since it says 'de rester sans connoissance' which means 'to remain unconscious, to faint'.
83. *had the goodness to*: Absent from the French, this is another instance of Brooke interpreting the French in addition to translating it.
84. *if you write to him*: The French says the opposite: 's'il vous écrit' ('if he writes to you').
85. *But why should his loss be a reason for reproaching me*: This is a mistranslation of the French 'mais pourquoi sa perte nous rapprocheroit-elle?', more accurately translated as 'But why should his loss bring us together?' Brooke undoubtedly thought of the French 'reprocher' meaning 'to reproach'.
86. *Adieu, my Lord*: Unlike Riccoboni, Brooke reminds readers that this very long letter XIV is addressed to Lord Castle-Cary.
87. *cannot help making*: Brooke leaves out the following sentence from the French: 'Qu'il s'éleve de singuliers mouvemens dans l'ame!' ('What singular feelings arise in the soul!').
88. *Spectator*: Riccoboni admired the *Spectator*, the daily English periodical founded in 1711 by Joseph Addison and Richard Steele; she had copies in her library (9 vols in 12; E. Crosby p. 171). In 1761, she wrote an anonymous letter to the editor of *Le Monde comme il est*, Jean-François de Bastide, in which she told him she was going to create a magazine in the image of the *Spectator* when she learned he had already done so. When he ceased its publication after two issues, she resumed her idea and created *L'Abeille*, after which she heard he would continue his *Monde comme il est* after all, but under a different title: *Le Monde* (pp. 9–10). She was annoyed with him, but decided to send him her texts, which he published anonymously (in 1761, volumes 3 and 4), together with the letters they exchanged. In her correspondence, Riccoboni also makes a reference to the *Spectator* in a letter dated 28 April 1773 and addressed to her Scottish friend Robert Liston: 'En compilant tous les voyageurs, il [l'abbé Rénal] a pris de vieux contes par-ci et par-là, et gâté celui de la négresse tuée par ses deux amants, qu'il a volé à votre *Spectateur* ...' ('In compiling all the travellers, he [Rénal] has taken old tales here and there and has spoiled

the one on the negress who was killed by her two lovers, which he stole from your *Spectator* ...'), *Mme Riccoboni's letters* p. 304).

In 1765, L'Abeille was included in Riccoboni's *Recueil de pieces détachées* (Paris: Humblot) without the correspondence with de Bastide, the anonymity and the *Lettres de la marquise de Sancerre à Monsieur le Comte de Nancé* which the author revised and published separately in 1766 as the novel *Lettres d'Adélaïde de Dammartin, Comtesse de Sancerre, à Monsieur le Comte de Nancé, son ami*. She added a new short story to the material from *L'Abeille* entitled *Lettres de la Princesse Zelmaïde au Prince Alamir, son époux*, of which I published a modern edition in 2009 (Paris: Éditions Indigo-Côté femmes). This short story concludes *L'Abeille* and Riccoboni interrupts her narrator at the end with a reference to Joseph Addison: 'Pour continuer un ouvrage de ce genre, il faudroit n'avoir jamais lu les admirables feuilles de Monsieur Addison. Je m'examine, je me juge & je m'arrête' ('In order to continue this type of work, one should never have read Mr. Addison's admirable pages. I examine myself, I judge myself and I fall silent') (p. 278). For a narratology-based feminist interpretation of this ending, see the article by S. S. Lanser, 'In a Class by Herself: Self-Silencing in Riccoboni's *Abeille*', in *Fictions of Authority: Women Writers and Narrative Voice* (Ithaca, NY and London: Cornell University Press, 1992), pp. 45–60. Based on an analysis of *L'Abeille* and other texts by Riccoboni as well as texts by Françoise de Graffigny but not the one included in this volume, H. Bostic has argued recently that 'women writers of the French eighteenth century claimed reason and contributed to Enlightenment' in *The Fiction of Enlightenment. Women of Reason in the French Eighteenth Century* (Newark, DE: University of Delaware Press, 2010), p. 17.

89. *Sir James Williams*: 'Sir Williams' in the French edition.

90. *See the danger of reading*: Eighteenth-century readers were well aware of this purported connection: authors like Madame de Lambert (1647–1733) warned girls and young women of the dangers of reading novels and naturally Rousseau wrote in the preface to his 1761 *Julie, ou la nouvelle Héloïse* that 'Jamais fille chaste n'a lu de romans' ('No chaste girl has ever read any novels'). Reading was also supposedly detrimental to one's vision, as Riccoboni illustrates in Letter IV: 'Lady Howard ... does not read for fear of spoiling her eyes.' On this and Riccoboni's own opinion of novels and periodicals, see also the article by S. van Dijk, 'Lire ou broder: Deux occupations féminines dans l'oeuvre de Mmes de Graffigny, Riccoboni et de Charrière', in J. Herman and P. Pelckmans (eds), *L'Epreuve du lecteur: Livres et lectures dans le roman d'Ancien Régime* (Louvain, Belgium: Peeters, 1995), pp. 351–60.

91. *Thursday, midnight*: The French edition specifies that it is still the same day: 'Toujours jeudi à minuit' ('still Thursday at midnight').

92. *explore my pity*: A more accurate translation of the French 'me demander ma pitié!' would be 'implore my pity!', which in fact appears starting with the 1769 edition.

93. *narcissuses*: The French 'semidoubles' refers to all flowers whose outermost stamens have been converted into petals while the inner ones remain perfect. So while Riccoboni uses a very general term, Brooke selects a specific type of flower. The narcissus can in fact be semi-double.

94. *those we make suffer*: The French edition adds 'même sans le vouloir' ('even without desiring to do so').

95. *snuff*: powdered tobacco that is not smoked but rather sniffed up the nostril. The custom started in the early seventeenth century in Europe. By the mid-eighteenth century, it had

become quite popular with both men and women and especially among the aristocracy. Snuff was usually carried in snuffboxes.

96. *Can Lord Ossory be in this country*: Brooke omits the following French sentence: 'Je voudrois qu'il me vint des aîles' ('I wish I had wings').

97. *Sunday night*: The French specifies both the exact time and the fact that it is still the same day: 'Toujours dimanche à minuit' ('Still Sunday at midnight').

98. *resentment*: Brooke omits two other emotions mentioned in the French: 'punir, se venger' ('to punish, to take revenge').

99. *that faithful friend*: Brooke omits 'cette femme sensible & vraie' ('that sensitive and true woman') from the French.

100. *Lady Catesby*: 'Lady Juliette' in the French edition.

101. *LETTER XXIII*: In the French edition, Letter XXII still contains the following two paragraphs. Because of this, the numbering of the letters in English no longer corresponds to that in the French edition from this point on.

102. *Monday, past midnight*: The French edition specifies both the exact time and the fact that it is still the same day: 'Toujours lundi à minuit' ('Still Monday at midnight').

103. *Two o'clock*: The French specifies that it is still the same day: 'Toujours lundi à deux heures' ('Still Monday at two o'clock').

104. *I erase*: The French edition adds 'je déchire' ('I tear up').

105. *torment myself*: The French edition adds 'me fatiguer' ('tire myself').

106. *they will not be restrained*: These words are absent from the French edition.

107. *and though ... my heart too easily gives it admittance*: This sentence is absent from the French edition.

108. *to reason*: absent from the French edition.

109. without thinking with the least degree of pleasure of my unworthy lover: Brooke has elaborated from the French which states simply 'sans me plaire à penser à vous' ('without pleasing myself by thinking of you').

110. *swoons away like a woman*: For an analysis of Sir Harry's role in the novel, among other things, see A. Sol, 'Violence and Persecution in the Drawing Room: Subversive Textual Strategies in Riccoboni's *Miss Juliette Catesby*', in S. Woodward (ed.), *Public Space of the Domestic Sphere/Espace public de la sphère domestique* (London, Ontario: Mestengo; 1997), pp. 65–76.

111. *he will come here no more*: The correct translation of the French 'il n'en reviendra pas' would be 'he will not recover from it'.

112. *at least, that he will find some other place to faint in. Adieu*: This sentence is absent from the French edition.

113. *Thursday, Winchester*: Brooke adds 'Winchester' here.

114. believe: Brooke may have mistaken the French 'écrire' ('write') for 'croire' ('believe') here.

115. *appear*: The correct translation of the French 'parez-vous' is 'adorn yourself'.

116. *tranquill*: Brooke omits '& presque contente' ('and almost happy').

117. *Egberth*: 'Seymour' in the French edition.

118. *Westbury*: 'Gage' in the French edition.

119. *friends*: The French 'compatriotes' might have better been left the same in English since Riccoboni talks about how men should risk their lives only for their country.

120. *Lady Catesby*: 'Lady Juliette' in the French edition.

121. *Charles Halifax*: 'Halifax' in the French edition.

122. *four*: The French states 'quinze' ('fifteen').

123. *my woman*: 'Betty' in the French edition.

124. *perplexing*: absent from the French edition.
125. *My Lord*: 'le pauvre malade' ('the poor patient') in the French edition.
126. *the weakness of my heart is what restrains me*: Brooke inserts this sentence presumably for clarification.
127. *Sally*: 'Sara' in the French edition.
128. *Jew*: 'arabe' ('Arab') in the French edition. According to the fourth edition of the *Dictionnaire de l'Académie française* (1762), 'arabe' was used at the time not to designate an inhabitant of a certain nation, but rather someone who is very insistent on getting what he is due.
129. *an attachment I have found such reason to regret*: simply 'tout' ('everything') in the French edition.
130. *domino*: see n. 54.
131. *Adieu*: This word is absent from the French edition, but the previous sentence ends in a comma, so it may have been a printing oversight.
132. *Hampstead*: 'Amstead' in the French edition.
133. *sorrow*: Brooke omits 'Hélas, ce chagrin étoit le triste présage du malheur qui devoit m'arriver! ...' ('Alas, that sorrow foreshadowed the misery which was to befall me! ...').
134. *let love again spread a veil before your eyes*: Love is blind. A favourite phrase of Shakespeare's, its mythological origin lies in the fact that Eros (Greek god of erotic love and beauty) sometimes had his eyes covered so he acted blindly.
135. *on the road*: Riccoboni specifies it was in 'Midlesex'.
136. *Anderson*: 'Andson' in the French edition.
137. *I drank freely*: absent from the French edition.
138. *flushed with wine*: absent from the French edition.
139. *school*: In this context, 'maison' would be better translated as 'convent'. Through Miss Montford, who proves that 'the most simple were the most amiable', Riccoboni criticizes the education girls received in convents, based on her personal experience. In a letter dated 2 January 1772 and addressed to her English friend David Garrick (1717–79; playwright, actor and theatre manager), she writes: 'I was raised as a girl whose only resort was the convent. They didn't teach me anything, they made me into a good little devout girl, who was capable only of praying to God ...' (*Mme Riccoboni's Letters* p. 227).
140. *infinitely attractive*: Riccoboni merely says 'offroient quelque chose de touchant' ('were somewhat touching').
141. *Miss Montford*: 'Miss Jenny' in the French edition.
142. *pictures*: Riccoboni may have intended for 'piéces' [*sic*] to mean 'rooms' in this context.
143. *to the garden*: Brooke omits 'nous nous orientâmes de notre mieux' ('we tried to get our bearings').
144. *the unhappy victim of my crime*: Brooke criminalizes the act whereas Riccoboni simply says 'Miss Jenny revenue à elle-même' ('Miss Jenny, come to').
145. *confessing my crime*: Brooke criminalizes the act while Riccoboni says 'lui apprendre mon malheur' ('tell him of my misfortune').
146. *in violation of all the sacred laws of hospitality and friendship*: Absent from the French edition.
147. *my crime*: Brooke criminalizes the act while Riccoboni calls it 'mon égarement' ('my having gone astray').
148. *and remorse*: absent from the French edition.
149. *Derbyshire*: 'le Comté d'Herney' in the French edition.
150. *Preston*: 'Exeter' in the French edition.

151. *Her amiable resignation*: absent from the French edition.
152. to afflict you: Brooke omits 'Faut-il que j'excite votre douleur!' ('Is it necessary that I cause you grief').
153. *Doctor Lewin, and Doctor Harrison*: R. Chai Elsholz sees a connection between these two doctors' names and Richardson's *Clarissa* (1748), a book of which Riccoboni did indeed possess a copy in English (see E. Crosby, p. 172): 'The name that Brooke changed from "Lereins" to "Lewin", while leaving unaltered Riccoboni's name for the other doctor, makes it more than likely that Brooke considered Jenny/Fanny as a kind of Clarissa' ('Textual Allusions and Narrative Voice', pp. 126–7). Dr Harrison already appeared in Letter XXX, curing Ossory.
154. *my crime*: 'tout' ('everything') in the French edition.
155. *Lady Bellville*: 'Duchesse de Neuchastel' in the French edition; see n. 81. Both Riccoboni and Brooke do not maintain the spelling of this name.
156. *how is it possible ... so hidden*: Brooke changes the order here: in the French edition, this sentence comes immediately after the one ending in 'hurried away by instinct'.
157. *I shall love her too*: The French omits the subject incorrectly ('je crois ... l'aime aussi'), but Brooke adds it.
158. *how happy is it that he has thus opened all his heart to me*: The French states instead 'Quel heureux avenir s'ouvre devant moi!' ('what a happy future opens up before me!')
159. *LETTER XXXIX*: In the French edition, this text is included in the preceding letter.
160. *nothing to say to you*: For a narratology-based feminist interpretation of Ossery's appropriation of Juliette's pen, see S. Lanser, 'The Rise of the Novel, the Fall of the Voice: Juliette's Catesby's Silencing', *Fictions of Authority: Women Writers and Narrative Voice* (Ithaca, NY and London: Cornell University Press, 1992), pp. 25–41. In April 1759, the *Correspondance Littéraire* already disliked this scene as well, but for different reasons: 'elle est commune et trop légère pour un homme qui a essuyé tant de contrariétés. Il faut qu'il soit plus sensible et plus touché de son bonheur, afin de devenir pour nous enore plus intéressant' ('it is common and too shallow for a man who has suffered so much. He ought to be more affected and more touched by his happiness in order to become even more interesting to us', p. 99).
161. *snare*: This word, both in French and in English, reminds readers of the reference to Milton's snake, see n. 40.
162. *the marriage is valid*: For an interpretation of this marriage in the context of Hardwicke's Marriage Act, see Chai-Elsholz, 'Textual Allusions and Narrative Voice', pp. 133–40.

## *The Peruvian Letters*

## Volume I

1. *PERUVIAN LETTERS*: The original French title is *Lettres d'une Péruvienne*, translated as *Letters written by a Peruvian princess* for Roberts's first volume. The second volume, which contains only three letters by the Peruvian princess (out of twenty-nine), is entitled *Letters to and from a Peruvian Princess*. *Peruvian Letters* thus refers to the two volumes together.
2. *Translated from the French*: It is one among several eighteenth-century translations of this novel into various languages as described by J. Mallinson in 'Reconquering Peru: Eighteenth-century translations of Graffigny's *Lettres d'une Péruvienne*', *SVEC*, 6 (2007), pp. 291–310. For a more detailed analysis of this particular English translation, see the

two articles by A. Rivara: 'Les *Lettres d'une Péruvienne* Traduites en Angleterre et en France', in J. Mallinson (ed.), *Françoise de Graffigny, femme de lettres: Ecriture et réception* (Oxford: Voltaire Foundation, 2004), pp. 272–87, and 'Les *Lettres d'une Péruvienne* de Mme de Graffigny et leur traduction par Miss Roberts (1774)', in A. Cointre, A. Rivara, F. Lautel-Ribstein (eds), *La Traduction du discours amoureux 1660–1830* (Metz: Centre d'Etudes de la Traduction, Université de Metz, 2006), pp. 65–77.

3.   *R. Roberts*: Although she had already published the texts that follow, this is the first one to which Roberts put her name (see 'Preface').

4.   *Translator … Millot*: Roberts published four moral tales by Marmontel in *Select Moral Tales translated from the French by a lady* in 1763 (Gloucester: R. Raikes), including 'The Good Mother', 'The Shepherdess of the Alps', 'The Happy Divorce' and 'The Partial Mother'. In 1770, she published *Sermons written by a Lady* (London: Dodsley) which she herself calls 'of an extraordinary kind for a woman's pen' (p. iii). Apologetic for her work, she states: 'When patriotism and loyalty engage all the wits of the age, it is no wonder that a Woman should take the lower department, and venture to write moral essays. The candid will remember that it is the work of a Woman, and will not be very severe in their criticism; the censure of others I am not solicitous to deprecate, as I think too highly of the Public to suppose it can influence their judgment' (pp. xi–xii). The text contains seven sermons on such topics as revenge, filial duty and children's educa-tion. In 1771, Roberts published *Elements of the History of France* (London: Dodsley and Cadell) in three volumes.

5.   *PREFACE*: The following Preface is by Roberts: it replaces the French eight-page 'Aver-tissement' ('Preface') in which Graffigny's fictional editor expresses the concern that French readers will not be receptive to the novel because of their prejudice against other nations. In order to illustrate this, Graffigny quotes the famous line from Montesquieu's *Lettres persanes* (*Persian Letters*) (1721) 'Comment peut-on être Persan?' ('How can one possibly be Persian?'). As a result of the partial elimination of the original edito-rial apparatus, the 'history of the letters' transformation from private documents into published texts' allowing us to read them as 'allegories of the Republic of Letters' (E. H. Cook, *Epistolary Bodies: Gender and Genre in the Eighteenth-Century Republic of Letters* (Stanford, CA: Stanford University Press, 1996), p. 26) is no longer included. Thus, English readers no longer have access to Zilia's life 'after' Graffigny's text which, the fictional editor implies, consists of writing and translating: 'Nous devons cette traduc-tion au loisir de Zilia dans sa retraite' (p. vi) ('We owe this translation to Zilia's leisure time in her retreat'). For a feminist interpretation of this activity, see M. Kaplan, 'Epis-tolary Silence in Françoise de Graffigny's *Lettres d'une Péruvienne* (1747)', *Atlantis: A Women's Studies Journal / Revue d'Études sur les Femmes* 29.1 (2004), pp. 106–12. Also due to this replacement by Roberts, English readers do not know that the fictional editor has supposedly edited Zilia's 'original' letters: 'On s'est contenté de supprimer (sur tout dans les premieres Lettres) un grand nombre de termes & de comparaisons Orientales …' ('We merely deleted (especially in the first letters) a large number of Oriental terms and comparisons', p. vii) and 'On a cru aussi pouvoir donner une tournure plus intelligible à de certains traits métaphysiques …' ('We also thought we could offer a clearer interpreta-tion for certain metaphysical features', p. viii). Through the replacement of the Preface, Roberts thus deletes part of the feminist context of Graffigny's text and posits her and her own text no longer as fiction attempting to pass for real correspondence, but rather as pure fiction.

6.   *three times offered my works to the Public*: see n. 4 for titles.

7. *many years since*: It was published in 1747. Calling Graffigny's text the 'first volume of the Peruvian Letters', Roberts implies that it is incomplete and thus justifies a continuation.

8. *the novel kind of writing*: Roberts has not written novels before (see n. 4).

9. *hurt the young female mind*: see *Letters from Juliet Lady Catesby*, n. 90 on the dangers young women face when reading.

10. *when all the transitory pleasures of this life shall be able to give none*: that is the moment of death.

11. *Dr. Hawkesworth ... person*: Dr John Hawkesworth, Roberts's dedicatee, had died 17 November 1773. Born *c.* 1715, Hawkesworth published during the Age of Johnson and was indeed a friend of Samuel Johnson. He edited the *Gentleman's Magazine*, Swift's works and Captain Cook's *Voyages* (1773), which caused him to be criticized by the public. Like Riccoboni, he had frequent (epistolary) contact with David Garrick.

12. *LETTERS WRITTEN BY A PERUVIAN PRINCESS*: see n. 1.

13. *the tender Zilia*: The French specifies 'ta' ('your') instead of 'the'. Roberts may have misread 'la' ('the') for 'ta'.

14. *are dissipated*: preceded in the French edition by 's'exhalent &' ('arise and').

15. *expect from thy love a redemption from my slavery*: The French uses the metaphor 'vienne briser les chaînes de mon esclavage' ('come break the chains of my slavery'). Although Roberts translates 'chaînes' as 'chains' several times in the novel ('the chain of time' (Letter I), 'the chains that were to unite us' (Letter II) and 'the chains of love' (Letter IV)), in this very first paragraph she selects 'redemption' which carries more obvious religious overtones.

16. *equally deaf to my language, and to the cries of my despair*: The French edition indicates a causal relationship here in 'sourds à mon langage, ils n'entendent pas mieux les cris de mon désespoir' ('deaf to my language, they do not hear the cries of my despair any better').

17. *cruel masters of the thunder, and of the power to extract it*: The French edition reads 'Maîtres Dyalpor' with the latter explained in a footnote as 'Name of the Thunder'. Roberts incorporates the concept of thunder directly into her translation, rather than its Peruvian personification, and explains in her footnote that it alludes to the cannon. The French 'la puissance d'exterminer' would be better translated as 'the power to kill'.

18. *Quipos*: While the French edition uses the past tense to define Quipos, Roberts uses the present tense, possibly to make the information appear more factual. She frequently makes this change in the footnotes.

19. *the groans of fear, the cries of rage*: in the French edition merely 'les cris de la fureur' ('the cries of rage').

20. *brought me at last to a sense of my misery*: The French 'm'ôterent jusqu'au sentiment de mon malheur' states the contrary 'took away even a sense of my misery' which is more logical given the following sentence 'Revenue à moi-même' ('Having recovered my senses').

21. *how did I then tremble*: The French 'j'en frémis encore' would be better translated as 'I continue to tremble at the remembrance' and indicates that the narrator, Zilia, is reliving the event when knotting her Quipos (and later translating them, according to the French original, see n. 5), rather than just describing how she felt at the particular moment.

22. *a daughter of the Sun*: 'la fille du Soleil' ('the daughter of the Sun') in the French edition, implying that there was only one.

23. *will inform me of your destiny*: Roberts has corrected the French 'm'instruiront de mon sort' ('will inform me of my destiny').

24. *I hope*: absent from the French edition, which portrays the narrator as convinced rather than hopeful.

25. *the pious citizen*: The French edition is more elaborate with 'la famille du pieux Citoyen' ('the family of the pious citizen').
26. *Pacha-Camac*: Roberts changes this name from the French 'Pachammac'.
27. *all hope*: 'ma joie' ('my joy') in the French edition.
28. *transmitted betwixt us the lively intelligence of hearts*: Roberts writes 'transmitted betwixt the lively intelligence of hearts' but based on the French 'nous transmettre cette vive intelligence des cœurs' ('transmitted to us the lively intelligence of hearts'), I have inserted 'us'.
29. *Caciputas*: Roberts changes this name from the French 'Cucipatas'.
30. *a Divinity*: In the French edition, 'lui' ('him') refers back to the Sun in the same sentence.
31. *child of the Sun*: In the French edition, the asterisk referring to the footnote is overlooked, but Roberts restores it to its rightful place.
32. *I judge to be large*: Although the French edition uses the past tense here ('j'ai jugé'), Roberts changes to the present tense, possibly in order to stress the fact that Zilia is still in the same location and of the same opinion when communicating this information to Aza.
33. *Ticai-Viracocha*: one word in the French edition, 'Ticaiviracocha'.
34. *Some days passed*: The French is less specific here in 'Un tems assez long s'étoit écoulé' ('A rather long time had passed').
35. *horror*: The French specifies it is a 'horreur secrette' ('unknown horror, that is produced by an unknown source').
36. *the whole creation*: Instead of 'all of nature' as a translation for 'la nature entiere', Roberts selects 'the whole creation' which carries more obvious religious overtones. She omits 'Je croyois le péril universel' ('I believed the danger to be universal') from the French.
37. *by their aspect*: absent from the French edition.
38. *unknown regions*: The French includes a definite article here in 'les regions inconnues' ('the unknown regions') implying that the unknown regions were known as such, but in the footnote uses an indefinite article in 'des lieux inconnues' ('unknown regions'). Roberts retains the latter.
39. *which I thought I beheld not far off*: absent from the French and redundant because of the word 'approaching'.
40. *disfigured image*: The French includes 'privée de sentimens' ('deprived of sentiments').
41. *the sun*: 'du Midi' ('the South of France') in the French edition. Roberts makes the reference more generic for English readers.
42. *uneasiness*: 'le poison des regrets' ('the poison of regrets') in the French edition.
43. *from being continually offended ... so many torments*: In the French edition, this applies to 'mon âme' ('my soul').
44. *Pachacamac*: Roberts retains the French spelling, unlike before, see n. 26.
45. *materials*: 'métaux' ('metals') in the French edition.
46. *sufficient matter*: 'l'air & le feu' ('air and fire') in the French edition.
47. *great deal of respect*: The French edition includes 'je crois, à sa façon' ('I believe, in his manner').
48. *ceremony*: The 'physic' Roberts mentions in her footnote refers to medicine.
49. *my tears*: 'bien des larmes' ('abundant tears') in the French edition.
50. *they*: 'on' ('we') in the French edition.
51. *entertainment*: 'désert' ('deserted place') in the French edition.
52. *Ramai*: Roberts changes this name from the French 'Raymi'. In the footnote, she translates the French 'les Prêtres' ('the priests') as 'Indians'.
53. *great Name*: for the footnote, see n. 44.

54. *sacred Diadem*: In the footnote, Roberts changes the French 'Manco-capa' to 'Manco-capac'. Being in England and not Roman Catholic, she also translates 'nous baisons les reliques de nos Saints' ('we kiss the relics of our saints') as 'the Roman catholics kiss the relics of their saints').

55. *soft, distinct, and harmonious*: All three words are preceded by the comparative in the French edition, 'plus doux, plus distinct, plus mesuré'.

56. *Mancocapac*: See n. 54. In the footnote, Roberts retains Graffigny's reference to the *History of the Incas*. Graffigny's subsequent 1752 edition contains various important changes – although the controversial ending remains the same in spite of reader criticism and continuations and rewrites – one of which is the inclusion of a multi-page 'Introduction historique aux *Lettres Péruviennes*' ('Historical introduction to the *Peruvian Letters*') in which the author discusses Peruvian culture and history as well as the country's destruction by the Spanish conquistadores; some of this information is included in the footnotes of the 1747 edition. In the introduction, Graffigny mentions El Inca Garcilaso de la Vega (1539–1616), the son of a Spanish aristocrat and an Inca princess who lived in both countries and spoke both languages. He wrote the *Comentarios reales de los incas y la historia general del Perú* (*'Royal Commentaries of the Incas and General History of Peru'*) in 1609, which was first translated into French in 1633 and of which a new translation had just appeared in 1744 (Paris: Prault fils). This intertextuality explains Graffigny's seemingly vast knowledge of a country and a culture she never visited.

57. *feel the same sentiments for women*: 'n'éprouvent-ils ces deux sentimens que pour les femmes' ('feel the same sentiments for women only') in the French edition.

58. *from my memory all my past misfortunes*: 'le souvenir de tant d'infortunes' ('the memory of all my past misfortunes') in the French edition.

59. *the sight of which*: 'dont la vûe seule' ('the sight of which alone') in the French edition.

60. *my future life*: The French edition adds that the life is 'infortunée' ('unhappy').

61. *and which I can no longer support*: absent from the French edition.

62. *and they shall cease to see any other object*: 'je ne veux plus vivre' ('I no longer wish to live') in the French edition.

63. *my dear Aza*: reinforced in the French edition as 'Non, mon cher Aza, non' ('No, my dear Aza, no').

64. *lends this voice*: 'emprunte ta voix' ('borrows your voice') in the French edition.

65. *a period*: 'une fin' ('an end') in the French edition.

66. *my miseries*: 'ses regrets' ('its regrets') in the French edition.

67. *a look*: preceded in the French edition by 'un mot' ('a word').

68. *repentance ... and contempt*: Both are followed in the French edition by 'only' ('que le repentir, & que le mépris').

69. *it*: The French edition specifies 'leurs fêtes' ('their festivities').

70. *their exclamations*: The French edition adds 'de joie' ('of joy').

71. *Mays*: For the footnote, see n. 56 on the *History of the Incas*. Although Roberts copies the reference to vol. 2 of the *History of the Incas*, she leaves off the page number (151). In the footnote, 'Mays is a liquor' is a mistranslation of 'Le Mays est une plante', which should be 'Mays is a plant'.

72. *he has delivered me from them ... any but himself*: 'il m'a délivrée de leurs regards importuns ... les siens' ('he has delivered me from their irksome looks ... any but his own') in the French edition.

73. *our thoughts*: followed in the French edition by 'mon cher Aza' ('my dear Aza').

74. *glanced over my heart*: The French continues the simile related to light: 'a porté sa clarté jusqu'au fond de mon cœur' ('carried its brightness to the bottom of my heart').

75. *fills my soul with good*: 'c'est mon unique bien' ('it is my only good') in the French edition.

76. *without being distinctly marked*: 'ou qu'elles ne soient pas sensiblement marquées' ('or are not distinctly marked') in the French edition.

77. *sunk by that total absence, that oblivion which is horrid to nature, the image of nothing*: 'dans cet abandon total (horreur de la nature, image du néant)' ('in that total oblivion (horror of nature, image of nothing)') in the French edition.

78. *The day*: 'les jours' ('the days') in the French edition.

79. *which conduces to my satisfaction*: 'qui m'étoient nécessaires' ('which were necessary to me') in the French edition.

80. *Cacique*: Roberts omits the following footnote here: 'Les Caciques étoient des espéces de petits souverains tributaires des Incas' ('The Caciques were a kind of petty sovereigns dependent on the Incas'), probably because the same term was already explained in the footnote on p. 78.

81. *time and observation*: 'l'habitude & ... la réflexion' ('custom and ... reflection') in the French edition.

82. *the custom*: 'un jeu à l'usage' ('a customary game') in the French edition. This distinction matters because it expresses the narrator's attitude towards what Deterville does.

83. *For example*: absent from the French edition.

84. *important concerns*: Roberts omits a sentence after these words: 'Je ne le puis, mon cher Aza, je cherche des lumieres avec une agitation qui me dévore, & je me trouve sans cesse dans la plus profonde obscurité' ('I can not do it, my dear Aza, I seek knowledge with an agitation which consumes me and I do not cease to find myself in the most profound darkness').

85. *The intelligence of tongues is that of the soul*: This sentence is a question in the French edition.

86. *this port*: 'cette Terre' ('this land') in the French edition.

87. *cannot throw off*: 'je ne cherche pas meme à me délivrer' ('I do not even seek to throw off') in the French edition.

88. *my surprise*: repeated in the French edition 'Quelle surprise, mon cher Aza, quelle surprise extrême' ('what a surprise, my dear Aza, what an extreme surprise').

89. *things*: 'prodiges' ('miracles') in the French edition.

90. *I see myself once more served by my own sex*: 'de revoir des femmes & d'en être servie' ('that I see women once again and am served by them') in the French edition.

91. *Cuzco*: 'Cuzcoco' in the French edition.

92. *brighter*: 'plus beau, plus pur' ('more beautiful, purer') in the French edition.

93. *Curaca*: 'Curacas' in the French edition.

94. *their manners*: 'les manieres de ces Sauvages' ('the manners of these savages') in the French edition.

95. *my dear Aza*: Roberts omits the following after these words: 'malgré leurs imperfections' ('in spite of their imperfections').

96. *begin my detail*: 'essayer de t'en instruire' ('try to begin my detail') in the French edition.

97. *the palace*: Roberts mistranslates 'Pallas', see footnote to p. 87.

98. *to be stared at*: This concept is reminiscent of the famous scene in Montesquieu's *Lettres persanes* (*Persian Letters*) in Letter XXX, where when Rica changes his original Persian clothes to Parisian ones, he is no longer the centre of attention and causes people to wonder 'Comment peut-on être Persan!' ('How can one possibly be Persian?'). See also n. 5.

99. *gazed at me some time*: 'nous regarda long-tems' ('gazed at us a long time') in the French edition.

100. *The effect they produced startled me*: 'Je ne sçais quel effet ils firent dans ce moment-là sur lui' ('I do not know what effect they produced on him that moment') in the French edition.

101. *respect her virtue*: 'le respect ... sa vertu' ('respect (noun) ... her virtue') in the French edition.

102. *one could not stand upright in it*: 'sans incommodité' ('without inconvenience') is omitted from the French.

103. *rove*: 'parcourent, embrassent & se reposent tout à la fois sur ...' ('simultaneously rove, embrace and rest on ...') in the French edition.

104. *this*: 'cette erreur' ('this error') in the French edition.

105. *order*: 'désordre' ('disorder') in the French edition.

106. *bias*: 'attrait intérieur' ('internal bias') in the French edition.

107. *odour*: followed by 'mais indéterminée' ('but unidentified') in the French edition.

108. *your idea the least of my curious desires*: 'ton idée dans le moindre de mes desirs curieux' ('your idea in the least of my curious desires') in the French edition.

109. *Quito*: 'Quitu' in the French edition.

110. *I drew to myself*: 'l'on m'a faite' ('they drew me') in the French edition.

111. *awe*: Roberts omits the following footnote here: 'Les filles, quoique du sang Royal, portoient un grand respect aux femmes mariées' ('Young girls, even if they were of royal blood, had great respect for married women'). The footnote explains Zilia's automatic respect for Deterville's mother.

112. *sternly*: absent from the French edition.

113. *Her presence seemed to me an essential good*: preceded by 'Dans la situation où j'étois' ('In the situation in which I found myself') in the French edition.

114. *pity itself*: 'la pitié de soi-même' ('pity for oneself') in the French edition.

115. *I related to her*: Roberts corrects Graffigny's mistake 'je lui comptois' ('I counted to her') to 'je lui contois' ('I related to her').

116. *I comforted myself with the thoughts*: 'Je crûs' ('I believed') in the French edition.

117. *sleep had not closed my eyes*: 'le sommeil n'avoit point encore tari mes larmes' ('sleep had not yet dried up my tears') in the French edition.

118. *Palace*: see n. 97.

119. *If I did not continue*: Roberts corrects Graffigny's mistake 'Si je continuois' ('If I continued') to 'Si je ne continuois' ('If I did not continue').

120. *sad thoughts*: 'tendres pensées' ('tender thoughts') in the French edition.

121. *light manners*: 'mœurs' ('manners') in the French edition.

122. *I see of*: 'je vis avec' ('I live with') in the French edition. This mistake can be explained by the fact that the French verb 'voir' ('to see') has a form 'vis' in the first person singular, passé simple tense.

123. *he treats me*: 'il me traite d'avance' ('he treats me in advance') in the French edition.

124. *chuse*: 'exige' ('demand') in the French edition.

125. *so weak am I*: absent from the French edition.

126. *thin substance*: 'matiere blanche & mince' ('white and thin substance') in the French edition.

127. *by gratifying the curiosity of others*: 'en excitant la curiosité des autres' ('by arousing the curiosity of others') in the French edition.

128. *fools and madmen*: 'les insensés & les méchans' ('madmen and wicked people') in the French edition.
129. *creatures like themselves*: The French edition adds 'autrefois' ('in the past').
130. *Our more favoured country*: The French edition adds 'de la nature' ('by nature').
131. *the sun has run half his course*: Roberts omits the following sentence after these words: 'Que cette double absence m'a paru longue' ('How long did this double absence appear to me!'). Also, at this point Zilia has run out of Quipos and writes to Aza in French. On the importance of this transition for both the epistolary and the travel narratives, see M. Kaplan 'Epistolary Silence in Françoise de Graffigny's *Lettres d'une Péruvienne* (1747)', *Atlantis: A Women's Studies Journal / Revue d'Études sur les Femmes*, 29:1 (2004), pp. 106–12.
132. *I exist anew*: 'je crois recommencer à vivre' ('I believe I am starting to exist anew') in the French edition.
133. *lest the kindness of Celina should decrease*: Roberts mistranslates 'que les bontés de Céline ne purent effacer' ('which Celina's kindness could not decrease').
134. *My fears were not ill-grounded*: absent from the French edition.
135. *because I have omitted to write them*: absent from the French edition.
136. *Among us, the Capa Inca ... their subjects*: Roberts's punctuation obscures this translation of 'Au lieu que le Capa-inca est obligé de pourvoir à la subsistance de ses peuples, en Europe les Souverains ne tirent la leur que des travaux de leurs sujets' ('Whereas among us, the Capa Inca is obliged to provide for the subsistence of his people, in Europe the sovereigns subsist only on the labours of their subjects').
137. *think it a shame*: 'cette nation insensée' ('this insane nation') is the subject of this verb in the French edition.
138. *By this method ... bestowing his liberality*: 'ce Souverain répand ses libéralités' ('This sovereign bestows his liberality') in the French edition.
139. *feeling*: 'souffrir' ('suffering') in the French edition.
140. *such men ever lived*: 's'ils vivent' ('whether they are alive') in the French edition.
141. *Cuzco*: 'Cozco' in the French edition, see n. 91.
142. *communicate*: 'me donner la confiance de communiquer' ('give me the confidence to communicate') in the French edition.
143. *could do much for me*: 'pourroit tout ce qu'il voudroit' ('could do anything he wished to do') in the French edition.
144. *without consulting him*: 'sans son consentement' ('without his approval') in the French edition.
145. *he appeared all rudeness and falsehood*: 'je n'ai trouvé que de la rudesse & de la fausseté dans tout ce qu'il m'a dit' ('I found only rudeness and falsehood in everything he said to me') in the French edition.
146. *other men*: 'le commun des hommes' ('ordinary men') in the French edition.
147. *a little*: absent from the French edition.
148. *haughty nation*: 'nation fastueuse' ('opulent nation') in the French edition.
149. *for bread*: 'pour vivre' ('in order to live') in the French edition.
150. *gravity*: 'séduction' ('seduction') in the French edition.
151. *an air of gaiety*: Roberts omits the following after these words: '& paroissant douter de la vérité de mes paroles' ('and while he appeared to doubt the truth of my words').
152. *but ... proved the sincerity of my heart*: 'mais à mesure que les expressions de mon cœur en prouvoient les sentiments' ('but as the expressions of my heart proved its sentiments') in the French edition.

153. *these words*: 'ces paroles insensées' ('these absurd words') in the French edition.
154. *his veracity*: 'la fausseté de ses paroles' ('the falsehood of his words') in the French edition.
155. *were it in my power*: absent from the French edition.
156. *in the truth and sincerity of my own heart*: absent from the French edition.
157. *so much*: 'de l'estime & de l'amitié' ('respect and friendship') in the French edition.
158. *me*: 'le' ('him') in the French edition.
159. *unwilling to interrupt me*: Roberts omits the following after these words: 'je ne sçais quel trouble me saisit' ('I do not know what inquietude seized me').
160. *and embarrassed*: absent from the French edition.
161. *earnestness*: 'avidité' ('ardent desire') in the French edition.
162. *it is only momentary*: absent from the French edition.
163. *character*: 'mon caractère' ('my character') in the French edition.
164. *friendship*: 'sentiments' ('sentiments') in the French edition.
165. *but should that not be the case, and I should sink under it:* absent from the French edition.
166. *alone*: The French edition adds 'sans oser paroître' ('afraid to appear').
167. *all*: 'tant de contrarieté & de la peine' ('such difficulties and pain') in the French edition.
168. *continual importunity*: 'disputer avec Céline' ('fighting with Céline') in the French edition.
169. *from what I had experienced before of Deterville's generosity*: absent from the French edition.
170. *forced appearance*: 'espéce de' ('sort of') in the French edition.
171. *doubt*: 'crainte' ('fear') in the French edition.
172. *and confidence*: absent from the French edition.
173. *who overrun our country*: absent from the French edition.
174. *I shall think for you alone*: 'je ne penserai plus que par toi' ('I shall think through you alone') in the French edition.
175. *in my determination*: The French edition adds 'à t'attendre' ('to wait for you').
176. *Can I willingly ... much for me*: 'mais pourrois-je me résoudre à contracter volontairement un genre d'obligation, dont la honte va presque jusqu'à l'ignominie' ('but could I willingly contract a sort of obligation of which the shame almost extends to humiliation') in the French edition.
177. *would be sufficient*: The French edition adds 'pour te faire admirer' ('to be admired').
178. *it will be necessary to display those before them*: absent from the French edition.
179. *all necessary preparations are making for her marriage*: 'son mariage n'est retardé que par les aprêts qui y sont nécessaires' ('her marriage is delayed only by all the necessary preparations') in the French edition.
180. *she sent for me into her chamber*: 'elle est accourue dans ma chambre, m'a emmenée dans la sienne' ('she rushed to my chamber, took me into hers') in the French edition.
181. *and*: the French edition adds 'd'un air empressé' ('attentively').
182. *presents ... by them*: 'quand les bienfaits ne sont d'aucune utilité à ceux qui les reçoivent, la honte en est effacée. Attendez donc que je n'en aye plus aucun besoin pour exercer votre générosité' ('when presents are of no use to those who receive them, their shame is erased. So please wait with your generosity until I no longer need it') in the French edition.
183. *my letter interrupted*: The French edition adds 'hier' ('yesterday').
184. *for ever lost*: The French edition adds 'je n'y comptois plus' ('I no longer expected it').
185. *my error was confirmed*: 'ma surprise confirma mon erreur' ('my surprise confirmed my error') in the French edition.
186. *the sacred remains of our altars*: 'ces restes sacrés de notre culte & de nos Autels' ('those sacred remains of our worship and our altars') in the French edition.
187. *disdain of obligation*: 'vengeance' ('vengeance') in the French edition.

188. *that I was afraid to offer her any thing*: 'pour n'y pas chercher de l'adoucissement' ('not to seek any soothing') in the French edition.
189. *flowers made of shells*: 'de Coquillages de Poissons & de fleurs' ('shells, fish and flowers') in the French edition.
190. *several idols of the nations*: In the footnote, Roberts changes 'Huayna' to 'Huyna' and 'Rimace' to 'Rimaca'. The reference to the *History of the Incas* is to volume 1, p. 350, in the French edition.
191. *beasts of prey*: 'animaux courageux' ('courageous animals') in the French edition.
192. *vows of eternal love*: 'sermens' ('vows') in the French edition.
193. *birds*: The footnote starts with 'on a déjà dit' ('As mentioned previously') in the French edition.
194. *since the celebration of her marriage*: 'où son mariage fut célébré en y arrivant' ('where her marriage was celebrated upon our arrival') in the French edition.
195. *with the more anxiety*: Between this point and the beginning of Letter XXIX, Graffigny makes significant changes to the text in the 1752 edition, including the insertion of two new letters in which she criticizes the French love for the superfluous and the superficial.
196. *to ask to speak to him alone*: 'de l'obliger à me parler' ('to force him to speak to me') in the French edition.
197. *pleasing*: absent from the French edition.
198. *what it was*: 'quelle sorte d'impatience' ('what kind of impatience') in the French edition.
199. *in which I was educated*: Roberts mistranslates 'où j'ai été enlevée' ('whence I was abducted'), probably mistaking it for 'où j'ai été élevée' ('in which I was educated').
200. *when I thoroughly knew you*: absent from the French edition.
201. *my heart beat with pleasure*: 'une sorte de sérénité ne se répandît dans mon cœur' ('a sort of serenity spread in my heart') in the French edition.
202. *adore your idea*: The French edition adds 'loin de vous' ('far from you'), referring to Deterville's upcoming departure.
203. *our beauty*: 'la beauté du visage & de la taille' ('the beauty of our face and our waist'). For a study of the changing concept of beauty and the use of cosmetics in eighteenth-century France, see M. Martin's *Selling Beauty. Cosmetics, Commerce, and French Society, 1750–1830* (Baltimore, MD: Johns Hopkins University Press, 2009).
204. *our sufferings*: absent from the French edition. The French includes only positive features.
205. *our sex*: 'les femmes' ('women') in the French edition. Since Zilia writes this letter to Aza, 'our' rather than 'my' indicates that Roberts includes herself here.
206. *I endeavoured ... shewed it me*: 'j'en cherchois la cause dans leurs bonnes qualités, lorsqu'un accident me l'a fait découvrir parmi leurs défauts' ('I endeavoured to find the cause of it among their good qualities when an accident made me uncover it among their shortcomings') in the French edition.
207. *conceal his malice with his shame*: Between this point and the final paragraph of this letter, Graffigny makes significant changes to the text in the 1752 edition, including the insertion of a new letter in which she criticizes how the French treat women.
208. *who have the art ... like virtues*: 'd'ailleurs charmante' ('otherwise charming') in the French edition.
209. *standish*: a stand for holding writing equipment.
210. *into the dining-room*: The French edition adds 'selon la coustume' ('following the custom').
211. *bason*: basin.
212. *at her feet*: 'dans ses bras' ('in her arms') in the French edition.

213. *and which belonged to a door in that room*: absent from the French edition.
214. *place*: 'solitude' ('solitude') in the French edition.
215. *Every piece of furniture it contained was equally elegant*: '& des meubles commodes assortis aux peintures' ('and comfortable furniture matching the paintings') in the French edition.
216. *this I took no notice of*: 'quoique je me gardasse bien d'en parler' ('although I took care not to speak of it') in the French edition.
217. *beaufet*: buffet.
218. *dinner*: The main meal of the day, here served at midday, and followed later in the day by the supper, the evening meal.
219. *Malta*: Note the all-important change in addressee and in his location. Deterville has joined the order of the Knights of Malta, a fact already mentioned in Letter XIX: 'From the same cruel motive, she ('Madam Deterville') has forced Deterville to enter into a particular order, from which he can not be disengaged, after he has pronounced certain words called vows.' The Knights took vows of poverty, chastity and obedience. They had been at Malta since 1530 and at Rhodes and Jerusalem before that (since 1048). The Order had a hospitaller mission and defended the Christian world against invaders.
220. *by your departure*: Roberts omits the following after these words: 'par des motifs de reconnoissance si pressans' ('for such pressing reasons of gratitude').
221. *despair for your absence*: 'à votre desespoir & à votre absence' ('your despair and your absence') in the French edition.
222. *the future days of your sister*: 'vos jours & ceux de votre sœur' ('the future days of you and your sister') in the French edition.
223. *to stab me with his sincerity*: 'que pour m'ôter la vie' ('to take my life') in the French edition.
224. *while life remains*: Roberts omits the following after these words: 'Ma vie lui appartient' ('My life belongs to him').
225. *to have fed her vanity*: absent from the French edition.
226. *and religion forbids him to think any more of me*: 'il m'abandonne, l'honneur l'y condamne' ('he abandons me, honour condems him to do so') in the French edition.
227. *which freely declare the sentiments of the heart, appear to me now to be crimes*: 'vous êtes donc des crimes quand l'occasion le veut?' ('so you are crimes when the occasion dictates it?') in the French edition.
228. *to that sweet power*: The French edition adds 'sans retour' ('forever').
229. *I place in you*: The French edition adds '& de l'état de mon ame' ('and the condition of my soul').
230. *to whom he was dear*: 'qui lui fut cher' ('who was dear to him') in the French edition. While Graffigny claims Zilia was dear to Aza, Roberts uses the reverse and more evident statement that Aza was dear to Zilia.
231. *I shall be ever faithful to them*: The French edition adds 'vous ne la partagerez avec personne, je vous les dois. Je vous les promets' ('you will not share them with anyone, I owe them to you. I promise them to you').
232. *so many people*: 'tant d'aveugles humains' ('so many blind people') in the French edition.
233. *I am, I live, I exist*: In her new study on aging and eighteenth-century French women writers including both Graffigny and Riccoboni, Joan Hinde Stewart argues that 'during the sixty-three years that she ('Graffigny') lived, she displayed an enduring fascination for life. Her attitude is reminiscent of her heroine's at the end of *Lettres d'une Péruvienne*, where the long-suffering but resilient Zilia invites Déterville to continue as her friend'

(*The Enlightenment of age: Women, Letters and Growing Old in Eighteenth-Century France* (Oxford: Voltaire Foundation, 2010), p. 243).

234. *Let us together renounce*: The French uses an imperative directed at Deterville only: 'Renoncez' ('Renounce').

235. *the loss of love*: For a feminist interpretation of this ending see E. J. MacArthur, 'Devious Narratives: Refusal of Closure in Two Eighteenth-Century Epistolary Novels', *Eighteenth-Century Studies*, 21 :1 (Autumn 1987), pp. 1–20.

# Volume II

1. *LETTERS TO AND FROM A PERUVIAN PRINCESS*: see Volume I, n. 1. The second volume consists of two continuations divided over twenty-nine letters. First, it contains Roberts's translation of the *Suite des Lettres d'une Péruvienne* (*Continuation to the Letters from a Peruvian Woman*), the first French continuation to the novel published in Paris in 1748. Although published anonymously, Graffigny attributed it to the chevalier de Mouhy (1701–84) and wrote in a letter dated 21 September 1748: 'Ah, poor chevalier de Mouhy, you have not disguised yourself well enough. You will not be mistaken for me' (*Letters of a Peruvian Woman*, trans. J. Mallinson (Oxford: Voltaire Foundation, 2009), p. 127). The *Suite* (*Continuation*) consists of seven letters, here Letters XXXIX–XLV, with several typographical errors. Roberts corrects them and also changes how the text is divided into paragraphs. Next, the second volume includes Roberts's own continuation to both Graffigny's 1747 novel and the 1748 *Suite* (*Continuation*), which is composed of twenty-two letters, Letters XLVI–LXVII.

2. *LETTER XXXIX*: As with Graffigny's Preface, Roberts deletes the 'Avis de l'éditeur' ('Notice from the editor') from the *Suite* (*Continuation*). In it, the editor says the success of Zilia's letters has been a surprise because they appeared 'too opposed to our country's prejudices' (p. iv). Yet, now that the public's taste has been tested, it is ready for the continuation of Zilia's letters in which it will see that she has made tremendous progress (p. v). In an effort to authenticate the letters, the editor adds that 'that is what the author thinks of them in a letter sent to me and which expresses a distinct partiality for this continuation' (p. vi). English readers may have thought that Roberts wrote these seven letters as they are included with her continuation in the second volume but without an indication of alternative authorship or their original title. See also Volume I, n. 5.

3. *Deterville's Answer to Zilia*: The French edition adds '& à la trente-huit & dernière Lettre imprimée' ('and to letter thirty-eight, the last one printed'). This is the first letter written by Deterville. Graffigny's text includes merely a note from him to Zilia in Letter XXVII; he functions as addressee for Zilia's final five letters with Aza being the addressee for her other thirty-three letters. In the *Suite* (*Continuation*) however, Zilia writes merely two letters, while Deterville composes three; she receives three letters, he two. Celina, Deterville's sister who was passively present in Graffigny's text, also becomes a new letter writer. From Graffigny's text to this continuation, the major formal transformation thus consists in monovocality becoming polyphony, already apparent from the second volume's title.

4. *I did all in my power to gratify your passion for him*: 'je respectois votre passion pour lui' ('I respected your passion for him') in the French edition.

5. *his inconstancy*: 'son changement' ('his change') in the French edition is less accusatory.

6. *the desire you had to make him happy*: The French 'du désir de couronner sa flâme' ('the desire you had to reward his fervour') implies love on Aza's part.

7. *those knots*: 'ces nœuds fortunés' ('those fortunate knots') in the French edition.

8. *would not have rejoiced in*: 'n'eût pas repris' ('would not have resumed') in the French edition.

9. *and rather than not do that*: absent from the French edition.

10. *my desire*: 'mon sort' ('my destiny') in the French edition.

11. *which will never be less than it is now*: 'dont le respect égalera toujours la vivacité' ('of which the respect will always match the ardour') in the French edition.

12. *Zilia to Celina*: Zilia has not written to Celina before, she is a new addressee.

13. *not philosopher enough to reconcile my mind to them*: 'manquant d'expérience' ('lacking experience') in the French edition.

14. *charming solitude seems to offer*: At the end of her novel, Graffigny leaves Zilia content with her 'charming solitude', in a 'room of her own', enjoying intellectual pursuits such as translating her Quipos into French and reading. Zilia reconsiders that situation in this *Suite* (*Continuation*), a step towards increased social interaction and assimilation. J. Mallinson calls Zilia 'ready to be integrated' ('Reconquering Peru' p. 298).

15. *the fates' decree*: According to Greek mythology, the Fates or Moirai (Parcae in Roman mythology) are three goddesses named Clotho, Lachesis and Atropos, who determine the course of every human being's life and destiny.

16. *acquaintance with others*: 'dépendance des autres' ('dependence on others') in the French edition.

17. *he can never hope*: 'il ne se flattoit plus' ('he no longer hoped').

18. *your religion*: Graffigny exposes Zilia to religion in her text and in spite of having an initially positive reaction to it, Zilia ends up rejecting its representative: among other things, he tells her about incest's incompatibility with Christianity (Letter XXII). Zilia now reconsiders Christianity and is portrayed as being open to assimilation into French society.

19. *Celina's answer to Zilia*: Like her brother, Celina becomes a letter writer in the *Suite* (*Continuation*). She writes two letters and receives two, but loses her voice again in Roberts's own continuation. Being both Deterville's sister and of the same age and sex as Zilia, Celina serves as an intermediary between the two.

20. *Aza would still fill a place in your heart*: 'Aza occupoit seul encore votre cœur' ('Aza alone would still fill your heart') in the French edition.

21. *you was incapable of*: 'n'étoient point entrés dans votre liaison' ('had not entered into your relationship') in the French edition.

22. *without any trial of his*: '& surtout point de concurrent' ('and especially no rival') in the French edition.

23. *but he does not feel it the less*: 'Uniquement occupé d'une passion aussi tendre que respectueuse' ('Feeling only a passion as tender as it is respectful') in the French edition.

24. *arguments*: 'des secours, des conseils' ('assistance, counsel') in the French edition.

25. *prejudice*: see Volume I, n. 5 and Volume II, n. 2. Whereas prejudice was previously associated with the French, Zilia is now said to possess it as well.

26. *it should be done*: 'vos deux cœurs soient à l'unisson' ('your two hearts be in unison') in the French edition.

27. *such a passion was not easily conquered*: 'un cœur véritablement épris, ne peut suffire qu'à un seul amour' ('a heart truly in love can only satisfy one love') in the French edition.

28. *authorised by duty ... a tender passion should be formed between them*: 'unis par le goût et le devoir, & par la vertu qui annoblit l'un & l'autre' ('close through inclination and duty and through that virtue which ennobled both their souls') in the French edition.

29. *to last for ever*: Graffigny implies at the end of her novel that Zilia will continue to love Aza forever even though she knows he will never be hers. Here a seed of doubt is planted regarding that assertion.

30. *the hands of love*: The French edition adds 'fait uniquement pour tromper les yeux jaloux' ('made solely for deceiving jealous eyes').

31. *most tender passion*: 'une passion des plus tendres & des plus légitimes' ('most tender and legitimate passion') in the French edition.

32. *vows*: The French edition uses 'nœuds' here which carries the double meaning of 'knots' and 'bonds'.

33. *a letter addressed to you*: This is the letter we just read. The presence of multiple correspondents here allows for this kind of epistolary device, a letter addressed to one person falling in the hands of another, who responds to it. It illustrates what J. G. Altman calls the 'epistolary mosaic': 'Multiple versions of the same reality are a common occurrence in epistolary narrative with multiple correspondents' (*Epistolarity: Approaches to a Form* (Columbus, OH: Ohio State University Press, 1982), p. 176). In her letter to Zilia (Letter XLI), Celina tells her to forget Aza, never mention him to Deterville and enjoy friendship with the latter, while she tells her brother to accept Zilia's friendship because it will undoubtedly turn into love (Letter XLIII).

34. *so alike*: 'si variées' ('so varied') in the French edition.

35. *ties*: see Volume II, n. 32.

36. *make our destiny perfectly happy*: a reiteration of the offer of friendship instead of love made by Zilia to Deterville in the final paragraph of Graffigny's text.

37. *crown them by our gratitude*: 'en couronnerons notre innocence' ('crown our innocence with them') in the French edition.

38. *most submissive homage*: This constitutes the end of Roberts's translation of the *Suite* (*Continuation*). Its ending resembles Graffigny's in that Zilia refuses to marry Deterville who accepts her offer of friendship. E. Showalter considers the *Suite* (*Continuation*) 'une tentative hâtive d'exploiter le succès des *Lettres d'une Péruvienne*' ('a hasty attempt to exploit the success of *Lettres d'une Péruvienne*') ('Les *Lettres d'une Péruvienne*: composition, publication, suites', *Archives et bibliothèques de Belgique*, 54: 1–4 (1983), p. 25).

39. *LETTER XLVI*: This is the first letter written (not translated) by Roberts. In her continuation to the preceding texts, Roberts lends Deterville a dominant epistolary voice as the writer of nineteen out of twenty-two letters, because he plays an active and important role in achieving the two objectives she mentions in her Preface, namely that 'the Indian Princess should become a convert to Christianity, through conviction; and that so generous a friend as Deterville might be as happy as his virtues deserved.' The foundation for both of these objectives has been laid in the *Suite* (*Continuation*). In Roberts's continuation, Zilia writes only one letter, while Deterville composes nineteen; they each receive three letters. A new female character named Maria St Clare is introduced who writes and receives two letters, as well as a new male addressee, Dubois, the recipient of fourteen letters. Compared to Graffigny's text, Zilia and Deterville trade places as primary letter writers. Based on what J. G. Altman calls the 'metonymic' function of the letter, according to which the letter represents the body of the letter writer (*Epistolarity*, p. 19), Zilia's body, dominant in Graffigny's text, is taken over by Deterville's now and becomes the object of negotiation by others. For an analysis of the same phenomenon in a 1772 epistolary novel by Riccoboni, see M. Kaplan 'Marie Jeanne Riccoboni's *Lettres d'Elisabeth Sophie de Vallière*: A Feminist Reading', *Women in French Studies*, 13 (2005), pp. 25–36. On a thematic level, these changes allow Roberts to accomplish her goals, but it happens

at the expense of Graffigny's Zilia's intellectual, emotional and spiritual independence. This may explain why Roberts chooses to base her translation on Graffigny's 1747 text, and not the 1752 version which is of course also available when she starts to write her continuation: the later text reaffirms Zilia's decision to remain single in the face of widespread reader opposition and includes new criticism of the way in which the French treat women, particularly after marriage (see Volume 1, n. 207).

40. *To the Chevalier Dubois*: Roberts introduces a new male character, the Chevalier Dubois. He is an addressee only, like Aza (and Deterville) in Graffigny's text. Dubois receives fourteen letters, all from Deterville.

41. *our French ladies*: another sign of Zilia's assimilation into French culture.

42. *SONG*: These three stanzas of six verses in iambic tetrameter follow the rhyming scheme ABABCC. I was unable to find a direct source for the song, but found allusions to Delia and love in numerous seventeenth- and eighteenth-century poems. Delia is another name of Artemis, the Greek goddess of hunting and wild animals, which explains the song's pastoral aspect. Obviously, the reference here is to Zilia and how Deterville is enchanted by her. The themes of nature, mythology and lyric poetry illustrate to readers that when Roberts writes her continuation, twenty-seven years after Graffigny's original text, Romanticism is much more evident in literature.

43. *votary*: devoted follower, often used with religious overtones.

44. *Platonick love*: Roberts labels - but Graffigny does not use - this term for the friendship Zilia offers Deterville, a strong affectionate friendship without sexual component that according to him, does not exist.

45. *asunder*: apart.

46. *choiristers*: choristers, members of a choir, here composed of birds.

47. *jessamine*: jasmine.

48. *woodbines*: honeysuckles.

49. *romantic*: see Volume II, n. 42. Consider the references to the senses: smell (flowers), hearing (birds), taste (dinner) and sight (river and hills). Nature has a profound impact on the characters and Roberts's Deterville is more lyrical and sentimental than Graffigny's.

50. *enlighten my mind*: see Volume II, n. 18.

51. *to be convinced*: As Roberts states in her Preface, she wants Zilia to be converted 'through conviction'.

52. *revenge*: One of Roberts's 1770 *Sermons by a Lady* also deals with revenge, Sermon II.

53. *Madamoiselle St. Clare*: a new female character introduced by Roberts as both a writer and an addressee of two letters.

54. *statuary*: sculptor.

55. *a turn*: a natural ability.

56. *by Zilia*: The six stanzas of four verses in iambic pentameter follow the rhyming scheme ABAB. The poem, in which Maria St Clare addresses her soul, describes how hurt by love, Maria wishes to turn to religion, God and death for salvation. It carries an exemplary lesson for Zilia, see n. 58 below.

57. *the base Judean*: Aza is compared to Judas, the apostle who betrayed Jesus.

58. *my love has died away*: This process of Zilia's ill-fated love for Aza being replaced by her devotion to religion resembles what Maria St Clare describes in her poem, see Volume II, n. 56.

59. *her story*: As stated, Graffigny includes a note from Deterville to Zilia in Letter XXVII from Zilia to Aza; Roberts incorporates this very lengthy letter written by Maria St Clare to Celina in this letter by Deterville to Dubois. This mise-en-abyme of the letter,

where a letter contains a smaller version of itself, offers an interesting variation on what J. G. Altman considers one of the essential features of epistolary literature: 'By its very *mise-en-abyme* of the writer-reader relationship, the epistolary form models the complex dynamics involved in writing and reading' (*Epistolarity*, p. 212). Including a letter from someone else to someone else in your own clearly complicates those dynamics even further, raising issues of authenticity and authority. Laclos uses this tool quite aptly in his *Liaisons dangereuses* (*Dangerous Liaisons*) in 1782.

60.  *genteel*: respectable.

61.  *beauty is of no consequence in a man*: M. Martin disputes this by claiming that the 'so-called Great Masculine Renunciation (according to which men aimed at being useful rather than beautiful) was nowhere near complete' and that 'Men were very much part of the consumer market created in the eighteenth century and very much part of the marketing campaigns of sellers of cosmetics' (*Selling Beauty*, p. 155).

62.  *guile never yet dwelt*: The Incas are also known for their inability to lie: 'It passes for certain, that no Peruvian ever told a lye' (footnote to p. 75).

63.  *post-horses*: horses that were kept at an inn or post house for mail couriers which could also be rented.

64.  *St. Far fleeting … grasped a shadow*: Note the aptness of St Far's name.

65.  *To the Chevalier St. Far*: see Volume II, n. 59. This constitutes a further mise-en-abyme of the letter (within the letter within the letter).

66.  *your loved Maria*: This illustrates what E. Pollak says: 'A striking number of English prose fiction narratives written between 1684 and 1814 predicate their plots on the tabooed possibility of incest' (*Incest and the English Novel, 1684–1814* (Baltimore, MD and London: Johns Hopkins University Press, 2003), p. 1). Maria's inserted narrative about her ill-fated relationship with St Far carries yet another exemplary lesson for Zilia whose love for Aza was also incestuous: 'The laws of the Indians oblige the Incas to marry their sisters, and when they had none, to take the first princess of the blood of the Incas, that was a Virgin of the Sun' (footnote to p. 74). See also Volume II, n. 56.

67.  *a small jointure*: A jointure is an estate settled on a wife for the period that she survives her husband; St Far's maternal grandmother was a widow.

68.  *amour*: illicit love affair.

69.  *apoplexy*: sudden loss of consciousness and death, sometimes as a result of a stroke.

70.  *in the words it was couched*: The letter that follows, from St Far and Maria's father to St Far's mother, represents a fourth level of mise-en-abyme of the letter. Within the letter from St Far's mother to him included in Maria's letter to Celina which Deterville forwards to Dubois, it represents the family genealogy and thus indirectly the incest. Just like Maria's letter was passed from Celina to Deterville, from sister to brother, the intercalated letter was passed from St Far to Maria, from brother to sister.

71.  *Count de —*: The dashes replacing the last name constitute a common tool in epistolary fiction aimed at concealing and thus protecting someone's identity. It reminds readers that real people supposedly wrote the letters they are reading.

72.  *twenty thousand crowns*: A crown equals five shillings, so 100,000 shillings, a very substantial amount of money.

73.  *bringing another person into being*: With the letter representing the body of the letter writer (see Volume II, n. 39), it is no coincidence that St Far's mother mentions her pregnancy right after her (epistolary) body has been penetrated by St Far's father.

74.  *Lady R*: Using an initial rather than a complete name is another tool in epistolary fiction for safeguarding someone's identity; see Volume II, n. 71.

75. *an unlawful marriage*: Since St Far's parents were married ('a marriage, so very private that there were no witnesses present at the ceremony'), his father's second marriage was unlawful, bigamy being illegal in eighteenth-century France. This makes Maria, offspring from the second marriage, technically illegitimate. A real-life example of this can be found in the biography of Marie Jeanne Riccoboni, whose father married her mother and was then forced to return to his first wife, leaving the author an orphan.

76. *wonted*: usual.

77. *the monks of La Trappe*: The Order of Cistercians of the Strict Observance, a Roman Catholic order following the Rule of St Benedict located in the La Trappe Abbey in Soligny-la-Trappe, Orne, France. According to the Rule, the monks pursue peace, prayer and work. They do not take a vow of silence, but speak only when necessary.

78. *your friendship*: that is Celina's friendship, for this letter was originally written by Maria to Celina.

79. *sprightly*: lively.

80. *chaunts*: chants.

81. *at Malta*: Note the parallel between St Far joining the monks of La Trappe and Deterville returning to the Order of the Knights of Malta in order to retreat from love.

82. *an idol*: commonly used in a religious context and denoting a representation of a god used as an object of worship. Through its use here, Roberts indicates why religion may provide the cure for ill-fated love.

83. *Muses*: inspiration for creative activity.

84. *Ovid*: Roman poet (b. 43 BC; d. c. AD 17) best known for his love and erotic poems, particularly *The Art of Love* in which he teaches readers how to love and how to seduce.

85. *hapless*: unfortunate.

86. *slavery*: The Slavery Abolition Act abolishes slavery in 1833 in the United Kingdom.

87. *his darts*: Love's darts. Love (also known as Eros and Cupid in Greek and Roman mythology, respectively) is personified here. When he shoots a dart at someone's heart, that person falls in love.

88. *œconomy*: careful management of available resources.

89. *the disease*: The idea that love is a disease can be traced back to Ovid, see Volume II, n. 84.

90. *saunter*: leisurely stroll.

91. *Deterville to Zilia*: Having written twelve letters to Dubois, Deterville now writes to Zilia since he is rejoining Dubois and therefore needs a new addressee.

92. *Turks*: Also known as the Ottomans, who ruled most areas surrounding the Mediterranean at the time, the Turks laid siege to Malta in 1565, but were repulsed by the Knights of Malta assisting the Maltese.

93. *Grand Master*: head of the Order of the Knights of Malta.

94. *loaded*: in debt.

95. *nominal*: in name only.

96. *clear*: debt-free.

97. *she loves Deterville*: Celina's role as letter writer and addressee having declined, Maria now becomes the intermediary between Deterville and Zilia.

98. *chid*: chided.

99. *a dispensation*: Since the Knights of Malta take a vow of chastity, Deterville would need dispensation in order to get married; see Volume I, n. 219.

100. *visitants*: visitors.

101. *England is really a fine country*: Roberts praises her own country and that of her readers. The fact that Deterville travels to England in Roberts's continuation is significant

because it duplicates Graffigny's original premise of Zilia coming to France as an exotic Other and observing French society from an outsider's perspective. However, whereas Zilia has mostly criticism for France and particularly for the way women are treated there, Deterville admires England and its people.

102. *countrywomen*: What Deterville admires in the English women are the qualities he loves in Zilia.

103. *vow I have taken*: see Volume II, n. 99.

104. *a dispensation from vows*: The Pope in Rome was the only one who could grant this dispensation since the Grand Master of the Knights of Malta was answerable only to him.

105. *durst*: dared.

106. *beautiful in the highest degree*: see Volume II, n. 101.

107. *most justly admired*: This description is reminiscent of the scene in Graffigny's text where Zilia goes to the theatre in Letter XVI.

108. *their works of genius*: Deterville's experience is that of the foreign Other here; like Zilia in France, he learns the new language and the foreign literature through the language. The French admired England a great deal in the eighteenth century, notably Voltaire who was exiled to England for three years and published the *Lettres philosophiques sur les Anglais* (*Philosophical Letters on the English*) (1734) where he praises English religion, politics, trade, science, etc.

109. *Deterville to Zilia*: Deterville writes this letter from Rome. With him visiting both London and Rome and discussing art and culture, Deterville's trip reminds readers of the Grand Tours commonly undertaken by upper-class wealthy young men before settling down in society.

110. *Zilia to Deterville*: Zilia finally picks up her pen again for her last letter after eighteen letters by Deterville and two by Maria St Clare. Again, with the letter representing the body of the letter writer (see Volume II, n. 39), Zilia accepts to give her body to Deterville here (marry him) in response to the two previous letters being invitations by him to do so. This letter confirms that Roberts has achieved her two goals of marriage and conversion for Zilia, see Preface.

111. *halcyon*: blissful.

112. *white Indian taffety*: taffeta is silk. Note all the references to Zilia's virginity on her wedding day: '... the *innocence* of whose countenance made her still appear like a *virgin* of that luminary. The *simplicity* of her dress corresponded with her looks; it was of *white* Indian taffety' ('I emphasize'). 'Indian' is of course also frequently used to refer to Zilia.

113. *a day or two after our marriage*: The timing of St Far's death reinforces the exemplary lesson that incestuous love, such as that between Maria and St Far and Zilia and Aza, ends not only in heartbreak but also in death, whereas 'healthy' love such as Zilia and Deterville's ends in marriage and bliss. See Volume II, n. 66.

114. *your faithful Deterville*: In the context of this book which juxtaposes Riccoboni's *Letters from Juliet Lady Catesby* and Roberts's *Letters To and From a Peruvian Princess*, one can not fail to notice the final parallel between the two texts. With the protagonists barely married, Juliet writes in a letter to her friend Henrietta: 'You are expected here with impatience– No feasts, no balls, without my dear Henrietta; I should have said, no happiness, if the person whose eyes follow my pen, was not already a little jealous of my tender friendship' while Deterville writes to his friend Dubois: 'We long, my dear friend, for that visit which you have promised us. Come and share the happiness of a little circle of friends, who at present feel no wish ungratified, except that of seeing you once more joined with your faithful Deterville'. Due to the epistolary novel's formal requirements,

the married, reunited protagonists need an addressee outside of the couple. In both cases this addressee is a friend and in both cases the author implies that happiness, marital happiness, is incomplete without same-sex friendship. While her new husband appropriates Juliet's pen in the final letter, Zilia abandons her pen altogether in the two final letters, ceding it and her voice to Deterville. See also Introduction.

# TEXTUAL VARIANTS

## *Letters from Juliet Lady Catesby*

3a my destiny seemed wrote,] my destiny seems wrote *1763, 1764*; my destiny seems written *1769, 1780, 1786*

3b produced by the same cause] produced by the same case *1763*

4a This couple seemed to me,] This couple seem to me *1769, 1780, 1786*

5a that escape me,] that escaped me; *1769, 1780, 1786*

5b Heaven! what a look!] Heavens! What a look! *1769, 1780, 1786*

5c It is my letter which puts him] It is my letter which put him *1764, 1769, 1780, 1786*

5d be so good to use yourself to it.] be so good as to use yourself to it. *1769, 1780, 1786*

7a agreeable silly creature] agreeably silly creature *1763, 1764, 1769, 1780, 1786*

7b knowledge of] knowledge of the *1760a* (listed in Errata *1760a*)

8a nor can] how can *1760a* (listed in Errata *1760a*); nor how can *1760b, 1763, 1764, 1769, 1780, 1786*

9a all Olympus,] and Olympus, *1760b, 1763, 1764, 1769, 1780, 1786*

11a duties of this trust,] duties of his trust, *1769, 1780, 1786*

11b the idol of all our ladies,] the idol of our ladies *1769, 1780, 1786*

11c his jealous furies] his zealous furies *1763, 1764, 1769, 1780, 1786*

11d How bitter is it] How bitter it is *1769, 1780, 1786*

12a thirty.] thirty? *1760a; corrected in later editions*

15a conversations] conversation *1760a* (listed in Errata *1760a*)

15b unbounded confidence] undoubted confidence *1763, 1764, 1780, 1786*] undoubed *1769*

16a to confess to him my weaknesses.] at confessing to him my weaknesses. (listed in Errata *1760a*); to confess to him my weakness *1760b, 1763, 1764, 1769, 1780, 1786*

16b you were,] you was, *1760a* (listed in Errata *1760a*)

16c you were] you was *1760a* (listed in Errata *1760a*)

16d rose] arose *1760b, 1763, 1764, 1769, 1780, 1786*

16d cannot be] cannot but be *1760a* (listed in Errata *1760a*)

17a subject no farther.] subject no further. *1764, 1769, 1780, 1786*

18a have been very light to another.] have been light to another. *1786*

18b Pall-Mall] Pall-mall *1760a; corrected in later editions*

19a to ask the reason] to ask him the reason *1760b, 1763, 1764, 1769, 1780, 1786*

19b to address to me] to address me *1760b, 1763, 1764, 1769, 1780, 1786*

20a in him;] in in him; *1760a; corrected in later editions*

22a to which I had been till then] to which I was till then *1760a* (listed in Errata *1760a*) to which I had been then *1760b, 1763, 1764, 1769, 1780, 1786*

22b    and at night wrote to each other] and at night we wrote to each other *1780, 1786*

22c    to read in his] to read in him *1760a* (listed in Errata *1760a*)

24a    we were agreed on all points,] we were agreed in all points, *1764, 1769, 1780, 1786*

24b    had sat down to write.] had set down to write. *1769, 1780, 1786*

26a    My faintings] Faintings *1760b, 1763, 1764, 1769, 1780, 1786*

26b    succeeded each other] succeeded each *1760a* (listed in Errata *1760a*)

26c    whether he shared my tenderness;] whether he had shared my tenderness; *1769, 1780, 1786*

27a    the weight of my chagrins,] the weight of my chagrin, *1780, 1786*

28a    I always remembered I had loved.] I always remembered I *had* loved *1769, 1780, 1786*

28b    made a thousand efforts] have a thousand efforts *1760a* (listed in Errata *1760a*)

28c    loved no longer,] loved no person, *1760a* (listed in Errata *1760a*)

28d    Penshurst] Penshunt *1760a* (listed in Errata *1760a*)

28e    least I should betray myself.] lest I should betray myself *1763, 1764, 1769, 1780, 1786*

28f    on his return,] on his return. *1760a* (listed in Errata *1760a*)

29a    whom he knew,] who he knew, *1760a* (listed in Errata *1760a*)

29b    Ah! God!] Ah! my God! *1769, 1780, 1786*

29c    console] consider *1760a* (listed in Errata *1760a*)

29d    Sir Harry] Sir Henry *1760a; corrected in later editions*

30a    as flourishing a state of health] as nourishing a state of health *1763, 1764, 1769, 1780, 1786*

30b    I hate to seek for reasons] I have to seek for reasons *1763, 1764, 1769, 1780, 1786*

30c    profit of those seeds] profit those seeds *1760a* (listed in Errata *1760a* with incorrect page number)

31a    Sir Harry] Sir Henry *1760a; corrected in later editions*

31b    which chance had now given him—] which chance had given him— *1769, 1780, 1786*

32a    Sir Harry] Sir Henry *1760a; corrected in later editions*

32b    to explore my pity!] to implore my pity! *1769, 1780, 1786*

33a    to return] to come to return *1760a* (listed in Errata *1760a*)

35a    is it possible for a man] is it possible for man *1786*

35b    of which kind they are:] of what kind they are: *1769, 1780, 1786*

36a    by those impetuous passions] by these impetuous passions *1786*

36b    they consider only the pleasures] they consider only the pleasure *1764, 1769, 1780, 1786*

37a    became *unjust*] become *unjust* *1760b, 1763, 1764, 1769, 1780, 1786*

37b    offers itself readily to my mind] offers itself ready to my mind *1786*

37c    my silence a consent to see him—] my silence as a consent to see him— *1769, 1780, 1786*

38a    to whom I am obliged] to whom I obliged *1760a* (listed in Errata *1760a*)

39a    I once fancied myself mistress of,] I once fancied myself mistress; *1760a* (listed in Errata *1760a*)

39b    and of all those blessings] and of all other blessings *1763, 1764, 1769, 1780, 1786*

40a    its horrors] it's horrors *1760a, 1760b, 1763; corrected in later editions*

41a    friend's sake] friends sake *1760a; corrected in later editions*

41b    LETTER XXVII] LETTER XVI *1760a; corrected in later editions*

41c    blackest kind;] blackest kind? *1760a* (listed in Errata *1760a*)
41d    eager acceptance;] eager acceptance? *1760a* (listed in Errata *1760a*)
41e    Insupportable insolence] Insupportable. Insolence *1760a* (listed in Errata *1760a*)
42a    disturb my peace of mind,] disturb the peace of mind, *1764, 1769, 1780, 1786*
44a    How shall I find out] How shall I find it out *1760b, 1763, 1764, 1769, 1780, 1786*
44b    the erring heart of the other,] the erring heart of the other. *1760a* (listed in Errata *1760a*)
44c    either to listen to] either to hasten to *1760a* (listed in Errata *1760a*)
45a    this too lively emotion] this lively emotion *1760b, 1763, 1764, 1769, 1780, 1786*
47a    its empire] it's empire *1760a, 1760b, 1763; corrected in later editions*
47b    where I often go] where I go often *1760b, 1763, 1764, 1769, 1780, 1786*
49a    lift my eyes up] lift up my eyes *1760b, 1763, 1764, 1769, 1780, 1786*
49b    you tell me I *ought to have seen him,*] yet tell me I *ought to have seen him*, *1764, 1769, 1780, 1786*
50a    who have never had any thing to pardon] who had never any thing to pardon *1769, 1780, 1786*
51a    the farther end of the terrace] the further end of the terrace *1764, 1769, 1780, 1786*
51b    which every body expresses] which every one expresses *1786*
53a    reconcile me in that amiable sex] reconcile me to that amiable sex *1763, 1764, 1769, 1780, 1786*
53b    in recollecting those first moments] in correcting those first moments *1763, 1764*
53c    which give birth to love] which gave birth to love *1769, 1780, 1786*
53d    you yielded to give me your hand] you yielded to give me your hands *1764*
54a    and often, even in breaking to pieces] and often in breaking to pieces *1769, 1780, 1786*
54b    each other's throats] each others throats *1760a, 1760b, 1763, 1764; corrected in later editions*
55a    her sex, and blooming season of life] her sex, her blooming season of life *1760b, 1763, 1764, 1769, 1780, 1786*
55b    its motions] it's motions *1760a, 1760b, 1763; corrected in later editions*
56a    apartment being almost as new] aparment being almost as new *1760a* (listed in Errata *1760a*)
56b    we both took a great deal of pains] we both took a deal of pains *1769, 1780, 1786*
59a    she is become haughty] she has become haughty *1786*
59b    Amiable little innocence!] Amiable little innocent! *1763, 1764, 1769, 1780, 1786*
59c    possession of ?] possession off ? *1760a; corrected in later editions*
59d    to procure for her pleasures] to procure for her peasures *1760a* (listed in Errata *1760a*)
59e    pleasures which I was incapable of partaking] pleasures of which I was incapable of partaking *1763, 1764, 1769, 1780, 1786*
60a    inform you of my reasons] inform you of my reason *1769, 1780, 1786*
60b    the most lively inquietudes] the most lively inquietude *1760b, 1763, 1764, 1769, 1780, 1786*
61a    bathing it with her tears,] bathed it with her tears. *1764, 1769, 1780, 1786*
61b    I wish, continued she, that the person] I wish, continued she, that person *1769, 1780, 1786*
61c    my ardent prayers] my ardent prayer *1769, 1780, 1786*
61d    of which she had had but too much sensibility] of which she had but too much sensibility *1769, 1780, 1786*

61e    how terrible is it] how terrible it is *1769, 1780, 1786*
62a    threw me into a despair] threw me into despair *1769, 1780, 1786*
63a    It is then true] Is it then true *1763, 1764, 1769, 1780, 1786*
63b    She who banished you the heart of your husband,] She who banished the heart of
       your husband, *1760b, 1763, 1764, 1769, 1780, 1786*
64a    He has given a reason] He has given a a reason *1760a; corrected in later editions*
65a    If there is, it is not however at Hertford,] If there is, is it not however at Hertford
       *1764, 1769, 1780, 1786*
66a    I believe it now perfect,] I believe it is now perfect; *1769, 1780, 1786*

## *The Peruvian Letters*

No variants.

# SILENT CORRECTIONS

### *Letters from Juliet Lady Catesby*

### *The Peruvian Letters*

### *Volume II*